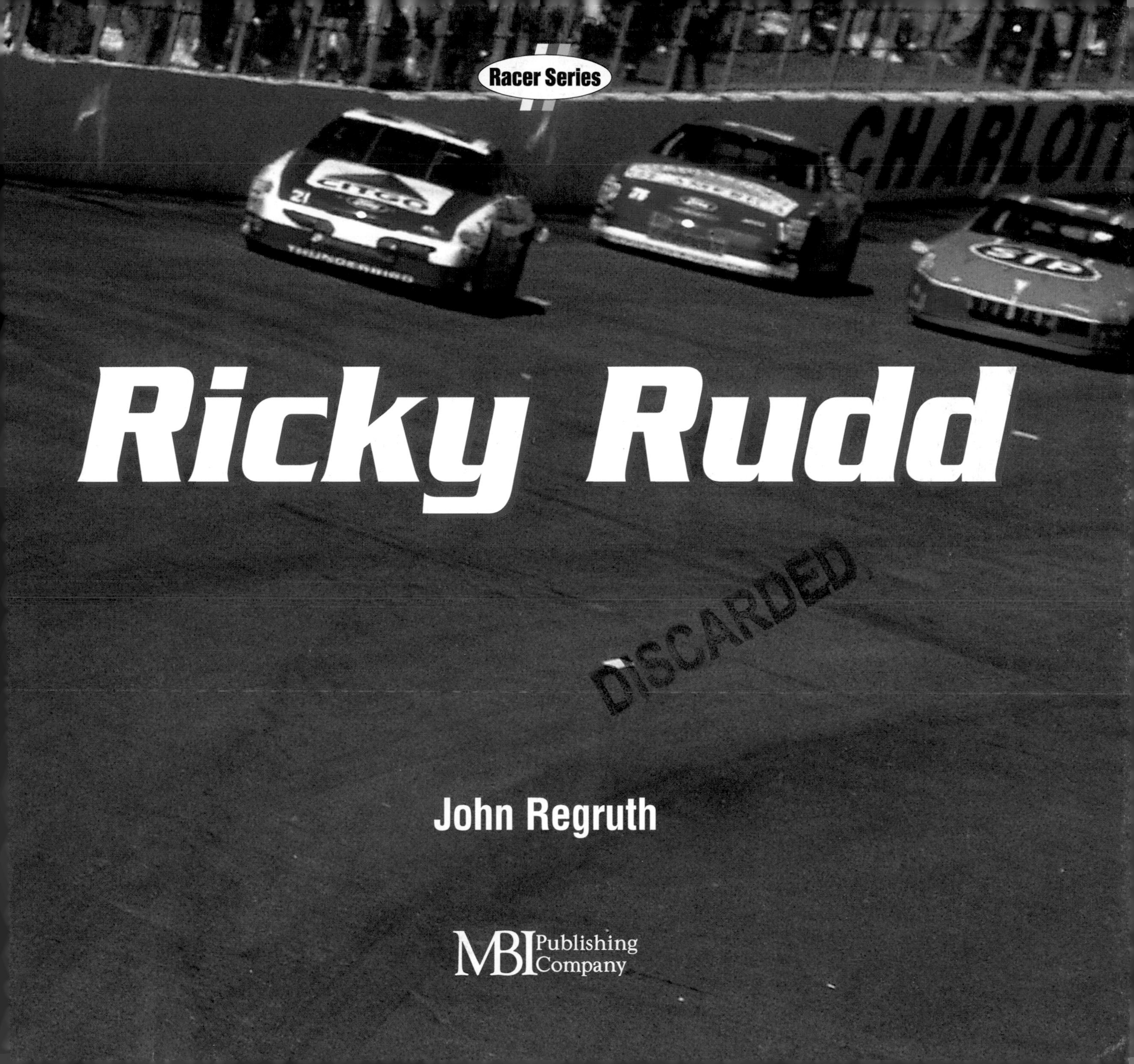

CHARLOTT

Ricky Rudd

John Regruth

MBI Publishing Company

First published in 2002 by MBI Publishing Company, Galtier Plaza, Suite 200, 380 Jackson Street, St. Paul, MN 55101-3885 USA

MBI Publishing Company books are also available at discounts in bulk quantity for industrial or sales-promotional use. For details write to Special Sales Manager at Motorbooks International Wholesalers & Distributors, Galtier Plaza, Suite 200, 380 Jackson Street, St. Paul, MN 55101-3885 USA.

Library of Congress Cataloging-in-Publication Data Available

ISBN 0-7603-1327-X

On the front cover 1: After walking away from car ownership in 1999, Ricky Rudd signed on with Robert Yates Racing, a move that put him back in a very competitive car and gave him one of his best seasons in 2000.

On the front cover 2: Rudd's determination and strength, which have carried him through decades of NASCAR competition, show through in this thoughtful shot from the Pennzoil 400 at Homestead-Miami Speedway in 2000.

On the frontispiece: A well-earned smile caught up with Rudd at the 1997 Brickyard 400--but no stock car driver did. He celebrates his biggest career victory to date with his wife, Linda.

On the title page: Racing his own car, which Tide's sponsorship made possible, Rudd leads the pack into a turn in the UAW/GM 500 at Pocono Raceway.

On the back cover: Drivers--especially owner-drivers, like Rudd--know that their pit crews are as important to the race's outcome as anything they do at the wheel. Here, Rudd's crew shakes a leg to get him back on the track at the Pop Secret Popcorn 400 at Rockingham in 1999.

Edited by Amy Glaser
Designed by Dan Perry

Printed in China

Contents

Quick Facts about Ricky Rudd's Winston Cup Career

Number of races run before 1st victory	161
Most consecutive victories	1 (22 times)
Most consecutive races without a victory (after getting first win)	89 (Race 27 of 1998 through Race 15 of 2001)
Most consecutive Top 5 finishes	5 (1981)
Most consecutive Top 10 finishes	8 (twice – 1979 & 2000)
Fewest points earned in a race	34 - twice (1998 at Rockingham, 1999 at Las Vegas)
Number times earned maximum 185 points	6 - 1983 (2 times), 1986 (2), 1987 (1), 1989 (1)
Most wins in a season	2 – 5 times (1983, 1986, 1987, 1997, 2001)
Most DNFs in a season	13 – 1982
Fewest DNFs in a season	1 (three times) – 1991, 1996, 2000
Largest single-race prize	$571,000 (1997 Brickyard 400)
Smallest single-race prize	$345 (1975 Gwyn Staley Memorial/North Wilkesboro)
Number of poles	27
Worst starting position	41st (4 times) - (1997 – DieHard 500/Talladega; 1998 – Pepsi 400/Daytona;1999 – Cracker Barrel 500/Atlanta; TranSouth Financial 400/Darlington)
Worst finish	43rd - twice (1998 Goodwrench Service 400/Rockingham, 1999 Las Vegas 400/Las Vegas)
Lowest position in point standings (full-time seasons only)	43rd (Week 2 – 1998)
Lowest finish in point standings (full-time seasons only)	31st – 1999
Number of times led the most laps	19 – 1981 (1 time), 1983 (2), 1984 (1), 1986 (3), 1987 (1), 1988 (3), 1989 (1), 1990 (1), 1991 (2), 1992 (1), 1993 (1), 1995 (1), 2000 (1)
Most laps led in a single race	380 of 500 (1983 Goody's 500/Martinsville)
Highest percentage of laps led, race	82.4 – 61 of 74 (1989 Banquet Frozen Foods 300/SearsPoint)
Most laps led in a season	871 (1983)
Least number of laps completed in a race	2 of 119 (1981 Winston Western 500/Riverside)
Tracks where Rudd has won	Atlanta, Darlington, Dover, Indianapolis, Martinsville, Michigan, New Hampshire, Phoenix, Pocono, Richmond, Riverside, Rockingham, Sears Point, Watkins Glen
Tracks where Rudd has not won	Bristol, California, Charlotte, Chicagoland, Daytona, Homestead, Kansas, Las Vegas, Nashville*, North Wilkesboro*, Ontario*, Talladega, Texas, Texas World*, Watkins Glen
Tracks where Rudd has won a pole	Bristol, Charlotte, Daytona, Dover, Indianapolis, Las Vegas, Martinsville, Nashville, North Wilkesboro, Pocono, Richmond, Riverside, Rockingham, Sears Point
Tracks where Rudd has not won a pole	Atlanta, California, Chicagoland, Darlington, Daytona, Homestead, Kansas, Michigan, New Hampshire, Ontario*, Phoenix, Talladega, Texas, Texas World*, Watkins Glen
Track where Rudd has won most often	Dover (4)
Track where Rudd won the most poles	Dover, Martinsville, Sears Point (4)
Most lucrative track, career	Daytona - $1,354,520
Worst-to-First: Worst starting spot in an eventual victory	29th (1995 Dura-Lube 500/Phoenix)
First-to-Worst: Worst finish after starting from the pole	30th (1999 Dura-Lube/Kmart 400/Rockingham)
Favorite starting spot in victories	4th (five victories)
No. of times won from the pole	1

* -- Tracks no longer on the Winston Cup schedule.

Career Overview

When Ricky Rudd signed to drive for Robert Yates in September 1999, it wasn't the first time the two NASCAR legends had crossed paths. Nearly 20 years earlier, in 1981, a young Yates—then the lead engine builder for the ultrapowerful DiGard Racing team—wooed a 24-year-old Rudd to drive the No. 88 Gatorade Chevy. It was the first breakthrough opportunity for Rudd, and he responded admirably by accumulating 14 Top 5s and 17 Top 10s in 31 starts and contending for the Winston Cup Grand National title. For six weeks he was second in the points, before a late-season slump dropped him to sixth in the final standings.

For Rudd, thanks to Yates' confidence, the 1981 season was a giant leap forward and a confirmation of the promise he had shown in lesser rides after joining the series in 1975. For Rudd's owners, however, it was a giant step backward. Jim and Bill Gardner, the brothers who directed the DiGard powerhouse, were irritable for a championship. Developing a talent such as Rudd's required time and patience—two traits in short supply at DiGard.

The Gardners watched their perpetually unhappy superstar driver, Darrell Waltrip, depart in late 1980 to take over Junior Johnson's vaunted No. 11 ride. Waltrip's escape left DiGard Racing in a lurch. The top drivers in the series were already under contract for the following season. With Waltrip, they had come within 11 points of winning a title (in 1979, losing to Richard Petty). As their relationship with Waltrip broke down irrevocably in October

1980, Rudd caught Yates' eye at Charlotte. Driving his dad's Chevrolet, Rudd earned a front row starting spot for the National 500. When the green flag fell, he kept the No. 22 Al Rudd entry in the Top 5 and finished a career-best fourth.

Yates couldn't help noticing, and wondering. If the top drivers—Bobby Allison, Earnhardt, Yarborough—were unavailable, why not get the hotshot youngster from Chesapeake, Virginia?

Unfortunately, Rudd never really had a chance with DiGard. The Gardners, afflicted with Junior Johnson-envy, watched Waltrip march to the 1981 championship, while Rudd was merely developing into a force. If Rudd had been given the opportunity to continue in the No. 88 car, he may well have become a perennial threat to win the title. Instead, the Gardners axed Rudd after a single season and lured Bobby Allison away from Harry Ranier's No. 28 team. Allison flourished with DiGard, winning eight races in 1982 and the 1983 Winston Cup championship.

The mix of personalities, politics and events left Rudd out in the cold—and professionally embarrassed. In terms of victories, he went 0-for-31 with DiGard in 1981, one season after Waltrip had won five times and one season before Allison won eight times. Rudd was the meatless middle in a DiGard sandwich.

Eighteen years later, when Yates came calling again, a similar combination of cars—the No. 28 and the No. 88—was involved. And, once again, Yates offered one of the best cars in the series. This time the relationship

was built on greater stability. Rudd signed a guaranteed three-year deal and immediately reestablished himself among the top drivers in the Winston Cup series, one year after dropping to a career-worst 31st in the final 1999 point standings.

In his first official drive in the No. 28 Yates Ford, Rudd won the outside pole for the 2000 Daytona 500. Though he didn't win a race in 2000—he came achingly close five times—he finished fifth in the final standings. In 2001, he chased Jeff Gordon for the title before slumping late in the year and dropping to fourth in the points.

Diverse Career

The twisting, turning racing relationship with Yates is a mere fraction of the Ricky Rudd

Ecstatic Tide crew members celebrate their driver's victory in the 1997 Brickyard 400.

Rudd and his wife, Linda, celebrate winning the 1997 Brickyard 400.

story. A national go-kart champion, motorcross ace, road course master and history-making stock car racer, Rudd can safely be called a natural born racer. At age 4, he eased along the streets near his house in a go-kart built by his dad. Before reaching his teens, he was driving greater than 100 miles per hour in his go-kart on winding road courses. At 18, he started his first Winston Cup Grand National race at Rockingham (where he finished 11th).

Since then, he has scratched, clawed, and struggled his way into one of the most remarkable careers in NASCAR history. Few drivers can point to as diverse an experience in major league stock car racing as Rudd. In his nearly three decades on the Winston Cup circuit, he has driven for NASCAR elders (Junie Donlavey, Bud Moore), up-and-comers (Richard Childress, Rick Hendrick), never-made-its (Kenny Bernstein), established powers (DiGard, Robert Yates Racing) and family cars (his own and his dad's). He has driven a Ford, a Chevy, a Pontiac, a Mercury and a Buick. He has competed against Allison, Yarborough, Petty, Parsons, Earnhardt, Richmond, Wallace, Gordon, and Stewart.

Along the way, Rudd has seen it all and made an impression. He gave Childress his first victory as an owner. He set an unbreakable qualifying record at Riverside—in the track's final NASCAR event. He was Rick Hendrick's best driver for three years, before Gordon took over. He was the best driver-owner in the 1990s, contending for championships more seriously than the other independents (save the late Alan Kulwicki). He has bullied and cheapshoted with the best, never letting Earnhardt or any others intimidate him.

The sheer length of Rudd's career—700-plus races over 20-plus seasons—has spawned some staggering facts. In the Modern Era (i.e., since 1972), 780 different drivers have participated in Winston Cup events. Rudd has competed against 560 of them. Only two of those drivers—Waltrip, and Dave Marcis—have started more races than Rudd in the Modern Era. In NASCAR history (since 1949), only Petty, Waltrip, and Marcis can claim more starts. Even more mind-boggling, Rudd has driven 260,000 miles during his career—excluding testing, practice and qualifying—and has completed nearly 212,000 laps. Only Waltrip has run more circles in the Modern Era.

Career Odyssey

It's impossible to imagine an 18-year-old Virginian beginning a similarly rich career today in the same manner as Rudd in 1975. Armed only with a few practice laps, his first Winston Cup Grand National start (at Rockingham) was also his first stock car race. His second stock car race came at Bristol, one of the toughest tracks on the circuit. Amazingly, he finished both races without serious damage to himself or his car.

As he had throughout his youth, Rudd relied on his family to support his racing endeavors. His father, Al, bankrolled his early NASCAR ventures—essentially buying his son rides in 1975, 1976, and 1977. The 1977 season was a Rudd family road show. Al acted as owner, while Ricky's brother, Al Jr., was lead engine builder and crew chief. Rudd's sister, Carolyn, was the team's secretary. The family's efforts paid off, although not financially—Rudd won the 1977 Rookie-of-the-Year Award and nearly $70,000 . . . about $50,000 less than his dad spent.

When Rudd's award-winning season failed to win over a sponsor for the 1978 season, an uncomfortable reality of NASCAR racing became all too clear: Sometimes, solid results don't guarantee opportunity. As the defending Rookie-of-the-Year, he competed in just 13 races during the 1978 season. In 1979, he caught a break by joining forces with Junie Donlavey—and becoming a driver-for-hire for the first time—but his strong performance (17 Top 10s, 9th in the point standings) was again met with indifference. He competed in only 13 races in 1980 while hopping in and out of four different cars.

Rudd's perseverance in the face of indifference finally yielded an opportunity, however, when Yates took notice at Charlotte in October 1980. Yates helped sign Rudd to drive for DiGard Racing in 1981 and formally launched Rudd's career. Rudd has raced in every Winston Cup event since the 1981 Daytona 500. (Rudd entered the 2002 season with 644 consecutive starts, putting him in position to break Terry Labonte's all-time record of 655 in May at Charlotte.) He followed his unceremonious dumping from DiGard by latching on with Richard Childress before the start of the 1982 season. Newly retired as a driver, Childress became a full-time owner in 1981 when he hired a young Dale Earnhardt. Childress was a remarkably unsuccessful driver, failing to win or even finish second in 285 races, although he certainly had an eye for talent.

When he lost Earnhardt to Bud Moore after the 1981 season, Childress turned to Rudd to pilot his No. 3 Pontiac. Rudd stayed for two seasons, and in 1983 at Riverside gave Childress his first victory as an owner. The win came in Rudd's 161st Winston Cup start. Twelve races later, he scored again at Martinsville. It was the beginning of 16-year consecutive winning season streak, a Modern Era-record, that would become Rudd's signature accomplishment.

Following the 1983 season, Rudd and Earnhardt switched teams. Earnhardt joined Childress and began a beautiful NASCAR relationship. The two tough customers would combine to win six championships over the next 11 seasons. Rudd, meanwhile, provided Moore with four of his best seasons as a NASCAR owner. In 116 races in Moore's No. 15 Ford, Rudd won 6 times, nabbed 5 poles, had 41 Top 5s and 65 Top 10s, and never finished worse than seventh in the final point standings.

Rudd's tenure with Moore included the worst wreck of his career. In his first official drive in the No. 15 car, the 1984 Busch Clash, Rudd was nudged by Jody Ridley coming off of Turn 4 of Daytona's high-banked, high-speed 2.5-mile oval. Losing control of his car as it headed into the tri-oval, Rudd survived a rolling wreck that saw his car flip end-over-end seven times. He escaped without serious injury, but suffered two black eyes and significant bruising and swelling to his face. (He wore a faceless helmet in those days.) Though his eyes were nearly swollen shut, Rudd returned from his harrowing accident two days

Rudd awaits the start of the 1997 Goody's 500 at Martinsville.

later and practiced at nearly 195 miles per hour. He finished the Daytona 500 in seventh place seven days later. Then, in one of the highlights of his career, he won at Richmond just 14 days after the Busch Clash wreck.

Rudd left Moore following the 1987 season, choosing to join the still-young operations run by Kenny Bernstein. Rudd was the third person to steer the No. 26 King Motorsports Chevy in three years. Though he was under the tutelage of ace crew chief Larry McReynolds, Rudd couldn't overcome the growing pains at King Motorsports. Unreliable equipment—he suffered 17 DNFs in two seasons with the No. 26 team, 15 of which were the result of engine or mechanical problems—ruined Rudd's chances on a weekly basis. His chances in the Winston Cup point

standings took a predictable hit. He fell to 11th place in the final standings in 1988, and improved slightly to 8th in 1989.

In 1990, driver shuffling involving Junior Johnson's No. 11 once again helped Rudd land one of the most competitive rides of his career. This time, Geoffrey Bodine's departure from the strong No. 5 Hendrick Motorsports team to join Johnson created opportunity. Rudd signed with Hendrick for the first of four successful seasons. Though Hendrick Motorsports had yet to find the championship form that would make its cars so formidable in the late 1990s, it was powerful nonetheless. Bodine—Hendrick's original driver—was strong in the No. 5, winning 7 races and 22 poles in six seasons.

Rudd drove the tie-dyed Tide car at Martinsville in 1999.

Joining Hendrick provided another novelty in Rudd's career: Teammates Darrell Waltrip and Kenny Schrader were the other drivers in Hendrick's stable in 1990. Though Waltrip and Schrader were two of the best drivers on the circuit, Rudd immediately became Hendrick's top gun. He finished the 1990 season 7th in the final standings, easily bettering Schrader (10th) and Waltrip (20th, thanks to a midseason injury). In fact, Rudd was the best Hendrick driver for three consecutive seasons, a longer stretch of excellence than any driver in HMS history until Jeff Gordon's run beginning in 1995.

The pinnacle of Rudd's career came in 1991, when he made his best run at the Winston Cup title. He led the series for the first and only time in his career early that season, going a full month as the Winston Cup points leader. Dale Earnhardt ultimately retook the lead and ran away with the championship. But for four glorious weeks, Rudd looked to the top of the points list for his name. Only two other times has he approached the top spot in the point standings. In 1981 with DiGard, he was second in points for six weeks before slipping to sixth.

In 2001, he chased Gordon for three months before dropping to fourth.

Though unquestionably some of his best seasons, Rudd never seemed to enjoy his time at Hendrick Motorsports. Being an old-school driver, he didn't warm to the idea of teammates. He scuffled with Schrader at Martinsville in 1990 while the two battled for the lead—knocking both out of contention for the win. When Gordon signed with Hendrick in 1992 and quickly became the pride of Hendrick Motorsports, Rudd wasted little time in developing what had been a fanciful idea—leaving the No. 5 Chevy and creating his own team. He announced his plans to create Rudd Performance Motorsports for the 1994 season in June of 1993—much earlier than most other "silly season" announcements. After leaving Hendrick, Rudd didn't hesitate to express his unhappiness with the multiteam concept and leaked details of rampant in-house fighting.

Rudd's displeasure with Hendrick included a general disdain for Gordon. In 1994 at Charlotte, after being driven hard into the third turn by Gordon, Rudd tailgated the young driver through the 1.5-mile track's trioval before sending him into the wall entering Turn 1. After the race, Rudd declared that his actions were intentional, prompting a $10,000 fine from NASCAR. Rudd reacted to the punishment by claiming NASCAR was protecting Gordon and apologizing only for the damaged cars. Then Rudd made the preposterous statement that Gordon's lack of talent caused the accident. The animosity lived on in 2001, when Rudd and Gordon fought for the championship. While Gordon regularly complimented Rudd's talent and professionalism—particularly after their classic battle at Michigan—Rudd noted only that Gordon's points lead was due to an ability to avoid bad luck. When Gordon officially clinched the title late in the season, Rudd declined to offer congratulations in his postrace comments, choosing instead to complain about engine problems and inconsiderate lapped cars.

Going It Alone

Freed from Hendrick Motorsports in 1994, Rudd appeared to be in solid position for a solo run. He had lured the lucrative Tide sponsorship away from Hendrick and was locked into a stable deal for six seasons. He had joined forces with Ford, agreeing to drive its competitive Thunderbird. And his crew, led by Bill Ingle, was stocked with trusted talent whom Rudd had gotten to know during his travels on the Winston Cup circuit over the previous 13 seasons. For three years, he was independent and at the top of his game. He finished a strong fifth in the point standings in 1994, then followed with sixth in 1996.

Rudd started losing his grip in 1997, however. He wasn't prepared for NASCAR's changing landscape. What appeared to be a solid foundation in 1994 turned out to be an ideal situation for the 1980s. In the 1990s, the Winston Cup series' powerhouses were no longer the independent "mom-and-pop" organizations, but were instead the multicar corporations. Led by Hendrick Motorsports and Gordon, multiteam organizations ascended. Information and resource sharing provided competitive advantage; Rudd had neither. Even worse, the Tide sponsorship that looked so promising in 1994 transformed into an out-dated business arrangement that handcuffed Rudd with low-ball sponsor dollars, when the costs of fielding a NASCAR team ballooned in the late 1990s. Working with a noncompetitive budget, he could no longer attract the kind of talent necessary to remain among the best. Thus began Rudd's slide. In 1997, he fell to 17th in the standings, followed by 22nd in 1998. He hit rock bottom in 1999 when he plummeted to 31st.

Two racing legends—Rudd and A.J. Foyt (right)—share a laugh at Indianapolis in 1996.

Rudd awaits the start of the Goodwrench 400 at Rockingham in 1997.

Rudd is one of just three Winston Cup drivers to win on all three of the Modern Era road courses—Watkins Glen, Sears Point, and Riverside. Geoffrey Bodine and Rusty Wallace also won on each.

Disadvantaged, but not blind, Rudd tried everything to keep his team operating. He looked to buy another team, start up his own multicar effort or merge with a moneyed partner—none of which materialized. When Tide announced its decision not to renew with Rudd, his chances of salvaging Rudd Performance Motorsports were doomed. In September 1999,

he signed to drive for Yates. In December, he sold off his equipment at auction and shut down RPM's operations.

The demise of his team, of course, turned out to be a blessing in disguise. Rudd has flourished since joining Robert Yates Racing. He has returned to winning races and poles, and even contending for the Winston Cup title.

Phases

Coloring the timeline of Rudd's career have been various phases and accomplishments. During the early 1980s, he was a terrific qualifier, winning 13 poles and starting an average 9th or better for 5 seasons between 1981 and 1985. His average start of 6.6 in 1983 was the best among all Winston Cup

Grand National drivers. His reputation shifted from qualifying to fighting and road course virtuosity in the late 1980s and early 1990s. His interest in Winston Cup road courses started at the now-defunct Riverside International Raceway in 1983, when he won his first Winston Cup race. But his right-turn mastery blossomed in 1987 when he set the all-time track qualifying record at Riverside despite nursing an injured left leg (suffered in a crash at Charlotte). His record will never be broken—it was the last NASCAR event at the track. A year later, he won for the first time at Watkins Glen International. In 1989, he won the inaugural race at Sears Point and became the first driver to win at all three Modern Era road courses. He won three straight poles at Sears Point and added another win at Watkins Glen in 1990. At one point, he won three of five non-oval races. Only Rusty Wallace could keep up with Rudd on the road courses.

While he was becoming a road warrior, Rudd also began developing a reputation as a street fighter. He got into memorable paint-trading battles with Joe Ruttman, Sterling Marlin, Brett Bodine, and Derrike Cope. His tussles with Earnhardt, however, remain the most unforgettable. At North Wilkesboro in the fall of 1988, Rudd bumped Earnhardt to make a pass for the lead with 50 laps to go; Earnhardt responded a lap later by spinning Rudd out. NASCAR sent the two to the back of the field, where they continued their skirmish. Despite the shared hostilities, Rudd received the punishment when NASCAR fined him $6,000 for rough driving. The following season, the fighting persisted. In the spring race at Rockingham, Earnhardt took out Rudd, who was leading the race and trying to put Earnhardt a lap down. Instead, Earnhardt sent his rival into the wall and a 32nd-place finish.

Later in 1989, however, Rudd got revenge at the end of the Holly Farms 400 at North

In six seasons as owner of the No. 10 Tide Ford, Rudd won six races and four poles.

Wilkesboro—and may have cost Earnhardt the 1989 championship. On the race's final lap, Rudd got underneath Earnhardt as they headed into Turn 1. Earnhardt came down on Rudd—or Rudd bumped into Earnhardt, depending on your point of view—and the two cars slid out of the racing groove. Immobilized, Earnhardt and Rudd were passed by the remaining eight cars on the lead lap, including Rusty Wallace, who slipped by to finish seventh. Rudd recovered to finish in ninth, while Earnhardt limped to 10th. As a result of the incident, Earnhardt lost ground to Wallace in the points race, dropping 37 points back, instead of regaining the lead by 12 points. That 49-point swing proved to be decisive when Earnhardt lost the championship by 12 points.

Following his 1991 run for the title and eventual departure from Hendrick Motorsports, Rudd entered his "Independent" phase. Unfortunately, his decision to field his own cars proved to be completely out of step with NASCAR's new economic reality. Rudd's self-ownership coincided with the Winston Cup series' massive consolidation during the mid-1990s. Fewer and fewer owners began to control more and more of the sponsor dollars flowing into the sport. Rudd, meanwhile, played the "little guy" to perfection. In essence, he became Dave Marcis (except Rudd actually won a few races). As his performance deteriorated under an inadequate sponsor budget, he routinely decried the advantage enjoyed by multicar giants like Hendrick and Roush. His run as the "Independent" culminated

The Tide crew tends to Rudd's car at Pocono in 1997.

with the June 1999 announcement by Procter & Gamble not to continue its sponsorship of the No. 10 Ford. Rudd reacted by calling for NASCAR to implement franchise protections for owners—a rule that ran counter to everything the sport espouses. If Rudd's idea had been in force in 1975, a certain 18-year-old from Virginia almost certainly would never have gotten his stock car career started.

The Big Moments

Rudd's rough-driving tendencies during the late 1980s contributed to one of the most controversial moments in NASCAR history. At Sears Point in 1991, he crossed the finish line first, but was awarded second place after Winston Cup officials determined that he had been "unnecessarily rough" while passing Davey Allison. With two laps to go in the Banquet Frozen Foods 300, Rudd bumped race-leader Allison in the track's tight Turn 11. Rudd's shot knocked Allison out of shape and allowed Rudd's No. 5 Tide Chevy to pass. Rudd took the lead as the white flag flew, but when he came around to the finish line, he was presented with the black flag instead of the checkered. Allison recovered and followed four seconds behind Rudd and was shown the checkered flag.

In an unprecedented move, NASCAR penalized Rudd five seconds—essentially giving the win to Allison and installing Rudd in the second position. Rudd claimed

a simple misjudgment of speed and bad brakes going into the fateful 11th turn as reasons for the contact. NASCAR, however, noted that the placement of Rudd's bump—in Allison's rear bumper, rather than his right-rear quarter panel—indicated malicious intent.

Even more unforgettable—and tragic—was Rudd's pit-road accident at Atlanta in 1990. In the season's final race at Atlanta, he lost control of his car as he entered pit road and spun into Bill Elliott's car, which was being tended to by his over-the-wall crew. Elliott's rear tire changer, Mike Rich, got caught in the tangle. He was rushed to a nearby hospital, but died a short time later of cardiac arrest. Also injured were Tommy Cole, the team's jackman, and Dan Elliott, Elliott's brother and front tire changer. Each survived the incident. The tragedy inspired NASCAR to experiment with its pit-road rules. Chief among the regulations that emerged from the accident was a pit-road speed limit.

NASCAR's enforcement of a pit-road speed limit played into the greatest highlight of Rudd's career—his victory in the 1997 Brickyard 400. In one of the biggest upsets in recent memory, he used fuel mileage to claim the richest victory of his career. Aiding his effort was a stop-and-go penalty imposed on Jeff Burton for speeding down pit road. Burton appeared to have the best car late in the race, but became a nonfactor after the penalty. Rudd took advantage and beat second-place Bobby Labonte to the line by two car lengths. His take from the Brickyard was $571,000—a single-race prize that exceeded his earnings from entire seasons earlier in his career. At the time, the check was the second largest prize ever handed out at a NASCAR event. (Jeff Gordon's 1994 Brickyard prize of $613,000 was the largest.)

Rudd had 60 Top 5s and 102 Top 10s in his first 187 starts on tracks measuring less than a mile.

What's Missing

Despite the successes and the unforgettable, exhilarating, and tragic moments, it's impossible to ignore the overriding question mark in Ricky Rudd's career: why hasn't he won a Winston Cup championship? The answer is somewhat understandable and partly uncomfortable. On the one hand, it is certainly true that for much of his career, Rudd has not occupied the driver's seat of a championship car. His years in the family car, with Junie Donlavey, Bud Moore, the young Richard Childress, Kenny Bernstein, and, ironically, his own Rudd Performance Motorsports—totaling 16 seasons—qualify as "noncompetitive"

years. The uncomfortable side of the answer is the fact that on three occasions, Rudd's ride became championship caliber shortly after his departure. Allison led DiGard Racing to a championship in 1983, two seasons after Rudd was let go. Earnhardt won a title in Childress' car in 1986, three seasons after switching rides with Rudd. In 1996, Terry Labonte drove the No. 5 Chevy to the championship three seasons after Rudd took off for his solo venture. In other words, while Rudd can point to less than favorable conditions, the uncomfortable reality is that three of Rudd's teams won titles shortly after he left.

Rudd's career is similarly barren when talk turns to NASCAR's major races. In his first 75 attempts to win the Daytona 500, the Coca-Cola 600 at Charlotte, and the Southern 500 at Darlington, he has been shut out. In fact, he has yet to finish second.

Ultimately, such questions miss the point. The bottom line is, Ricky Rudd is a racer, and a damn good one. His career includes accomplishments that few drivers can ever hope to achieve. Since his dad built that first go-kart for him at age four, all he's ever wanted to do is race. Nearly a half-century later, he's still at it—and doing it pretty well.

Career Statistics

A Statistical Breakdown of Ricky Rudd's Career Performance

The following section offers the bottom-line statistical view of Ricky Rudd's career. Year-by-year and career totals are listed, including wins, Top 5s, Top 10s, poles, average start and finish, DNFs, total championship and bonus points, points per race, total winnings, races led, percentage of laps led, and lead-lap finishes.

· Career Start-Finish Breakdown—A complete breakdown of Rudd's starts and finishes throughout his career
· Career Poles—A complete listing of Rudd's pole starts
· Career Wins—A complete listing of Rudd's victories
· Career Performance by Track—Rudd's career totals at each track, broken out by track type

Rudd ranks fourth all-time in the number of Winston Cup starts. Only Richard Petty, Dave Marcis, and Darrell Waltrip have started more races.

Ricky Rudd's Career Statistics

Year	Final Standing	Races Run	Wins	Top 5's	Top 10's	Poles	Avg. Start	Avg. Finish	DNF's	Total Points	Bonus Points	Points Per Race	Total Winnings	Races Led	Laps Led	Pct. Led	On Lead Lap	Miles Driven
1975	53rd	4	0	0	1	0	26.0	18.5	2	431	0	107.8	4,345	0	0	0.0	0	883
1976	56th	4	0	0	1	0	23.0	20.5	2	407	0	101.8	7,525	0	0	0.0	0	1,527
1977	17th	25	0	1	10	0	16.6	17.5	11	2,810	15	112.4	68,448	3	13	0.2	0	7,509
1978	32nd	13	0	0	4	0	16.5	22.8	7	1,264	25	97.2	49,610	5	16	0.4	0	4,327
1979	9th	28	0	4	17	0	11.5	12.1	6	3,642	20	130.1	146,302	4	22	0.2	1	9,917
1980	32nd	13	0	1	3	0	14.0	21.1	6	1,319	10	101.5	50,500	2	7	0.2	1	4,146
1981	6th	31	0	14	17	3	7.6	13.8	9	3,988	65	128.6	381,968	12	443	4.3	7	9,879
1982	9th	30	0	6	13	2	7.6	16.4	13	3,542	40	118.1	201,130	8	140	1.4	5	8,680
1983	9th	30	2	7	14	4	6.6	15.3	8	3,693	75	123.1	257,585	13	871	8.5	7	9,907
1984	7th	30	1	7	16	4	8.7	12.5	6	3,918	45	130.6	476,602	8	566	5.5	7	10,584
1985	6th	28	1	13	19	0	7.9	10.5	5	3,857	30	137.8	512,441	6	329	3.5	8	10,281
1986	5th	29	2	11	17	1	12.7	12.7	7	3,823	50	131.8	671,548	7	525	5.5	13	10,193
1987	6th	29	2	10	13	0	13.8	13.5	9	3,742	65	129.0	653,508	12	505	5.4	12	9,891
1988	11th	29	1	6	11	2	14.9	15.7	12	3,547	95	122.3	410,954	16	695	7.1	10	10,428
1989	8th	29	1	7	15	0	16.3	14.4	5	3,608	40	124.4	534,824	7	247	2.5	11	11,075
1990	7th	29	1	8	15	2	14.1	14.6	5	3,601	40	124.2	573,650	7	180	1.9	12	10,392
1991	2nd	29	1	9	17	1	12.0	9.5	1	4,092	75	141.1	1,093,765	13	425	4.4	11	11,427
1992	7th	29	1	9	18	1	9.5	13.3	4	3,735	50	128.8	793,903	9	331	3.4	11	10,269
1993	10th	30	1	9	14	0	10.9	15.5	6	3,644	40	121.5	752,562	7	136	1.4	11	10,265
1994	5th	31	1	6	15	1	17.1	12.3	2	4,050	50	130.6	1,044,441	10	192	1.9	14	12,046
1995	9th	31	1	10	16	2	11.2	16.0	6	3,734	60	120.5	1,337,703	11	368	3.7	13	10,834
1996	6th	31	1	5	16	0	20.5	14.6	1	3,845	60	124.0	1,503,025	12	150	1.55	13	11,400
1997	17th	32	2	6	11	0	20.3	20.6	6	3,330	15	104.1	1,975,981	3	72	0.7	13	11,623
1998	22nd	33	1	1	5	0	20.2	23.2	7	3,131	20	94.9	1,602,895	4	256	2.6	9	11,590
1999	31st	34	0	3	5	1	20.3	26.2	7	2,922	15	85.9	1,632,011	3	21	0.2	8	12,033
2000	5th	34	0	12	19	2	12.7	11.5	1	4,575	75	134.6	2,974,970	14	362	3.6	24	13,011
2001	4th	36	2	14	22	1	13.1	13.2	4	4,706	80	130.7	4,878,027	16	569	5.2	26	13,846
Totals		**731**	**22**	**179**	**344**	**27**	**13.6**	**15.4**	**158**	**88,956**	**1,155**	**121.7**	**24,590,223**	**212**	**7,441**	**3.1**	**247**	**257,963**

Career Start Breakdown

Career Finish Breakdown

Career Start Breakdown				Career Start Statistics		
Pos. Pole	No. of Starts	Pct.		Total Races	731	
1	27	3.69		Average Start	13.6	
2	42	5.75		Front Row (Pct.)	69	(9.4)
3	31	4.24		Top 5	170	(23.3)
4	40	5.47		Top 10	335	(45.8)
5	30	4.10		Top 20	570	(78.0)
6	34	4.65		Top 30	670	(91.7)
7	40	5.47		Pos. 31 - 43	61	(8.3)
8	34	4.65				
9	26	3.56				
10	31	4.24				
11	25	3.42				
12	20	2.74				
13	40	5.47				
14	35	4.79				
15	23	3.15				
16	21	2.87				
17	17	2.33				
18	24	3.28				
19	12	1.64				
20	18	2.46				
21	15	2.05				
22	17	2.33				
23	11	1.50				
24	7	0.96				
25	15	2.05				
26	9	1.23				
27	9	1.23				
28	6	0.82				
29	6	0.82				
30	5	0.68				
31	5	0.68				
32	3	0.41				
33	12	1.64				
34	10	1.37				
35	8	1.09				
36	5	0.68				
37	5	0.68				
38	2	0.27				
39	6	0.82				
40	1	0.14				
41	4	0.55				
42	0	--				
43	0	--				

Career Finish Breakdown				Career Finish Statistics		
Pos. Win	No. of Finishes	Pct.		Average Finish	15.4	
1	22	3.01		Top 2 (Pct.)	49	(6.7)
2	27	3.69		Top 5	179	(24.5)
3	41	5.61		Top 10	344	(47.1)
4	49	6.70		Top 20	489	(66.9)
5	40	5.47		Top 30	630	(86.2)
6	36	4.92		Pos. 31 - 43	101	(13.8)
7	35	4.79		DNFs	158	(21.6)
8	34	4.65				
9	30	4.10				
10	30	4.10				
11	28	3.83				
12	17	2.33				
13	19	2.60				
14	21	2.87				
15	12	1.64				
16	10	1.37				
17	7	0.96				
18	9	1.23				
19	15	2.05				
20	7	0.96				
21	12	1.64				
22	11	1.50				
23	12	1.64				
24	15	2.05				
25	16	2.19				
26	11	1.50				
27	19	2.60				
28	21	2.87				
29	10	1.37				
30	14	1.92				
31	18	2.46				
32	11	1.50				
33	4	0.55				
34	10	1.37				
35	5	0.68				
36	9	1.23				
37	10	1.37				
38	7	0.96				
39	6	0.82				
40	6	0.82				
41	8	1.09				
42	5	0.68				
43	2	0.27				

Listing of Ricky Rudd's Career Pole Starts

Year	Career Race	Pole No.	Track - Race	Speed	Fin.
1981	96	1	Martinsville -- Virginia 500	89.056	3
	98	2	Nashville -- Melling Tool 420	104.409	5
	112	3	Dover -- CRC Chemicals 500	136.757	5
1982	142	4	Dover -- CRC Chemicals 500	139.384	11
	145	5	Martinsville -- Old Dominion 500	89.132	2
1983	149	6	Daytona -- Daytona 500	198.864	24
	150	7	Richmond -- Richmond 400	93.439	28
	151	8	Rockingham -- Warner W. Hodgdon Carolina 500	143.413	6
	155	9	Martinsville -- Virginia National Bank 500	89.910	5
1984	183	10	Bristol -- Valleydale 500	111.390	6
	184	11	North Wilkesboro -- Northwestern Bank 400	113.487	3
	189	12	Dover -- Budweiser 500	140.807	8
	195	13	Nashville -- Pepsi 420	104.120	16
1986	246	14	Dover -- Budweiser 500	138.217	4
1988	302	15	Martinsville -- Pannill Sweatshirts 500	91.328	18
	306	16	Riverside -- Budweiser 400[1]	118.484	3
1990	354	17	Richmond -- Pontiac Excitement 400	119.617	3
	364	18	Sears Point -- Banquet Frozen Foods 300	99.743	3
1991	393	19	Sears Point -- Banquet Frozen Foods 300	90.634	2
1992	422	20	Sears Point -- SaveMart 300	90.985	4
1994	498	21	Rockingham -- AC Delco 500	157.099	4
1995	510	22	Sears Point -- SaveMart Supermarkets 300	92.132	4
	528	23	Charlotte -- UAW-GM Quality 500	180.578	4
1999	629	24	Rockingham -- Dura-Lube/Big Kmart 400	157.241	30
2000	664	25	Las Vegas -- Cardirect.com 400	172.563	12
	681	26	Indianapolis -- Brickyard 400	181.068	21
2001	710	27	Pocono -- Pocono 500	170.503	1

1 -- Denotes track record

Pole Statistics

No. of Poles	27
Avg. Finished after Pole Starts	8.70
Wins from the Pole	1
No. of Track Records	1
Fastest Pole Speed	198.864
Slowest Pole Speed	89.056

Year	Career Race	No.	Track - Race	Start Pos.	Laps/Led	Pct. Led	Money
1983	161	1	Riverside -- Budweiser 400	4	95/57	60.0	24,530
	173	2	Martinsville -- Goody's 500	2	500/380	76.0	31,395
1984	180	3	Richmond -- Miller High Life 400	4	400/36	9.0	31,775
1985	236	4	Riverside -- Winston Western 500	4	119/27	22.7	37,875
1986	244	5	Martinsville -- Sovran Bank 500	4	500/163	32.6	40,850
	259	6	Dover -- Delaware 500	11	500/141	28.2	51,500
1987	269	7	Atlanta -- Motorcraft Quality Parts 500	6	328/7	2.1	62,400
	288	8	Dover -- Delaware 500	13	500/373	74.6	54,550
1988	312	9	Watkins Glen -- The Bud at the Glen	6	90/4	4.4	49,625
1989	335	10	Sears Point -- Banquet Frozen Foods 300	4	74/61	82.4	62,350
1990	370	11	Watkins Glen -- The Bud at the Glen	12	90/20	22.2	55,000
1991	386	12	Darlington -- TranSouth 500	13	367/69	18.8	62,185
1992	433	13	Dover -- Peak AntiFreeze 500	6	500/32	6.4	64,965
1993	453	14	Michigan -- Miller Genuine Draft 400	2	200/19	9.5	77,890
1994	485	15	New Hampshire -- Slick 50 300	3	300/55	18.3	91,875
1995	530	16	Phoenix -- Dura-Lube 500K	29	312/63	20.2	78,260
1996	560	17	Rockingham -- AC Delco 400	2	393/81	20.6	90,025
1997	574	18	Dover -- Miller 500	13	500/31	6.2	95,255
	581	19	Indianapolis -- Brickyard 400	7	160/15	9.4	571,000
1998	621	20	Martinsville -- NAPA Autocare 500	2	500/198	39.6	102,575
2001	710	21	Pocono -- Pocono 500	1	200/23	11.5	158,427
	721	22	Richmond -- Chevrolet Monte Carlo 400	9	400/88	22.0	158,427

Mixing it up on the track has been a Rudd hallmark. In his long career, he has had intense battles with Joe Ruttman, Dale Earnhardt, Brett Bodine, Derrike Cope, Sterling Marlin, Rusty Wallace, and Kevin Harvick.

Victory Statistics

No. of Victories	22
Avg. Starting Pos.	7.14
Favorite Starting Spot in Victories	4 (5 times)
Total Victory Earnings	$2,052,734
Laps Led (Pct.)	1,943 (27.65)
Fewest Laps Led in a Win	4
Most Laps Led in a Win	380
Highest Pct. Led	82.4
Lowest Pct. Led	2.1

Ricky Rudd's Career Performance on Current and Former Winston Cup Tracks

Track	Track Length	No. of Races	Wins	Win Pct.	Top 5s	Top 10s	Poles	Avg. Start	Avg. Finish	DNFs	Total Winnings	Races Led	Laps Led	Pct. Led	Total Points	Points/ Race
Short Tracks																
Bristol	.533	48	0	0.0	13	28	1	12.5	13.1	11	$1,016,990	9	604	2.6	6,158	128.3
Martinsville	.526	45	3	6.7	12	17	4	10.6	15.6	11	980,499	17	1,569	7.0	5,490	122.0
Nashville	.596	12	0	0.0	5	8	2	7.4	10.8	2	55,275	2	246	4.9	1,628	135.7
N. Wilkesboro	.625	36	0	0.0	11	23	1	11.1	10.1	4	415,675	9	653	4.5	4,987	138.5
Richmond	.750	46	2	4.3	19	26	2	14.7	12.1	7	1,121,229	15	762	4.2	6,135	133.4
Short Track Totals		**187**	**5**	**2.7**	**60**	**102**	**10**	**12.0**	**12.7**	**35**	**$3,589,668**	**52**	**3,834**	**4.6**	**24,398**	**130.5**
1-mile Ovals																
Dover	1.0	47	4	8.5	14	26	4	11.8	13.0	11	$1,287,644	16	935	4.1	6,105	129.9
New Hampshire	1.058	14	1	7.1	6	9	0	19.4	13.7	2	819,194	3	123	2.9	1,787	127.6
Phoenix	1.0	14	1	7.1	3	5	0	13.4	18.9	2	537,452	5	387	9.0	1,562	111.6
Rockingham	1.017	49	1	2.0	12	19	3	10.7	16.5	14	1,033,430	17	478	2.1	5,806	118.5
1-mile Oval Totals		**124**	**7**	**5.6**	**35**	**59**	**7**	**12.4**	**15.1**	**29**	**$3,677,720**	**41**	**1,923**	**3.6**	**15,260**	**123.1**
Speedways (less than 2 miles)																
Atlanta	1.54	48	1	2.1	7	22	0	17.3	16.0	10	$1,062,909	11	94	0.6	5,695	118.6
Charlotte	1.5	51	0	0.0	8	24	1	16.8	15.8	8	1,256,699	8	255	1.4	6,072	119.1
Chicagoland	1.5	1	0	0.0	1	1	0	3.0	3.0	0	112,600	1	25	9.4	170	170.0
Darlington	1.366	50	1	2.0	7	25	0	14.5	15.8	12	986,753	15	239	1.4	5,971	119.4
Homestead-Miami	1.5	3	0	0.0	0	1	0	6.3	22.7	1	201,322	1	49	6.1	295	98.3
Las Vegas	1.5	4	0	0.0	0	0	1	19.8	21.5	1	306,522	1	1	0.0	399	99.8
Kansas	1.5	1	0	0.0	1	1	0	8.0	3.0	0	138,947	1	20	0.1	170	170.0
Texas	1.5	5	0	0.0	1	2	0	17.6	19.6	2	606,197	2	35	2.1	539	107.8
Speedway Totals		**163**	**2**	**1.2**	**25**	**76**	**2**	**16.0**	**16.1**	**34**	**$4,671,949**	**40**	**718**	**1.3**	**19,311**	**118.5**
SuperSpeedways (2 miles or greater)																
California	2.0	5	0	0.0	2	3	0	21.4	13.0	1	$373,747	2	12	1.0	655	131.0
Daytona	2.5	50	0	0.0	6	20	1	17.9	17.0	11	2,125,288	12	46	0.5	5,749	115.0
Indianapolis	2.5	8	1	12.5	1	3	1	14.8	17.3	1	1,278,297	3	33	2.6	927	115.9
Michigan	2.0	50	1	2.0	9	21	0	13.8	17.9	13	1,115,096	16	344	3.5	5,679	113.6
Ontario, CA	2.0	2	0	0.0	0	2	0	12.0	9.0	0	11,375	2	4	1.0	286	143.0
Pocono	2.5	45	1	2.2	9	20	1	11.2	16.4	10	1,104,379	12	132	1.5	5,319	118.2
Talladega	2.66	50	0	0.0	9	12	0	16.9	20.3	15	1,063,326	10	79	0.8	5,258	105.2
Texas World	2.0	2	0	0.0	0	0	0	9.0	26.0	2	8,550	0	0	0.0	170	85.0
Superspeedway Totals		**212**	**3**	**1.4**	**36**	**81**	**3**	**15.1**	**17.8**	**53**	**$7,080,058**	**57**	**650**	**1.6**	**24,043**	**113.4**
Road Courses																
Riverside, CA	2.63	16	2	12.5	8	9	1	5.9	13.8	4	$225,500	9	147	8.6	2,094	130.9
Sears Point	1.99	13	1	7.7	8	9	4	6.7	11.3	1	554,937	6	114	10.2	1,801	138.5
Watkins Glen	2.45	16	2	12.5	7	8	0	10.1	14.1	2	520,857	7	55	3.9	2,049	128.1
Road Course Totals		**45**	**5**	**11.1**	**23**	**26**	**5**	**7.6**	**13.2**	**7**	**$1,301,294**	**22**	**316**	**7.5**	**5,944**	**132.1**

Ricky Rudd has made himself comfortable on NASCAR's short tracks. Through 2001, he had more Top 5s, Top 10s, poles, and laps led on short tracks than any other track type. His average finish in 187 starts at Bristol, Martinsville, Nashville, North Wilkesboro, and Richmond is also tops among the different track configurations in Winston Cup racing.

The trend that developed in Rudd's long career is relatively simple: The closer the short track is to Rudd's hometown of Chesapeake, Virginia, the better his performance. Richmond, the closest of the five tracks, has been Rudd's steadiest oval. When track owner Paul Sawyer introduced the new Richmond International Raceway in September 1988, Rudd's performance became even more consistent. He has more Top 5s at Richmond than any other track.

Virginia's other short track—Martinsville Speedway—was the site of Rudd's first-ever oval victory in 1983. Three months after getting win No. 1 on the road course at Riverside International Raceway, he piloted Richard Childress' No. 3 Chevy to Victory Lane at Martinsville. The .526-mile track was also the site of his first career pole in 1981 and his stirring 1998 victory, which set a new Modern Era record for consecutive winning seasons (16).

Bristol, located near the Tennessee-Virginia line, has accounted for more Top 10s in Rudd's career (28) than any other track. Along with North Wilkesboro, another consistently solid Rudd track, Bristol was the stage for some of the veteran's fiercest on-track fights. Legendary battles with Dale Earnhardt, Sterling Marlin, and Brett Bodine marked Rudd as a lesser-known Intimidator.

Nashville, meanwhile, proved that even away from home, Rudd was comfortable racing nose-to-tail with stock car racing's biggest names. He won two poles at the Tennessee half-mile and on more than one occasion showed he could keep up with the greats.

Short Track Stats Chart

Short Track Record Book - Modern Era (min. 25 starts)

Category	Rudd's Total	Rudd's Rank	Modern Era Short Track Leader
Starts	187	5th	Darrell Waltrip -- 225
Total Points[1]	24,398	4th	Darrell Waltrip -- 31,149
Avg. Start	12.0	19th	Cale Yarborough -- 4.1
Avg. Finish	12.7	13th	Cale Yarborough -- 6.4
Wins	5	12th	Darrell Waltrip -- 47
Winning Pct.	2.7	26th	Cale Yarborough -- 35.4
Top 5s	60	8th	Darrell Waltrip -- 113
Top 10s	102	6th	Darrell Waltrip -- 141
DNFs	35	6th	J.D. McDuffie -- 61
Poles	10	7th	Darrell Waltrip -- 35
Front Row Starts	20	9th	Darrell Waltrip -- 57
Laps Led	3,834	8th	Darrell Waltrip -- 14,840
Pct. Laps Led	4.6	16th	Cale Yarborough -- 37.6
Races Led	52	9th	Darrell Waltrip -- 133
Times Led	114	7th	Darrell Waltrip -- 343
Times Led Most Laps	10	6th	Darrell Waltrip -- 37
Bonus Points[1]	310	8th	Darrell Waltrip -- 840
Laps Completed	75,285	4th	Darrell Waltrip -- 92,033
Pct. Laps Completed	90.1	23rd	Bobby Labonte -- 95.8
Points per Race[1]	130.5	13th	Cale Yarborough -- 157.9
Lead-Lap Finishes	65	4th	Darrell Waltrip—101

[1] -- Since implementation of current point system in 1975

Short Track Definition

What is a short track?

A short track is an oval track measuring less than 1 mile in length.

Which tracks are short tracks?

Bristol
Martinsville
Nashville*
North Wilkesboro*
Richmond

* -- No longer on the Winston Cup schedule

On Winston Cup short tracks, Rudd has 5 victories and 10 poles.

Rudd on the 1-Mile Ovals

Barring early retirement or other unforeseen developments, Ricky Rudd will become the most prolific driver in Modern Era history on 1-mile ovals. If his performance remains steady, he should take over most of the "longevity" records—starts, total points, and laps completed. With a little luck, he may also take over one of the "performance" records, too; with 9 more Top 10s, he'll break Dale Earnhardt's Modern Era record of 68.

Rudd's imminent arrival at the top of the heap is not all that surprising. One-mile ovals are his best track configuration—this side of road courses, of course—and have been throughout his three-decade career. His seven victories on one-milers is tops in his career for any track type. His most successful 1-mile track is Dover, where he has four wins and four poles. Whether asphalt or concrete, the Delaware track has been receptive to Rudd's driving style.

New Hampshire has been a bigger Martinsville for Rudd, and his performance has been similar to that on the tiny Virginia short track. He showed early strength with four Top 10s and a win in NHIS's first four Winston Cup races—then cooled off. With Robert Yates Racing, Rudd's fancy for the New England track has returned. He nearly won the summer race in 2001 before being upstaged by teammate Dale Jarrett.

Phoenix, meanwhile, is Rudd's "What Might Have Been" track. He was good enough to win there five times, but only visited Victory Lane in 1995. His other chances to win have been offset by countervailing, and sometimes bizarre luck. A blown engine denied him a win in 1988, while bad pit stops hurt his finishes in 1994 and 1999. The worst of his luck came in 2001, when he got caught up in a wreck between lapped cars, preventing a sure victory.

Rudd willed his way to a victory at Rockingham simply by ignoring his crew. He skipped pit road during the final caution in the 1996 fall race and held off the rest of the field on old tires to win. It was his only win at the Rock, the track where his career got started in 1975. Rudd has seen a lot since that first race. He was 18 years old when he strapped into a stock car for the very first time. Whatever he learned that day stuck. Now in his late 40s, he is on the verge of becoming one of the most durable NASCAR drivers ever.

One-Mile Oval Stats Chart

One Mile Oval Record Book - All-Time (min. 25 starts)

Category	Rudd's Total	Rudd's Rank	All-Time One Mile Oval Leader
Starts	124	2nd	Darrell Waltrip -- 133
Total Points[1]	15,260	2nd	Dale Earnhardt -- 15,405
Avg. Start	12.4	16th	David Pearson -- 5.1
Avg. Finish	15.1	13th	Cale Yarborough -- 11.1
Wins	7	8th	Jeff Gordon -- 11
Winning Pct.	5.6	18th	David Pearson -- 31
Top 5s	35	4th	Dale Earnhardt -- 39
Top 10s	59	2nd	Dale Earnhardt -- 68
DNFs	29	5th	J.D. McDuffie -- 43
Poles	7	5th	M. Martin, R. Wallace -- 11
Front Row Starts	13	4th	Mark Martin -- 19
Laps Led	1,923	16th	Cale Yarborough -- 4,951
Pct. Laps Led	3.6	20th	David Pearson -- 25.9
Races Led	41	6th	Dale Earnhardt -- 63
Times Led	87	14th	Dale Earnhardt -- 181
Times Led Most Laps	3	16th	Cale Yarborough -- 13
Bonus Points[1]	220	7th	Dale Earnhardt -- 350
Laps Completed	47,730	2nd	Darrell Waltrip -- 53,580
Pct. Laps Completed	88.5	23rd	Jeff Gordon -- 95.5
Points per Race[1]	123.1	12th	Cale Yarborough -- 139.7
Lead-Lap Finishes	34	6th	Mark Martin -- 50

[1] -- Since implementation of current point system in 1975

One-Mile Oval Definition

Which tracks are one-mile ovals?

Dover
New Hampshire
Phoenix
Rockingham

On Winston Cup 1-mile ovals, Rudd has seven wins and seven poles.

As the tracks get longer in NASCAR, the driver often appears to be the lesser factor in a winning car. Aerodynamics, horsepower, chassis setups—the factors that can be purchased—become ascendant on Winston Cup ovals measuring greater than a mile. For Ricky Rudd, this tendency has always played to his weakness. Rarely the occupant of a dominant car, he has relied on skill, experience, luck, and guile to earn top finishes. On NASCAR's speedways, wins and top finishes have been difficult to secure.

Rudd's speedway performance counterbalances his stepped-up effort on road courses, short tracks, and 1-mile ovals (on which he has 17 wins). In his first 163 races on tracks between a mile and 2 miles in length, he has just 2 wins. His difficulty on speedways is best illustrated by his career at Lowe's Motor Speedway in Charlotte, where he owns the Modern Era record for most starts without a victory (51).

Rudd's two wins were typical of his reliance on external factors falling into order. At Darlington, he won in 1991 after Michael Waltrip, who dominated, was stopped by an extra long pit stop and Davey Allison had to visit pit road out of sequence for a final splash of gas. At Atlanta in 1987, Rudd took the checkered flag after leading just seven laps (the second fewest laps led by a winner in the track's Modern Era history). He was the beneficiary of Dale Earnhardt's late-race mechanical problems and a late caution that bunched up the field.

Now that Rudd can draw from the deep pockets of Robert Yates Racing, his long-track performance may pick up. For one of the few times in his career, he can count on the kind of top-notch backing from chassis specialists, engine experts and research and development engineers that other top drivers have enjoyed for years. As if to show what may lie in store, he celebrated his second year with Yates by scoring 6 Top 10s in 10 speedway races during the 2001 season.

Speedways Stat Chart

Speedway Record Book - Modern Era (min. 25 starts)

Category	Rudd's Total	Rudd's Rank	Modern Era Speedway Leader
Starts	163	2nd	Darrell Waltrip -- 175
Total Points[1]	19,314	3rd	Bill Elliott -- 20,287
Avg. Start	16.0	22nd	David Pearson -- 4.4
Avg. Finish	16.1	14th	Dale Earnhardt -- 12.0
Wins	2	20th	Dale Earnhardt -- 23
Winning Pct.	1.2	32nd	Jeff Gordon -- 20.3
Top 5s	25	16th	Dale Earnhardt -- 61
Top 10s	76	3rd	Dale Earnhardt -- 83
DNFs	33	14th	Dave Marcis -- 68
Poles	2	24th	David Pearson -- 25
Front Row Starts	8	17th	David Pearson -- 35
Laps Led	718	25th	Dale Earnhardt -- 6,818
Pct. Laps Led	1.3	34th	David Pearson -- 15.1
Races Led	40	19th	Dale Earnhardt -- 90
Times Led	70	21st	Dale Earnhardt -- 362
Times Led Most Laps	2	24th	Dale Earnhardt -- 24
Bonus Points[1]	210	17th	Dale Earnhardt -- 570
Laps Completed	49,500	2nd	Darrell Waltrip -- 51,148
Pct. Laps Completed	89.8	15th	Tony Stewart -- 96.7
Points per Race[1]	118.5	15th	Dale Earnhardt -- 136.7
Lead-Lap Finishes	40	8th	Dale Earnhardt—68

[1] -- Since implementation of current point system in 1975

Speedway Definition

What is a speedway?
A speedway is a track longer than 1 mile, but shorter than 2 miles.

Which tracks are speedways?
Atlanta
Charlotte
Chicagoland
Darlington
Homestead-Miami
Las Vegas
Kansas
Texas

On Winston Cup speedways, Rudd has two wins and two poles.

Rudd on the SuperSpeedways

Ricky Rudd has been around for a long time. NASCAR's big tracks—the superspeedways—have sometimes made it feel even longer. The superspeedways are Rudd's least successful track type, though the sky's turned brighter now that he's with the powerful Robert Yates Racing team. With just 3 wins in 212 starts, the Winston Cup series' biggest tracks have given the veteran driver his biggest headaches.

Talladega and Daytona have been the most difficult ovals for Rudd. Through 2001, he raced at the two fast tracks a combined 100 times without scoring a victory—an amazing feat, considering Rudd's competitiveness over the years. Restrictor plates, introduced in 1988, had no effect on his luck. He was 0-for-44 before the speed-limiting device was imposed by NASCAR, and 0-for-56 after. What's more amazing than his winless streak? He hasn't even finished second. Rudd's best finish at both tracks is third.

At Michigan and Pocono, Rudd can happily point to victories—he's got one at each track, though he has been in position to win more often. Five times at Michigan, some kind of mishap or turn of events has diverted a potential visit to Victory Lane. His most recent near-miss produced one of the best MIS races in recent memory. Rudd and Jeff Gordon traded the lead on the white flag lap of the Kmart 400, with Gordon pulling ahead, thanks to a strong move on the outside in Turn 1. The loss marked the seventh time Rudd had just missed winning his first race with Yates.

A week later, he finally secured that victory at Pocono. Rudd passed his teammate, Dale Jarrett, to take the popular win—the No. 28 car's first in nearly four years and Rudd's first in almost three. It was fitting that he experienced his breakthrough at Pocono. Rudd can safely say he is one of the best Winston Cup drivers to race at the 2.5-mile Pennsylvania track. While not a repeat winner, he has been consistently good, and ranks fourth in track history in Top 10 finishes.

Perhaps the best superspeedways news for Rudd has been the introduction of Indianapolis and California to the Winston Cup schedule. He has successfully transferred his strength at Michigan to the new 2-mile track in Fontana, California. In his first five starts at California, he has two Top 5 finishes, but was strong in all five races. Indianapolis, meanwhile, supplied the biggest victory of Rudd's career. His improbable Brickyard 400 win in 1997—which he earned through fuel mileage and smart track-position strategy—created the largest payday in his life: $571,000. That single-race sum was greater than his earnings in seven different seasons and was a far cry from the check he received after his first race at North Wilkesboro in 1975: $345.

SuperSpeedways Stats Chart

Superspeedway Record Book - Modern Era (min. 25 starts)

Category	Rudd's Total	Rudd's Rank	Modern Era Superspeedway Leader
Starts	208	3rd	Darrell Waltrip -- 213
Total Points[1]	23,587	4th	Bill Elliott -- 25,176
Avg. Start	15.2	19th	David Pearson -- 7.1
Avg. Finish	17.8	24th	Jeff Gordon -- 11.0
Wins	3	21st	Dale Earnhardt -- 18
Winning Pct.	1.4	33rd	David Pearson -- 22.7
Top 5s	36	14th	Dale Earnhardt -- 70
Top 10s	79	5th	Dale Earnhardt -- 114
DNFs	51	4th	Dave Marcis -- 64
Poles	3	25th	Bill Elliott -- 23
Front Row Starts	18	5th	Bill Elliott -- 41
Laps Led	646	21st	Dale Earnhardt -- 3,754
Pct. Laps Led	1.6	32nd	Jeff Gordon -- 17.2
Races Led	55	18th	Dale Earnhardt -- 122
Times Led	86	24th	Dale Earnhardt -- 505
Times Led Most Laps	2	22nd	Dale Earnhardt -- 22
Bonus Points[1]	290	16th	Dale Earnhardt -- 720
Laps Completed	34,500	3rd	Darrell Waltrip -- 34,703
Pct. Laps Completed	87.0	39th	Jeremy Mayfield -- 95.7
Points per Race[1]	113.4	25th	Jeff Gordon -- 142.1
Lead-Lap Finishes	78	7th	Dale Earnhardt -- 108

[1] -- Since implementation of current point system in 1975

SuperSpeedway Definition

What is a SuperSpeedway?

A SuperSpeedway in an oval measuring 2 miles or greater in length

Which tracks are SuperSpeedways?

California Speedway
Daytona International Speedway
Indianapolis Motor Speedway
Michigan International Speedway
Ontario (Calif.) Motor Speedway*
Pocono Raceway
Talladega SuperSpeedway
Texas World Speedway*

* -- No longer on the Winston Cup schedule

On Winston Cup superspeedways, Rudd has three wins and three poles.

In any short list of great Winston Cup road course racers—Bobby Allison, Darrell Waltrip, Geoffrey Bodine, Mark Martin, Rusty Wallace, Terry Labonte, Jeff Gordon, and Tim Richmond spring immediately to mind—the name Ricky Rudd must be inserted. Rudd revealed a natural ability for right-hand turns when he finally got a chance to race at Riverside in 1981. He raced 87 times over a six-year period before getting his first shot at a road course with DiGard Racing. He made the most of his first opportunity, qualifying third, and leading 19 laps before dropping out with engine trouble. Two years later, he won for the first time in his career at Riverside.

As his skills developed rapidly—and NASCAR added Watkins Glen in 1986 and Sears Point in 1989—Rudd became a dominant road course force. In the 10 road course events between 1988 and 1992, he won three times, had four poles, and finished in the Top 5 seven times. With two wins each at Riverside and Watkins Glen, and his win in the inaugural Sears Point event, Rudd is one of just three Winston Cup drivers, with Rusty Wallace and Geoffrey Bodine, to earn victories at all three Modern Era road courses.

Rudd holds the Modern Era record for Top 5s on road course tracks. He is near the top in a host of other statistical categories. Thanks to his new association with Robert Yates Racing, he has renewed his strength on NASCAR's nonovals. In the four road course races in 2000 and 2001, he finished in the Top 5 three times. With a few more solid seasons, he may find himself at the top once again.

Road Course Stats Chart

Road Course Record Book - Modern Era (min. 10 starts)

Category	Rudd's Total	Rudd's Rank	Modern Era Road Course Leader*
Starts	45	5th	Darrell Waltrip -- 53
Total Points[1]	5,944	4th	Darrell Waltrip -- 6,598
Avg. Start	7.6	6th	Cale Yarborough -- 3.8
Avg. Finish	13.2	8th	Cale Yarborough -- 7.4
Wins	5	3rd	Jeff Gordon -- 7
Winning Pct.	11.1	12th	Jeff Gordon -- 38.9
Top 5s	23	1st	(Dale Earnhardt -- 20)
Top 10s	26	2nd	Dale Earnhardt -- 31
DNFs	7	21st	Hershel McGriff -- 23
Poles	5	4th	Darrell Waltrip -- 9
Front Row Starts	10	3rd	Darrell Waltrip -- 16
Laps Led	316	10th	Bobby Allison -- 820
Pct. Laps Led	7.5	12th	Cale Yarborough -- 33.5
Races Led	22	2nd	Darrell Waltrip -- 23
Times Led	36	4th	Bobby Allison -- 69
Times Led Most Laps	2	11th	Jeff Gordon -- 7
Bonus Points[1]	120	3rd	Darrell Waltrip -- 140
Laps Completed	3,784	7th	Darrell Waltrip -- 4,743
Pct. Laps Completed	89.5	28th	Johnny Benson Jr. -- 99.6
Points per Race[1]	132.1	7th	Cale Yarborough -- 163.0
Lead-Lap Finishes	30	3rd	Dale Earnhardt -- 40

[1] -- Since implementation of current point system in 1975

* -- Second-place driver listed in parentheses if Rudd is category leader.

Road Course Definition

What is a road course?

A road course is an enclosed, non-oval track that requires both left and right turns. (Oval tracks require left turns only.)

Which tracks are road courses?

Riverside*
Sears Point
Watkins Glen

* -- Track closed in 1988

On Winston Cup road courses, Rudd has five wins and five poles.

The Record Book

Ricky Rudd's Standing in Winston Cup History—
All-Time and the Modern Era

In 1972, NASCAR entered its "Modern Era" after striking a new series sponsorship deal with the R.J. Reynolds tobacco company. Most fundamental among the changes implemented as a result of the new deal was a significant reduction in the number of races staged on a reduced number of racetracks. Accompanied by the 1975 introduction of the current point system—which rewards consistency more than victories—NASCAR embarked on a new era of stability that, in turn, increased competitiveness and sparked an unprecedented boom in popularity through the 1980s and 1990s.

From a statistical point of view, the 1972 demarcation makes historical comparison a tap dance. Judging Rudd's Modern Era career in light of the cross-era career of a racer such as Richard Petty is fruitless. In 1967, Petty won 27 times in 48 starts—nearly equaling the number of victories in Rudd's entire career. Petty was sometimes one of just a few Grand National regulars to enter a race, giving him an enormous advantage over the local Saturday night racers against whom he competed. Today's drivers face better competition in fewer events.

In recognition of these distinct eras and their fundamental differences, this section puts Rudd's career in both contexts, All-Time and Modern Era. All-Time records include all drivers who have competed since NASCAR's inception in 1949; the Modern Era includes only results from 1972 to the present.

Rudd had 36 Top 5s and 81 Top 10s in his first 212 starts on tracks measuring 2 miles or longer.

All-Time Records

Championships

1	Dale Earnhardt	7
	Richard Petty	7
3	Jeff Gordon	4
4	David Pearson	3
	Lee Petty	3
	Darrell Waltrip	3
	Cale Yarborough	3
8	Buck Baker	2
	Tim Flock	2
	Ned Jarrett	2
	Terry Labonte	2
	Herb Thomas	2
	Joe Weatherly	2
14	Bobby Allison	1
	Red Byron	1
	Bill Elliott	1
	Bobby Isaac	1
	Dale Jarrett	1
	Alan Kulwicki	1
	Bobby Labonte	1
	Benny Parsons	1
	Bill Rexford	1
	Rusty Wallace	1
	Rex White	1
	Ricky Rudd	**0**

Career Starts

1	Richard Petty	1,184
2	Dave Marcis	881
3	Darrell Waltrip	809
4	**Ricky Rudd**	**731**
5	Bobby Allison	718
6	Terry Labonte	709
7	Buddy Baker	699
8	Dale Earnhardt	676
9	Bill Elliott	659
10	J.D. McDuffie	653
11	Buck Baker	636
12	Kyle Petty	609
13	James Hylton	601
14	David Pearson	574
15	Rusty Wallace	562
16	Buddy Arrington	560
17	Cale Yarborough	559
18	Geoffrey Bodine	554
19	Sterling Marlin	539
20	Elmo Langley	536
21	Ken Schrader	528
22	Benny Parsons	526
23	Michael Waltrip	498
24	Neil Castles	497
25	Wendell Scott	495
26	Mark Martin	494
27	Morgan Shepherd	481
28	Harry Gant	474
29	Dale Jarrett	459
30	Jimmy Means	455
31	Cecil Gordon	450
32	Brett Bodine	442
33	Lee Petty	427
34	Jim Paschal	422
35	G.C. Spencer	415
36	Lake Speed	402
37	Frank Warren	396
38	Henley Gray	374
39	Jimmy Spencer	370
40	Neil Bonnett	363

Career Wins

1	Richard Petty	200
2	David Pearson	105
3	Bobby Allison	85
4	Darrell Waltrip	84
5	Cale Yarborough	83
6	Dale Earnhardt	76
7	Jeff Gordon	58
8	Lee Petty	54
	Rusty Wallace	54
10	Junior Johnson	50
	Ned Jarrett	50
12	Herb Thomas	48
13	Buck Baker	46
14	Bill Elliott	41
15	Tim Flock	39
16	Bobby Isaac	37
17	Fireball Roberts	33
18	Mark Martin	32
19	Dale Jarrett	28
	Rex White	28
21	Fred Lorenzen	26
22	Jim Paschal	25
	Joe Weatherly	25
24	**Ricky Rudd**	**22**
25	Benny Parsons	21
	Jack Smith	21
	Terry Labonte	21
28	Speedy Thompson	20
29	Buddy Baker	19
	Davey Allison	19
	Fonty Flock	19
32	Geoffrey Bodine	18
	Harry Gant	18
	Neil Bonnett	18
	Bobby Labonte	18
36	Curtis Turner	17
	Marvin Panch	17
	Jeff Burton	17
39	Ernie Irvan	15
40	Dick Hutcherson	14
	LeeRoy Yarbrough	14

All-Time Records

#	Winning Pct.		#	Money Won		#	Top 5s	
1	Herb Thomas	20.87	1	Jeff Gordon	45,008,022	1	Richard Petty	555
2	Tim Flock	20.86	2	Dale Earnhardt	41,473,589	2	Bobby Allison	336
3	Jeff Gordon	19.80	3	Dale Jarrett	33,313,332	3	David Pearson	301
4	David Pearson	18.29	4	Rusty Wallace	29,432,672	4	Dale Earnhardt	281
5	Richard Petty	16.89	5	Mark Martin	28,832,697	5	Darrell Waltrip	276
6	Fred Lorenzen	16.46	6	Bill Elliott	26,973,793	6	Cale Yarborough	255
7	Fireball Roberts	16.02	7	Terry Labonte	26,478,470	7	Buck Baker	246
8	Junior Johnson	15.97	8	Bobby Labonte	25,631,984	8	Lee Petty	231
9	Cale Yarborough	14.85	**9**	**Ricky Rudd**	**24,590,223**	9	Buddy Baker	202
10	Ned Jarrett	14.20	10	Darrell Waltrip	22,493,879	10	Benny Parsons	199
11	Dick Hutcherson	13.59	11	Jeff Burton	22,191,614	11	Mark Martin	188
12	Lee Petty	12.65	12	Sterling Marlin	19,814,283	12	Ned Jarrett	185
13	Fonty Flock	12.34	13	Ken Schrader	17,931,458	13	Rusty Wallace	182
14	Rex White	12.02	14	Geoffrey Bodine	14,827,869	**14**	**Ricky Rudd**	**179**
15	Bobby Isaac	12.01	15	Kyle Petty	13,331,568	15	Terry Labonte	176
16	Bobby Allison	11.84	16	Michael Waltrip	13,280,246	16	Bill Elliott	160
17	Tony Stewart	11.54	17	Bobby Hamilton	12,738,653	17	Jim Paschal	149
18	Dale Earnhardt	11.24	18	Ward Burton	12,662,939	18	Jeff Gordon	147
19	Joe Weatherly	10.87	19	Jimmy Spencer	12,478,183	19	Dale Jarrett	141
20	Darrell Waltrip	10.38	20	Tony Stewart	11,736,303	20	James Hylton	140
21	Dick Rathmann	10.16	21	Jeremy Mayfield	11,634,821	21	Bobby Isaac	134
22	Speedy Thompson	10.10	22	Ernie Irvan	11,624,617	22	Harry Gant	123
23	Davey Allison	9.95	23	John Andretti	11,598,410	23	Herb Thomas	122
24	Rusty Wallace	9.61	24	Brett Bodine	10,143,780	24	Junior Johnson	121
25	Curtis Turner	9.24	25	Joe Nemechek	9,859,452	25	Rex White	110
26	Jack Smith	7.98	26	Johnny Benson	9,533,583	26	Joe Weatherly	105
27	Marvin Panch	7.87	27	Mike Skinner	9,142,142	27	Tim Flock	102
28	Buck Baker	7.23	28	Dale Earnhardt Jr.	8,782,033	28	Geoffrey Bodine	99
29	Paul Goldsmith	7.09	29	Rick Mast	8,760,049	29	Marvin Panch	96
30	LeeRoy Yarbrough	7.07	30	Morgan Shepherd	8,565,265	30	Dave Marcis	94
31	Tim Richmond	7.03	31	Richard Petty	8,541,218		Jack Smith	94
32	Jim Reed	6.60	32	Harry Gant	8,524,844	32	Fireball Roberts	93
33	Jeff Burton	6.56	33	Ted Musgrave	8,464,192	33	Bobby Labonte	84
34	Mark Martin	6.48	34	Kenny Wallace	7,846,028	34	Neil Bonnett	83
35	Bill Elliott	6.22	35	Bobby Allison	7,673,808	35	Jeff Burton	81
36	Bobby Labonte	6.12	36	Robert Pressley	7,238,534	36	Donnie Allison	78
37	Dale Jarrett	6.10	37	Dave Marcis	7,212,758		Speedy Thompson	78
38	Jim Paschal	5.92	38	Steve Park	6,985,233	38	Fred Lorenzen	75
39	Cotton Owens	5.63	39	Ricky Craven	6,744,566	39	Fonty Flock	72
40	A.J. Foyt	5.47	40	Jerry Nadeau	6,739,084	40	Sterling Marlin	71
54	**Ricky Rudd**	**3.01**						

All-Time Records

#	Top 10s		#	Poles		#	Laps Led		#	Races Led	
1	Richard Petty	712	1	Richard Petty	126	1	Richard Petty	52,194	1	Richard Petty	599
2	Bobby Allison	446	2	David Pearson	113	2	Cale Yarborough	31,776	2	Bobby Allison	414
3	Dale Earnhardt	428	3	Cale Yarborough	70	3	Bobby Allison	27,539	3	Dale Earnhardt	405
4	Darrell Waltrip	390	4	Bobby Allison	59	4	Dale Earnhardt	25,714	4	Darrell Waltrip	402
5	Buck Baker	372		Darrell Waltrip	59	5	David Pearson	25,425	5	Cale Yarborough	340
6	David Pearson	366	6	Bill Elliott	51	6	Darrell Waltrip	23,130	6	David Pearson	329
7	**Ricky Rudd**	**344**	7	Bobby Isaac	50	7	Rusty Wallace	18,823	7	Rusty Wallace	255
8	Terry Labonte	340	8	Junior Johnson	47	8	Bobby Isaac	13,229	8	Mark Martin	246
9	Lee Petty	332	9	Buck Baker	44	9	Jeff Gordon	13,018	9	Buddy Baker	242
10	Cale Yarborough	318	10	Mark Martin	41	10	Junior Johnson	12,651	10	Bill Elliott	241
11	Buddy Baker	311	11	Buddy Baker	40	11	Bill Elliott	10,495	11	Terry Labonte	237
12	James Hylton	301	12	Jeff Gordon	39	12	Mark Martin	9,760	12	Geoffrey Bodine	220
13	Bill Elliott	294		Tim Flock	39	13	Buddy Baker	9,748	**13**	**Ricky Rudd**	**212**
14	Mark Martin	293	14	Herb Thomas	38	14	Ned Jarrett	9,468	14	Jeff Gordon	201
15	Rusty Wallace	292	15	Geoffrey Bodine	37	15	Geoffrey Bodine	8,680	15	Dave Marcis	195
16	Benny Parsons	283	16	Rex White	36	16	Harry Gant	8,445	16	Benny Parsons	192
17	Ned Jarrett	239	17	Fireball Roberts	35	17	Fred Lorenzen	8,131	17	Harry Gant	192
18	Jim Paschal	230		Ned Jarrett	35	**18**	**Ricky Rudd**	**7,441**	18	Dale Jarrett	171
19	Dave Marcis	222		Rusty Wallace	35	19	Tim Flock	6,937	19	Bobby Isaac	155
20	Dale Jarrett	210	20	Fonty Flock	33	20	Benny Parsons	6,860	20	Neil Bonnett	155
21	Harry Gant	208		Fred Lorenzen	33	21	Terry Labonte	6,807	21	Sterling Marlin	144
22	Elmo Langley	193	**22**	**Ricky Rudd**	**27**	22	Dale Jarrett	6,515	22	Junior Johnson	138
23	Jeff Gordon	190	23	Terry Labonte	26	23	Neil Bonnett	6,383	23	Ken Schrader	136
24	Geoffrey Bodine	188	24	Alan Kulwicki	24	24	Herb Thomas	6,197	24	Bobby Labonte	130
25	Neil Castles	178		Jack Smith	24	25	Fireball Roberts	5,970	25	Ernie Irvan	124
	Sterling Marlin	178	26	Ken Schrader	23	26	Buck Baker	5,662	26	Ned Jarrett	111
27	Ken Schrader	176	27	Bobby Labonte	22	27	Ernie Irvan	5,484	27	Donnie Allison	105
28	Bobby Isaac	170		Dale Earnhardt	22	28	Davey Allison	4,991	28	Morgan Shepherd	104
29	Morgan Shepherd	168		Dick Hutcherson	22	29	Lee Petty	4,787	29	Buck Baker	103
30	Kyle Petty	167	30	Marvin Panch	21	30	Curtis Turner	4,771	30	Kyle Petty	99
31	Rex White	163	31	Benny Parsons	20	31	Fonty Flock	4,682	31	Davey Allison	97
32	Herb Thomas	156		Neil Bonnett	20	32	Donnie Allison	4,642	32	Jeff Burton	94
	Neil Bonnett	156	33	Ernie Irvan	19	33	Jim Paschal	4,591	33	Lee Petty	93
34	Joe Weatherly	153		Joe Weatherly	19	34	Rex White	4,583	34	Fireball Roberts	90
35	Dick Brooks	150	35	Donnie Allison	18	35	Jeff Burton	4,570	35	Michael Waltrip	85
36	Junior Johnson	148		Lee Petty	18	36	Dick Hutcherson	3,995	36	Herb Thomas	84
37	Wendell Scott	147		Speedy Thompson	18	37	Kyle Petty	3,848	37	Fred Lorenzen	83
38	Bobby Labonte	142	38	Curtis Turner	17	38	Speedy Thompson	3,667	38	Tim Flock	82
39	Jack Smith	141		Harry Gant	17	39	Joe Weatherly	3,487	39	Alan Kulwicki	77
40	G.C. Spencer	138	40	Dale Jarrett	14	40	LeeRoy Yarbrough	3,421	40	Jim Paschal	76
										Tim Richmond	76

Modern Era Records

(minimum 100 Career Starts)

	Championships				Starts				Victories	
1	Dale Earnhardt	7		1	Darrell Waltrip	809		1	Darrell Waltrip	84
2	Jeff Gordon	4		2	Dave Marcis	759		2	Dale Earnhardt	76
	Richard Petty	4		**3**	**Ricky Rudd**	**731**		3	Cale Yarborough	69
4	Darrell Waltrip	3		4	Terry Labonte	709		4	Richard Petty	60
	Cale Yarborough	3		5	Dale Earnhardt	676		5	Jeff Gordon	58
6	Terry Labonte	2		6	Bill Elliott	659		6	Bobby Allison	55
7	Bobby Allison	1		7	Richard Petty	619		7	Rusty Wallace	54
	Bill Elliott	1		8	Kyle Petty	609		8	David Pearson	45
	Dale Jarrett	1		9	Rusty Wallace	562		9	Bill Elliott	41
	Alan Kulwicki	1		10	Geoffrey Bodine	554		10	Mark Martin	32
	Bobby Labonte	1		11	Sterling Marlin	539		11	Dale Jarrett	28
	Benny Parsons	1		12	Ken Schrader	528		**12**	**Ricky Rudd**	**22**
	Rusty Wallace	1		13	Michael Waltrip	498		13	Terry Labonte	21
	Ricky Rudd	**0**		14	Mark Martin	494		14	Benny Parsons	20
				15	Morgan Shepherd	478		15	Davey Allison	19
				16	Bobby Allison	476		16	Geoffrey Bodine	18
				17	Harry Gant	474			Harry Gant	18
				18	Dale Jarrett	459			Bobby Labonte	18
				19	Jimmy Means	455			Neil Bonnett	18
				20	J.D. McDuffie	443		20	Jeff Burton	17
				21	Brett Bodine	442		21	Ernie Irvan	15
				22	Benny Parsons	441			Buddy Baker	15
				23	Buddy Arrington	426		23	Tim Richmond	13
				24	Lake Speed	402		24	Tony Stewart	12
				25	Buddy Baker	391		25	Sterling Marlin	8
				26	Jimmy Spencer	370			Kyle Petty	8
				27	Cale Yarborough	366		27	Dale Earnhardt Jr.	5
				28	Neil Bonnett	363			Alan Kulwicki	5
				29	Derrike Cope	355			Dave Marcis	5
					Rick Mast	355		30	Donnie Allison	4
				31	Bobby Hamilton	337			Bobby Hamilton	4
				32	Bobby Hillin Jr.	334			Ken Schrader	4
				33	James Hylton	325			Morgan Shepherd	4
				34	Ernie Irvan	313		34	Ward Burton	3
				35	Hut Stricklin	306			Jeremy Mayfield	3
				36	Cecil Gordon	300		36	Derrike Cope	2
				37	Ted Musgrave	299			A.J. Foyt	2
				38	Dick Trickle	298			Steve Park	2
				39	Bobby Labonte	294			John Andretti	2
				40	Jeff Gordon	293			Kevin Harvick	2
									Jimmy Spencer	2
									Joe Nemechek	2

Modern Era Records

#	Winning Pct.		#	Money Won		#	Average Start	
1	David Pearson	21.84	1	Jeff Gordon	$45,008,022	1	David Pearson	5.58
2	Jeff Gordon	19.80	2	Dale Earnhardt	41,473,589	2	Cale Yarborough	7.15
3	Cale Yarborough	18.85	3	Dale Jarrett	33,313,332	3	Bobby Allison	8.44
4	Bobby Allison	11.55	4	Rusty Wallace	29,432,672	4	Jeff Gordon	8.89
5	Tony Stewart	11.54	5	Mark Martin	28,832,697	5	Benny Parsons	9.05
6	Dale Earnhardt	11.24	6	Bill Elliott	26,973,793	6	Mark Martin	9.83
7	Darrell Waltrip	10.38	7	Terry Labonte	26,478,470	7	Donnie Allison	9.97
8	Davey Allison	9.95	8	Bobby Labonte	25,631,984	8	Buddy Baker	10.73
9	Richard Petty	9.69	**9**	**Ricky Rudd**	**24,590,223**	9	Neil Bonnett	11.93
10	Rusty Wallace	9.61	10	Darrell Waltrip	22,493,879	10	Alan Kulwicki	12.00
11	Tim Richmond	7.03	11	Jeff Burton	22,191,614	11	Davey Allison	12.38
12	Jeff Burton	6.56	12	Sterling Marlin	19,814,283	12	Tim Richmond	12.46
13	Mark Martin	6.48	13	Ken Schrader	17,931,458	13	Harry Gant	12.51
14	Bill Elliott	6.22	14	Geoffrey Bodine	14,827,869	14	Rusty Wallace	12.60
15	Bobby Labonte	6.12	15	Kyle Petty	13,331,568	15	Dale Earnhardt	12.90
16	Dale Jarrett	6.10	16	Michael Waltrip	13,280,246	16	Bill Elliott	13.12
17	Neil Bonnett	4.96	17	Bobby Hamilton	12,738,653	17	Geoffrey Bodine	13.33
18	Ernie Irvan	4.79	18	Ward Burton	12,662,939	18	Richard Petty	13.40
19	Benny Parsons	4.54	19	Jimmy Spencer	12,478,183	**19**	**Ricky Rudd**	**13.58**
20	Buddy Baker	3.84	20	Tony Stewart	11,736,303	20	Darrell Waltrip	13.71
21	Harry Gant	3.80	21	Jeremy Mayfield	11,634,821	21	Bobby Labonte	14.66
22	Geoffrey Bodine	3.25	22	Ernie Irvan	11,624,617	22	Coo Coo Marlin	15.04
23	**Ricky Rudd**	**3.01**	23	John Andretti	11,598,410	23	Ron Bouchard	15.12
24	Terry Labonte	2.96	24	Brett Bodine	10,143,780	24	Terry Labonte	15.34
25	Donnie Allison	2.52	25	Joe Nemechek	9,859,452	25	Ken Schrader	15.38
26	Alan Kulwicki	2.42	26	Johnny Benson	9,533,583	26	Lennie Pond	15.43
27	Steve Park	1.75	27	Mike Skinner	9,142,142	27	Tony Stewart	15.50
28	Sterling Marlin	1.48	28	Dale Earnhardt Jr.	8,782,033	28	Dick Brooks	15.92
29	Kyle Petty	1.31	29	Rick Mast	8,760,049	29	Ernie Irvan	16.21
30	Jeremy Mayfield	1.27	30	Morgan Shepherd	8,565,265	30	Dale Jarrett	16.72
31	Ward Burton	1.20	31	Harry Gant	8,524,844	31	Joe Ruttman	17.39
32	Bobby Hamilton	1.19	32	Ted Musgrave	8,464,192	32	Sterling Marlin	17.96
33	Morgan Shepherd	0.84	33	Kenny Wallace	7,846,028	33	Morgan Shepherd	17.96
34	Joe Nemechek	0.79	34	Robert Pressley	7,238,534	34	Richard Childress	18.43
35	John Andretti	0.76	35	Steve Park	6,985,233	35	Mike Skinner	18.45
36	Ken Schrader	0.76	36	Ricky Craven	6,744,566	36	Jody Ridley	18.53
37	Dave Marcis	0.66	37	Jerry Nadeau	6,739,084	37	Ward Burton	18.82
38	Derrike Cope	0.56	38	Davey Allison	6,689,154	38	Joe Nemechek	19.30
39	Jimmy Spencer	0.54	39	Wally Dallenbach Jr.	6,144,988	39	Rick Wilson	19.74
			40	Derrike Cope	6,104,549	40	Bruce Hill	19.77

Modern Era Records

	Average Finish			Top 5s			Top 10s	
1	Dale Earnhardt	11.06	1	Dale Earnhardt	281	1	Dale Earnhardt	428
2	Cale Yarborough	11.45	2	Darrell Waltrip	276	2	Darrell Waltrip	390
3	Bobby Allison	11.58	3	Richard Petty	221	**3**	**Ricky Rudd**	**344**
4	Jeff Gordon	11.63	4	Bobby Allison	217	4	Terry Labonte	340
5	Tony Stewart	11.74	5	Cale Yarborough	197	5	Richard Petty	311
6	Mark Martin	12.74	6	Mark Martin	188	6	Bobby Allison	300
7	David Pearson	13.45	7	Rusty Wallace	182	7	Bill Elliott	294
8	Rusty Wallace	14.05	**8**	**Ricky Rudd**	**179**	8	Mark Martin	293
9	Richard Petty	14.15	9	Terry Labonte	176	9	Rusty Wallace	292
10	Davey Allison	14.25	10	Benny Parsons	172	10	Benny Parsons	239
11	Benny Parsons	14.39	11	Bill Elliott	160	11	Cale Yarborough	231
12	Terry Labonte	14.73	12	Jeff Gordon	147	12	Dale Jarrett	210
13	Bill Elliott	14.75	13	Dale Jarrett	141	13	Harry Gant	208
14	Bobby Labonte	14.77	14	Buddy Baker	128	14	Buddy Baker	199
15	Darrell Waltrip	15.12	15	Harry Gant	123	15	Jeff Gordon	190
16	Tim Richmond	15.18	16	David Pearson	108	16	Geoffrey Bodine	188
17	**Ricky Rudd**	**15.37**	17	Geoffrey Bodine	99	17	Dave Marcis	180
18	Dale Jarrett	15.51	18	Bobby Labonte	84	18	Sterling Marlin	178
19	Buddy Baker	15.52	19	Neil Bonnett	83	19	Ken Schrader	176
20	Jeff Burton	15.75	20	Jeff Burton	81	20	Morgan Shepherd	168
21	Harry Gant	15.87	21	Dave Marcis	75	21	Kyle Petty	167
22	Alan Kulwicki	16.41	22	Sterling Marlin	71	22	Neil Bonnett	156
23	Neil Bonnett	16.52	23	Ernie Irvan	68	23	Bobby Labonte	142
24	Jody Ridley	16.58	24	Davey Allison	66	24	David Pearson	124
25	Richard Childress	17.21	25	Ken Schrader	64	25	Ernie Irvan	124
26	Ron Bouchard	17.23	26	Morgan Shepherd	63	26	Jeff Burton	119
27	Ken Schrader	17.25	27	Kyle Petty	51	27	Dick Brooks	108
28	James Hylton	17.34	28	Donnie Allison	42	28	Davey Allison	92
29	Ernie Irvan	17.35		Tim Richmond	42	29	Lennie Pond	88
30	Sterling Marlin	17.58	30	Tony Stewart	39	30	James Hylton	87
31	Lennie Pond	17.78		Lennie Pond	39	31	Michael Waltrip	85
32	Dick Brooks	17.80	32	Alan Kulwicki	38	32	Tim Richmond	78
33	Buddy Arrington	17.84	33	Jeremy Mayfield	33	33	Richard Childress	76
34	Cecil Gordon	17.84	34	Dick Brooks	30	34	Lake Speed	75
35	Geoffrey Bodine	18.08	35	Jimmy Spencer	25	35	Alan Kulwicki	75
36	Elmo Langley	18.12	36	Michael Waltrip	21	36	Cecil Gordon	71
37	Morgan Shepherd	18.24	37	Ward Burton	21	37	Jimmy Spencer	70
38	David Sisco	18.53	38	Ted Musgrave	20	38	Buddy Arrington	68
39	Donnie Allison	18.67	39	Bobby Hamilton	20	39	Donnie Allison	67
40	Walter Ballard	18.88	40	Cecil Gordon	20	40	Ward Burton	67

Modern Era Records

Poles

#	Driver	Poles
1	Darrell Waltrip	59
2	David Pearson	56
3	Bill Elliott	51
	Cale Yarborough	51
5	Mark Martin	41
6	Jeff Gordon	39
7	Geoffrey Bodine	37
8	Bobby Allison	36
9	Rusty Wallace	35
10	Buddy Baker	30
11	**Ricky Rudd**	**27**
12	Terry Labonte	26
13	Alan Kulwicki	24
14	Richard Petty	23
	Ken Schrader	23
16	Dale Earnhardt	22
	Bobby Labonte	22
18	Neil Bonnett	20
19	Ernie Irvan	19
	Benny Parsons	19
21	Harry Gant	17
22	Dale Jarrett	14
	Davey Allison	14
	Tim Richmond	14
25	Dave Marcis	12
26	Sterling Marlin	11
27	Donnie Allison	9
	Bobby Isaac	9
29	Kyle Petty	8
30	Morgan Shepherd	7
31	Jeremy Mayfield	6
	Joe Nemechek	6
	Ward Burton	6
34	Ted Musgrave	5
	Mike Skinner	5
	Lennie Pond	5
	Bobby Hamilton	5
	A.J. Foyt	5
	Brett Bodine	5

Front Row Starts

#	Driver	Starts
1	Darrell Waltrip	115
2	Cale Yarborough	96
3	Bill Elliott	91
4	Bobby Allison	87
6	Mark Martin	81
5	David Pearson	86
7	Geoffrey Bodine	79
8	Jeff Gordon	73
9	**Ricky Rudd**	**69**
10	Rusty Wallace	66
12	Dale Earnhardt	58
11	Richard Petty	60
14	Terry Labonte	54
15	Benny Parsons	52
16	Harry Gant	45
	Buddy Baker	58
17	Ken Schrader	39
	Neil Bonnett	38
18	Bobby Labonte	38
20	Alan Kulwicki	37
21	Ernie Irvan	36
22	Dale Jarrett	31
23	Davey Allison	27
	Tim Richmond	27
25	Sterling Marlin	23
26	Donnie Allison	21
27	Dave Marcis	18
28	Bobby Isaac	16
	Brett Bodine	16
30	Kyle Petty	14
	Morgan Shepherd	14
	Ward Burton	14
33	Joe Nemechek	11
	Joe Ruttman	11
	Bobby Hamilton	11
36	John Andretti	10
	Mike Skinner	10
38	Ricky Craven	9
	Jeff Burton	9
	A.J. Foyt	9

Total Points[1]

#	Driver	Points
1	Darrell Waltrip	96,545
2	Dale Earnhardt	93,962
3	**Ricky Rudd**	**88,956**
4	Terry Labonte	87,943
6	Rusty Wallace	71,977
5	Bill Elliott	81,834
7	Dave Marcis	69,550
8	Kyle Petty	65,619
9	Mark Martin	65,442
10	Richard Petty	65,333
12	Sterling Marlin	61,252
11	Geoffrey Bodine	62,845
14	Harry Gant	56,949
15	Dale Jarrett	56,187
16	Morgan Shepherd	53,234
13	Ken Schrader	60,389
17	Bobby Allison	53,199
19	Benny Parsons	44,146
18	Michael Waltrip	50,845
20	Neil Bonnett	43,072
21	Jimmy Means	42,573
22	Brett Bodine	42,386
23	Cale Yarborough	41,910
24	Lake Speed	40,791
25	Jeff Gordon	40,658
26	Buddy Arrington	39,861
27	Buddy Baker	39,546
28	Jimmy Spencer	37,442
29	Bobby Labonte	36,710
30	Ernie Irvan	36,434
31	J.D. McDuffie	35,061
32	Bobby Hamilton	34,344
33	Bobby Hillin Jr	33,690
34	Rick Mast	32,611
35	Derrike Cope	31,960
36	Jeff Burton	31,535
37	Ted Musgrave	31,240
38	Hut Stricklin	27,942
39	Dick Trickle	26,773
40	Dick Brooks	26,628

[1]—Since current point system was implemented in 1975

Modern Era Records

Points Per Race[1]				DNFs				Laps Led		
1	Dale Earnhardt	139.0		1	Dave Marcis	230		1	Cale Yarborough	27,260
2	Jeff Gordon	138.8		2	J.D. McDuffie	200		2	Dale Earnhardt	25,714
3	Cale Yarborough	138.3		3	Richard Petty	189		3	Darrell Waltrip	23,130
4	Bobby Allison	136.1		4	Darrell Waltrip	176		4	Rusty Wallace	18,823
5	Tony Stewart	135.6		5	Jimmy Means	172		5	Bobby Allison	18,502
6	Mark Martin	132.5		6	Buddy Baker	159		6	Richard Petty	16,902
7	Rusty Wallace	128.1		**7**	**Ricky Rudd**	**158**		7	Jeff Gordon	13,018
8	Davey Allison	127.5		8	Geoffrey Bodine	156		8	Bill Elliott	10,495
9	David Pearson	125.9			Benny Parsons	156		9	David Pearson	10,079
10	Benny Parsons	125.8		10	Kyle Petty	148		10	Mark Martin	9,760
11	Darrell Waltrip	125.5		11	Harry Gant	146		11	Geoffrey Bodine	8,680
12	Bobby Labonte	124.9		12	Morgan Shepherd	141		12	Harry Gant	8,445
13	Bill Elliott	124.2		13	Terry Labonte	140		**13**	**Ricky Rudd**	**7,441**
14	Terry Labonte	124.0		14	Neil Bonnett	138		14	Terry Labonte	6,807
15	Richard Petty	123.3		15	Lake Speed	128		15	Buddy Baker	6,580
16	Tim Richmond	123.0		16	Dick Brooks	126		16	Benny Parsons	6,552
17	Dale Jarrett	122.4		17	Derrike Cope	123		17	Dale Jarrett	6,515
18	Jeff Burton	121.8		18	Bobby Allison	122		18	Neil Bonnett	6,383
19	**Ricky Rudd**	**121.7**		19	Greg Sacks	118		19	Ernie Irvan	5,484
20	Harry Gant	121.2		20	Sterling Marlin	108		20	Davey Allison	4,991
21	Buddy Baker	120.6		21	Rusty Wallace	108		21	Jeff Burton	4,570
22	Neil Bonnett	119.3		22	Cale Yarborough	105		22	Kyle Petty	3,848
23	Alan Kulwicki	118.5		23	Michael Waltrip	104		23	Sterling Marlin	3,334
24	Richard Childress	117.9		24	Lennie Pond	103		24	Bobby Labonte	3,202
25	Jody Ridley	116.4		25	Bill Elliott	99		25	Tony Stewart	2,904
26	Ernie Irvan	116.4		26	Buddy Arrington	98		26	Alan Kulwicki	2,686
27	Dick Brooks	114.8		27	Ronnie Thomas	95		27	Tim Richmond	2,537
28	Ken Schrader	114.4		118	Dale Earnhardt	95		28	Ken Schrader	2,373
29	Donnie Allison	113.9		29	D.K. Ulrich	94		29	Dave Marcis	2,332
30	Ron Bouchard	113.9		30	Dick Trickle	94		30	Donnie Allison	2,297
31	Sterling Marlin	113.6		31	Dale Jarrett	93		31	Morgan Shepherd	2,141
32	Geoffrey Bodine	113.4		32	Ed Negre	90		32	Bobby Hamilton	1,975
33	Lennie Pond	112.9		33	Joe Ruttman	88		33	Jeremy Mayfield	1,697
34	Morgan Shepherd	111.4		34	Donnie Allison	87		34	Ward Burton	1,491
35	Buddy Arrington	109.8		35	Brett Bodine	86		35	Bobby Isaac	1,399
36	Kyle Petty	107.7		36	Richard Childress	85		36	Dale Earnhardt Jr.	1,194
37	James Hylton	107.3			Mark Martin	85		37	Jimmy Spencer	1,100
38	Cecil Gordon	105.4		38	Bobby Hillin Jr.	84		38	Brett Bodine	1,037
39	Johnny Benson Jr.	104.7		39	David Pearson	82		39	Mike Skinner	1,016
40	Joe Ruttman	104.6			Rick Wilson	82		40	Steve Park	963

[1]—Since current point system was implemented in 1975

Modern Era Records

	Pct. Led				Races Led				No. of Times Led	
1	Cale Yarborough	22.80		1	Dale Earnhardt	405		1	Dale Earnhardt	1,398
2	David Pearson	15.93		2	Darrell Waltrip	402		2	Darrell Waltrip	1,227
3	Jeff Gordon	14.33		3	Bobby Allison	306		3	Cale Yarborough	1,179
4	Dale Earnhardt	11.68		4	Richard Petty	289		4	Bobby Allison	1,112
5	Bobby Allison	11.55		5	Cale Yarborough	271		5	Richard Petty	975
6	Rusty Wallace	10.43		6	Rusty Wallace	255		6	Buddy Baker	720
7	Tony Stewart	9.32		7	Mark Martin	246		7	Rusty Wallace	671
8	Darrell Waltrip	8.65		8	Bill Elliott	241		8	David Pearson	663
9	Richard Petty	8.08		9	Terry Labonte	237		9	Jeff Gordon	607
10	Davey Allison	7.93		10	Geoffrey Bodine	220		10	Mark Martin	585
11	Mark Martin	6.16		**11**	**Ricky Rudd**	**212**		11	Bill Elliott	570
12	Jeff Burton	5.76		12	Jeff Gordon	201		12	Terry Labonte	501
13	Ernie Irvan	5.49		13	Harry Gant	192		13	Geoffrey Bodine	477
14	Neil Bonnett	5.34		14	Dave Marcis	183		14	Neil Bonnett	460
15	Harry Gant	5.30		15	Benny Parsons	182		15	Benny Parsons	457
16	Buddy Baker	5.14		16	Buddy Baker	178		16	Harry Gant	454
17	Bill Elliott	4.99		17	Dale Jarrett	171		**17**	**Ricky Rudd**	**397**
18	Geoffrey Bodine	4.81		18	Neil Bonnett	155		18	Dale Jarrett	382
19	Benny Parsons	4.53		19	Sterling Marlin	144		19	Dave Marcis	326
20	Dale Jarrett	4.46		20	David Pearson	140		20	Ernie Irvan	320
21	Donnie Allison	4.35		21	Ken Schrader	136		21	Ken Schrader	284
22	Tim Richmond	4.16		22	Bobby Labonte	130		22	Sterling Marlin	269
23	Alan Kulwicki	3.84		23	Ernie Irvan	124		23	Bobby Labonte	265
24	Bobby Labonte	3.51		24	Morgan Shepherd	104		24	Davey Allison	263
25	**Ricky Rudd**	**3.14**		25	Kyle Petty	99		25	Donnie Allison	252
26	Terry Labonte	2.95		26	Davey Allison	97		26	Jeff Burton	207
27	Steve Park	2.85		27	Jeff Burton	94		27	Morgan Shepherd	190
28	Jeremy Mayfield	2.34		28	Michael Waltrip	85		28	Tim Richmond	188
29	Ward Burton	1.95		29	Alan Kulwicki	77		29	Kyle Petty	171
30	Kyle Petty	1.94		30	Tim Richmond	76		30	Alan Kulwicki	157
31	Mike Skinner	1.94		31	Jimmy Spencer	74		31	Jeremy Mayfield	113
32	Sterling Marlin	1.94		32	Donnie Allison	69		32	A.J. Foyt	110
33	Bobby Hamilton	1.86		33	Brett Bodine	64		33	Tony Stewart	109
34	Ken Schrader	1.40		34	Ward Burton	55		34	Michael Waltrip	106
35	Morgan Shepherd	1.36		35	Lennie Pond	53		35	Bobby Hamilton	103
36	Jerry Nadeau	1.34		36	Bobby Hamilton	51			Ward Burton	103
37	Ricky Craven	1.22		37	Jeremy Mayfield	49		37	Jimmy Spencer	99
38	Joe Ruttman	1.15		38	John Andretti	46		38	Lennie Pond	93
39	Lennie Pond	1.12		39	Tony Stewart	45		39	Bobby Isaac	88
40	Jimmy Spencer	0.94		40	Mike Skinner	43		40	Brett Bodine	86

Modern Era Records

No. of Times Led Most Laps		Bonus Points		Laps Completed	
1 Cale Yarborough 88		1 Dale Earnhardt 2,445		1 Darrell Waltrip 237,772	
2 Dale Earnhardt 84		2 Darrell Waltrip 2,310		**2 Ricky Rudd 211,452**	
3 Darrell Waltrip 69		3 Rusty Wallace 1,595		3 Terry Labonte 208,187	
4 Rusty Wallace 64		4 Cale Yarborough 1,465		4 Dave Marcis 205,554	
5 Bobby Allison 61		5 Bobby Allison 1,400		5 Dale Earnhardt 202,888	
6 Jeff Gordon 53		6 Bill Elliott 1,395		6 Bill Elliott 193,282	
7 Richard Petty 41		7 Mark Martin 1,390		7 Richard Petty 175,097	
8 David Pearson 39		8 Terry Labonte 1,290		8 Kyle Petty 170,711	
9 Bill Elliott 37		9 Jeff Gordon 1,270		9 Rusty Wallace 163,524	
10 Mark Martin 32		10 Geoffrey Bodine 1,225		10 Geoffrey Bodine 155,915	
11 Buddy Baker 28		11 Richard Petty 1,220		11 Ken Schrader 154,252	
12 Geoffrey Bodine 25		**12 Ricky Rudd 1,155**		12 Sterling Marlin 153,362	
13 Harry Gant 23		13 Harry Gant 1,075		13 Mark Martin 144,686	
14 Ernie Irvan 22		14 Dale Jarrett 955		14 Michael Waltrip 141,407	
15 Terry Labonte 21		15 Dave Marcis 905		15 Bobby Allison 139,780	
16 Dale Jarrett 20		16 Benny Parsons 870		16 Harry Gant 133,628	
Jeff Burton 20		17 Neil Bonnett 855		17 Morgan Shepherd 129,983	
18 Ricky Rudd 19		18 Buddy Baker 795		18 Dale Jarrett 128,336	
19 Davey Allison 17		19 Sterling Marlin 775		19 Brett Bodine 124,953	
20 Neil Bonnett 16		20 Ernie Irvan 730		20 Buddy Arrington 123,604	
21 Benny Parsons 14		21 Ken Schrader 700		21 Benny Parsons 116,905	
22 Kyle Petty 11		22 Bobby Labonte 685		22 Jimmy Means 113,948	
Tim Richmond 11		23 Jeff Burton 580		23 J.D. McDuffie 105,874	
24 Tony Stewart 10		24 Davey Allison 570		24 Lake Speed 105,738	
Sterling Marlin 10		25 Kyle Petty 550		25 Jimmy Spencer 103,123	
26 Alan Kulwicki 7		26 Morgan Shepherd 535		26 Cale Yarborough 102,924	
Bobby Labonte 7		27 David Pearson 525		27 Rick Mast 100,128	
28 Dale Earnhardt Jr. 6		28 Tim Richmond 435		28 Bobby Hamilton 97,614	
29 Donnie Allison 5		29 Michael Waltrip 430		29 Buddy Baker 97,394	
Jeremy Mayfield 5		30 Alan Kulwicki 420		30 Neil Bonnett 96,119	
31 A.J. Foyt 4		31 Jimmy Spencer 380		31 Derrike Cope 90,783	
Ken Schrader 4		32 Brett Bodine 330		32 Bobby Hillin Jr. 90,070	
Mike Skinner 4		33 Ward Burton 290		33 James Hylton 89,291	
34 Morgan Shepherd 3		34 Donnie Allison 285		34 Ernie Irvan 88,656	
Steve Park 3		35 Tony Stewart 275		35 Ted Musgrave 88,104	
Ward Burton 3		36 Jeremy Mayfield 270		36 Bobby Labonte 85,296	
Bobby Isaac 3		Bobby Hamilton 270		37 Jeff Gordon 85,221	
Bobby Hamilton 3		38 Mike Skinner 235		38 Hut Stricklin 83,947	
		Lennie Pond 235		39 Dick Trickle 82,630	
		40 John Andretti 230		40 Cecil Gordon 80,137	

Modern Era Records

Pct. Of Laps Completed

1	Tony Stewart	95.25
2	Steve Park	93.83
3	Jeff Gordon	93.80
4	Bobby Labonte	93.50
5	Johnny Benson Jr.	93.12
6	Ted Musgrave	93.11
7	Elliott Sadler	92.87
8	Jeff Burton	92.31
9	Dale Earnhardt	92.14
10	Bobby Hamilton	92.03
11	Bill Elliott	91.93
12	Jerry Nadeau	91.72
13	Jeremy Mayfield	91.71
14	Mark Martin	91.37
15	Ken Schrader	91.26
16	Joe Nemechek	91.15
17	Kevin Lepage	90.83
18	Rusty Wallace	90.62
19	Mike Skinner	90.30
20	Terry Labonte	90.17
21	Steve Grissom	90.07
22	**Ricky Rudd**	**89.11**
23	Sterling Marlin	89.10
24	Davey Allison	89.04
25	Darrell Waltrip	88.94
26	Michael Waltrip	88.79
27	Ernie Irvan	88.74
28	Brett Bodine	88.69
29	Jimmy Spencer	88.23
30	Alan Kulwicki	88.09
31	Ward Burton	87.96
32	Wally Dallenbach Jr.	87.94
33	Dale Jarrett	87.86
34	John Andretti	87.84
35	Mike Wallace	87.47
36	Bobby Allison	87.29
37	Chad Little	86.80
38	Kenny Wallace	86.77
39	Rick Mast	86.75
40	Ricky Craven	86.46

Rudd became a happy man in 2000, when he joined Robert Yates Racing.

As the owner of his own team, Rudd was forced to assume responsibilities well beyond his driving duties.

## Chapter 3

The Seasons

A Season-by-Season Look at Ricky Rudd's Career

This section gets into the details of Rudd's career, season by season. Every race Rudd started since he joined the Winston Cup series full-time in 1987 is presented, listing his start, finish, total laps, laps completed, race-ending condition, and money won. His championship performance in each season is also charted, including championship and bonus points earned for each race, his position in the points standings, and how far he trailed the points leader. If Rudd is the points leader at any point, the second-place driver in the standings is listed in parentheses, along with the margin of Rudd's lead. The context of each race is also available in the "Career Race" column, which indicates the number of races in which Rudd competed at any point in his career.

Each season is given historical context with the inclusion of full statistics and a season summary. For each season, 20 statistical categories are cataloged. Rudd's total for each category is listed, along with his rank and that category's leader. If Rudd is the leader of a category, the second-place driver is listed in parentheses with his total. The season summary explores Rudd's accomplishments and memorable moments and is often accompanied by tables that provide greater insight into his career.

In his first three seasons as a car owner, Rudd thrived, finishing in the Top 10 in points three times.

1975-1976: Getting Started

After successful stints as a go-kart and motorcross racer—and after pestering his father long enough–18-year-old Ricky Rudd got an opportunity to race a stock car for the first time on NASCAR's Grand National circuit. Al Rudd Sr. purchased a ride for his son in the car owned by Bill Champion, whose NASCAR career stretched back to 1951—the stock car association's third season. An on-again, off-again driver, Champion competed in 289 races until 1976 and fielded cars as an owner until 1979.

In 1975, Champion was nearing the end of his career and was looking to sell his team. Rudd's brother—Al Jr.—talked the owner into giving his hot-shot brother a chance. On March 2, 1975, at Rockingham, Ricky Rudd started his first Winston Cup race. Despite 10 years of handling lightweight karts and motorcycles, he displayed a natural ability in a heavy stock car. He started the Carolina 500 in 26th and finished in 11th, 56 laps off the pace set by race winner Cale Yarborough.

The following week at Bristol, Rudd improved on his debut by finishing 10th. Just two races into his career, he had his first Top 10. He started two more races in Champion's car—at Atlanta and North Wilkesboro—though the results weren't nearly as strong. He failed to finish either race, finishing 25th at Atlanta and dead last in 28th at North Wilkesboro, after wrecking with Elmo Langley on the third lap.

Rudd's 1975 experience was enough to get the whole family hooked on NASCAR racing. Ricky's father purchased equipment and began fielding cars for his son. The owner of a salvage yard and a used auto parts business in Norfolk, Virginia, Al got Ricky started on racing by building his first kart when he was just four years old. With Al Sr. playing the owner, Al Jr. assumed engine-building and crew chief responsibilities, while Ricky took the wheel.

Starting up the No. 22 Al Rudd team, the Rudds challenged themselves in 1976 by entering four races at some of the toughest tracks on the Winston Cup circuit: Talladega, Dover, Daytona, and Charlotte. Once again, Ricky showed promise, finishing the Pepsi 400 at Daytona in 10th place.

With his family squarely behind him, Ricky Rudd entered the Winston Cup series full-time in 1977. The Rudds were about to make a splash.

1975–1976 Stats

Category	Rudd's Total
Money	$11,870
Starts	8
Total Points	838
Avg. Start	24.5
Avg. Finish	19.5
Wins	0
Winning Pct.	0.0
Top 5s	0
Top 10s	2
DNFs	4
Poles	0
Front Row Starts	0
Races Led	0
Laps Led	0
Laps Completed	1,901
Pct. Laps Completed	65.5
Points per Race	104.8
Lead-Lap Finishes	0

1975-1976 Performance Chart

Year	Career Race	Race. No.	Date	Race	St.	Fin.	Laps	Laps Completed	Laps Led	Condition	Money	Pts.	Bonus Pts.
1975[1]	1	4	Mar 2	Rockingham -- Carolina 500	26	11	492	436	0	Running	2,000	130	0
	2	5	Mar 16	Bristol -- Southeastern 500	23	10	500	456	0	Running	800	134	0
	3	6	Mar 23	Atlanta -- Atlanta 500	33	25	328	130	0	DNF - Engine	1,200	88	0
	4	7	Apr 6	North Wilkesboro -- Gwyn Staley Memorial	22	28	400	3	0	DNF - Crash	345	79	0
1976[2]	5	10	May 2	Talladega -- Winston 500	20	23	188	159	0	DNF - Mechanical	2,035	94	0
	6	12	May 16	Dover -- Mason-Dixon 500	17	33	500	247	0	DNF - Accident	555	64	0
	7	16	Jul 4	Daytona -- Firecracker 400	22	10	160	152	0	Running	2,590	134	0
	8	27	Oct 10	Charlotte -- National 500	33	16	334	318	0	Running	1,995	115	0

[1] -- Drove No. 10 Bill Champion Ford in all four 1975 starts
[2] -- Drove No. 22 Al Rudd Chevrolet in all four 1976 starts

1977: Rookie of the Year

The Rudd family competed against the Winston Cup giants in 1977 essentially with a single car and enough replacement parts to keep it running. The self-sponsored team operated on the barest of budgets, using family labor to save. Ricky's brother, Al Jr., built his engines and acted as crew chief. Ricky's sister, Carolyn, was the team's administrative assistant.

The Rudds also saved by limiting their schedule. They entered 25 of the season's 30 events, choosing to skip the two Riverside, California, races and save on the cost of coast-to-coast travel. They also missed or failed to qualify for races at Atlanta, North Wilkesboro, and Martinsville.

Otherwise, the Rudds and the No. 22 Chevrolet were part of the action, trying to keep up with the high-budget teams fielded by the Pettys, the Gardners, and Junior Johnson. Not surprisingly, the going was tough for the rookie team. Ricky failed to finish any of his 25 starts on the lead lap. In 8 of his first 11 starts, he parked his car early due to engine or mechanical problems.

At midseason, however, the Rudds' luck began to turn. Ricky finished 10th at Nashville in July. He followed with a 7th at Pocono and then claimed the first Top 5 of his career—4th at Talladega. He stretched his consecutive Top-10 streak to four races with a 7th-place finish at Michigan. Suddenly, Ricky found himself in position to win the Rookie-of-the-Year Award.

The Winston Cup Grand National rookie class was relatively light in 1977. No newcomer started all 30 races. In fact, Rudd ran the most races of any rookie that season. His main rookie competition consisted of Sam Sommers, Janet Guthrie, and Butch Hartman—none of whom raced regularly in the Winston Cup series after the 1977 season ended. Sommers, however, gave a solid run for the Rookie-of-the-Year Award and chased Rudd as the schedule reached its conclusion.

Once Rudd's chances of winning the rookie award began to build momentum, his family assured his presence at all of the remaining races—even the season-ending event in Los Angeles at the Ontario Motor Speedway, located just 20 miles from Riverside, which they had skipped earlier in the season. He closed the season with a strong run, finishing three of the final five races in the Top 10. He secured his Rookie-of-the-Year Award with an eighth-place run at Ontario.

Adding to his rookie title, Rudd led a Winston Cup race for the first time in 1977 when he paced the World 600 at Charlotte. He led two other events—at Michigan and Ontario—and finished with a modest 13 laps led for the year. In every season since 1977, Rudd has found his way to the front in at least two races.

1977 Stats Chart

Category	Rudd's Total	Rudd's Rank	1977 Leader
Money	$68,448	19th	Cale Yarborough -- 561,642
Total Points	2,810	17th	Cale Yarborough -- 5,000
Avg. Start	16.6	16th	Cale Yarborough -- 4.
Avg. Finish	17.5	17th	Cale Yarborough -- 4.5
Wins	0	--	Cale Yarborough -- 9
Top 5s	1	14th	Cale Yarborough -- 25
Top 10s	10	11th	Cale Yarborough -- 27
DNFs	11	8th	Ed Negre, Tighe Scott -- 15
Poles	0	--	Neil Bonnett -- 6
Front Row Starts	0	--	N. Bonnett, R. Petty, C. Yarborough -- 10
Laps Led	13	14th	Cale Yarborough -- 3,218
Races Led	3	12th	Cale Yarborough -- 28
Times Led	5	12th	Cale Yarborough -- 126
Miles Led	27	14th	Cale Yarborough -- 3,054
Times Led Most Laps	0	--	Cale Yarborough -- 12
Bonus Points	15	12th	Cale Yarborough -- 200
Laps Completed	6,233	17th	Cale Yarborough -- 9,747
Miles Completed	7,509	17th	Cale Yarborough -- 11,382
Points per Race	112.4	17th	Cale Yarborough -- 166.7
Lead-Lap Finishes	0	--	Cale Yarborough -- 19

In 1991, Rudd took over the Tide car after Darrell Waltrip left Hendrick Motorsports to start his own team.

1977 Performance Chart
No. 22 Al Rudd Chevrolet

Career Race	Race No.	Date	Race	St.	Fin.	Laps	Laps Completed	Laps Led	Condition	Money	Pts.	Bonus Pts.	Current Standing	Behind Leader	Current Leader
9	2	Feb 20	Daytona-- Daytona 500	21	22	200	135	0	DNF - Rear End	2,935	97	0	36	-268	Yarborough
10	3	Feb 27	Richmond -- Richmond 400	18	26	245	187	0	DNF - Rear End	400	85	0	22	-368	Yarborough
11	4	Mar 13	Rockingham -- Carolina 500	19	19	492	396	0	DNF - Engine	970	106	0	21	-417	Yarborough
12	7	Apr 3	Darlington -- Rebel 500	27	22	367	259	0	DNF - Engine	1,300	97	0	27	-795	Yarborough
13	8	Apr 17	Bristol -- Southeastern 500	14	10	500	465	0	Running	1,900	134	0	25	-846	Yarborough
14	10	May 1	Talladega -- Winston 500	36	28	188	110	0	DNF - Engine	1,585	79	0	27	-1,127	Yarborough
15	11	May 7	Nashville -- Music City USA 420	12	10	420	401	0	Running	1,815	134	0	26	-1,173	Yarborough
16	12	May 15	Dover -- Mason-Dixon 500	20	27	500	190	0	DNF - Mechanical	1,125	82	0	24	-1,271	Yarborough
17	13	May 29	Charlotte -- World 600	18	17	400	384	2	Running	2,960	117	5	24	-1,245	Yarborough
18	15	Jun 19	Michigan -- Cam 2 Motor Oil 400	13	28	200	131	8	DNF - Engine	950	84	5	23	-1,516	Yarborough
19	16	Jul 4	Daytona -- Firecracker 400	17	36	160	45	0	DNF - Transmission	910	55	0	24	-1,560	Yarborough
20	17	Jul 16	Nashville -- Nashville 420	17	10	420	404	0	Running	1,565	134	0	23	-1,591	Yarborough
21	18	Jul 31	Pocono -- Coca-Cola 500	12	7	200	198	0	Running	3,300	146	0	22	-1,608	R. Petty
22	19	Aug 7	Talladega -- Talladega 500	13	4	188	186	0	Running	8,000	160	0	21	-1,615	Yarborough
23	20	Aug 22	Michigan -- Champion Spark Plug 400	10	7	200	199	0	Running	2,000	146	0	20	-1,634	Yarborough
24	21	Aug 28	Bristol -- Volunteer 400	11	16	400	220	0	Running	590	115	0	20	-1,704	Yarborough
25	22	Sep 5	Darlington -- Southern 500[1]	18	7	367	360	0	Running	7,400	146	0	18	-1,718	Yarborough
26	23	Sep 11	Richmond -- Capital City 400	15	11	400	384	0	Running	2,540	130	0	18	-1,753	Yarborough
27	24	Sep 18	Dover -- Delaware 500	12	32	500	178	0	DNF - Engine	530	67	0	19	-1,856	Yarborough
28	25	Sep 25	Martinsville -- Old Dominion 500	14	27	500	84	0	DNF - Rear End	580	82	0	19	-1,959	Yarborough
29	26	Oct 2	North Wilkesboro -- Wilkes 400	14	7	400	388	0	Running	2,730	146	0	18	-1,988	Yarborough
30	27	Oct 9	Charlotte -- NAPA National 500	21	24	334	232	0	Running	1,750	91	0	19	-2,072	Yarborough
31	28	Oct 23	Rockingham -- American 500	16	25	492	234	0	DNF - Engine	920	88	0	19	-2,149	Yarborough
32	29	Nov 6	Atlanta -- Dixie 500	11	8	268	266	0	Running	6,150	142	0	17	-2,167	Yarborough
33	30	Nov 20	Ontario -- Los Angeles Times 500	16	8	200	197	3	Running	5,515	147	5	17	-2,190	Yarborough

[1] -- Relieved by Butch Hartman

The 1977 Rookie Class

Rudd won the 1977 Rookie-of-the-Year Award. A look at his competition that season.

Driver	Point Standing	Starts	Avg. Start	Avg. Finish	Top 10s	Laps Led	Points	Money
Ricky Rudd	17th	25	16.6	17.5	10	13	2,810	$68,448
Sam Sommers	21st	23	12.5	18.5	8	28	2,517	54,525
Janet Guthrie	25th	19	17.9	17.7	4	5	2,104	37,945
Butch Hartman	32nd	11	21.8	20.6	2	0	1,116	18,615

1978: No Reward for Hard Work

When Ricky Rudd lost his Tide sponsorship at the end of the 1999 season to a rookie owner with no Winston Cup experience (Cal Wells), his reaction was immediate and angry. Rudd took swipes at Procter & Gamble (the maker of Tide laundry detergent) and at Wells, then called on NASCAR to institute policies to protect veteran owners from the whims of fickle sponsors. Rudd's proposal was radical (and, ultimately, ignored). More than any other sport, NASCAR is a free-market capitalist's dream. Sponsors, car owners, and drivers enjoy more freedom to pursue their interests in the Winston Cup series than in any other sports league. In fact, Rudd took full advantage of those freedoms to get his career started. Other, more strictly controlled racing series certainly would have balked at allowing a driver as inexperienced as Rudd was in 1975 to race in its top division.

So, why would Rudd, one of NASCAR's most experienced veterans, ask the sport's governing body to reverse its policies so radically? Part of the reason is 1978, a year in which Rudd ran headfirst into NASCAR's harshest reality: sometimes, your performance doesn't count for much.

If on-track performance was the deciding factor, Rudd was on easy street after his Rookie of the Year season in 1977. Driving the same car in 25 races for a family-owned team operating on a shoestring budget, he had a Top 5 finish at Talladega, scored 10 Top 10 finishes and led three races. The conventional wisdom—if you want to race, win a sponsor over with top performances—didn't hold for Rudd. He and his dad failed to land a meaningful sponsorship for the 1978 season.

Without the necessary resources, Rudd couldn't run the same kind of schedule he had in 1977. He took his car to Daytona in February and looked to race his way into the Daytona 500. Instead, his nightmare scenario came to life when he was involved in a wreck just 21 laps into his Twin 125 qualifying race. Thanks to his solid qualifying effort (he had the 17th-fastest qualifying time) he was able to secure one of the final starting positions for the 500. Unfortunately, the damage to his car made even starting the race difficult. He wrestled the car for 21 laps in the Daytona 500 before exiting in 37th place.

With his car totaled and his father's bank account bereft, the 21-year-old Rudd entered events whenever possible. He started 12 races after the Daytona 500 in 1978, but finished only half of them. Remarkably, through the travails, he continued to post strong finishes. When not sidelined by a bad engine, he scored four Top 10 finishes at Darlington, Michigan, Pocono, and Atlanta. His qualifying efforts reached new heights when, for the first time in his career, he started in the Top 10 (seventh at Talladega and sixth at Rockingham). He also led five races.

In 46 races over a four-season span, Rudd had displayed the kind of budding talent that car owners and sponsors profess to treasure. Unfortunately, he could not secure the kind of deal that would have kept the family's racing enterprise afloat.

In 1979, Rudd hopped out of the Al Rudd Chevy and began working for hire. The cost of trying to do it his way had been too high. It's easy to see why the Tide-Cal Wells deal two decades later inspired such anger. In 1979, Rudd couldn't attract a sponsor despite a solid performance; in 1999, his long-time sponsor bolted for an owner with no performance.

1978 Stats Chart

Category	Rudd's Total
Money	$49,610
Starts	13
Point Standing	32nd
Total Points	1,264
Avg. Start	16.5
Avg. Finish	22.8
Wins	0
Winning Pct.	0.0
Top 5s	0
Top 10s	4
DNFs	7
Poles	0
Front Row Starts	0
Laps Led	16
Races Led	5
Times Led	5
Bonus Points	25
Laps Completed	2,535
Pct. Laps Completed	69.9
Points per Race	97.2
Lead-Lap Finishes	0

1978 Performance Chart
No. 22 Al Rudd Chevrolet

Career Race	Season Race	Date	Race	St.	Fin.	Total Laps	Laps Completed	Laps Led	Condition	Money	Pts.	Bonus Pts.	Point Standing	Behind Leader	Current Leader
34	2	Feb 19	Daytona -- Daytona 500	36	37	200	21	0	DNF - Handling	4,375	52	0	54	-308	Yarborough
35	7	Apr 9	Darlington -- Rebel 500	18	10	367	349	2	Running	5,290	139	5	40	-988	B. Parsons
36	10	May 14	Talladega -- Winston 500	13	27	188	150	1	DNF - Engine	3,355	87	5	38	-1,270	Marcis
37	12	May 28	Charlotte -- World 600	20	28	400	331	0	Running	3,430	79	0	37	-1,505	B. Parsons
38	15	Jun 18	Michigan -- Gabriel 400	11	9	200	195	0	Running	5,400	138	0	35	-1,867	Yarborough
39	16	Jul 4	Daytona -- Firecracker 400	25	21	160	143	0	DNF - Engine	2,970	100	0	33	-1,942	Yarborough
40	18	Jul 30	Pocono -- Coca-Cola 500	17	6	200	197	0	Running	5,745	150	0	33	-2,067	Yarborough
41	19	Aug 6	Talladega -- Talladega 500	7	39	188	22	0	DNF - Engine	2,580	46	0	35	-2,191	Yarborough
42	20	Aug 20	Michigan -- Champion Spark Plug 400	21	28	200	113	1	DNF - Engine	2,255	84	5	34	-2,287	Yarborough
43	22	Sep 4	Darlington -- Southern 500	13	36	367	122	1	DNF - Crash	3,025	60	5	35	-2,597	Yarborough
44	27	Oct 8	Charlotte -- NAPA National 500	13	23	334	308	0	Running	3,710	94	0	35	-3,305	Yarborough
45	28	Oct 22	Rockingham -- American 500	6	25	492	262	0	DNF - Engine	2,225	88	0	34	-3,402	Yarborough
46	29	Nov 5	Atlanta -- Dixie 500	15	8	328	322	11	Running	5,900	147	5	32	-3,402	Yarborough

Few drivers have seen as much on the Winston Cup circuit as Ricky Rudd. Here, he talks with one of NASCAR's newest stars, Tony Stewart.

1979: A Hired Gun

Driven to succeed on the Winston Cup Grand National circuit, but stung by his inability to attract the necessary sponsor dollars to sustain his own team, Ricky Rudd hired himself out for the first time in his career in 1979. In his first opportunity to drive full-time for someone other than his dad, he couldn't have picked a more established Winston Cup car owner. Rudd signed with Junie Donlavey, whose NASCAR roots stretched even farther back than Bill Champion's (Rudd's first patron in 1975).

Donlavey fielded a car for the first time at Martinsville in 1950—NASCAR's second year of existence. On that day, his driver, Runt Harris, finished in 19th place. In 1971, Donlavey became a full-time Grand National car owner. His incredible career continues today. Now in his 51st season, he fields the No. 90 cars driven by Rick Mast.

For Rudd in 1979, the opportunity was golden. For the first time in his career, he was in a competitive car on a weekly basis. His performance reflected his improved condition: He finished the season ninth in the final point standings, enjoyed the best Daytona 500 start of his short career, finished eight straight races in the Top 10 late in the year, and saw a dramatic improvement in his qualifying. Once again, Rudd proved an ability to produce solid results when given a chance.

It didn't last.

Donlavey, it turned out, was between drivers. After losing Dick Brooks after the 1978 season (to new owner Nelson Malloch), he hired Rudd to fill in. By the end of the 1979 season, Donlavey was grooming a young star named Jody Ridley. When the season ended, Rudd's ride became Ridley's. Donlavey's move wasn't completely off-base. Ridley in 1980 unfurled one of the best rookie seasons in NASCAR history and finished seventh in the point standings—an effort matched or bettered only by Dale Earnhardt and Tony Stewart in their rookie years. Ridley then finished fifth in the final standings in his sophomore season.

None of this made Rudd feel any better, of course. In consecutive seasons, he witnessed first-hand the fickle nature of sponsors and car owners. Results, it appeared, were not hard-and-fast reflections of talent; instead they were open to interpretation.

To the objective eye, Rudd's season was excellent. His average start and finish were career bests. He ranked 7th in the series in Top 10 finishes and 10th in Top 5 finishes. He earned a top position in the standings (9th) despite not racing in Riverside's two events (a cost-cutting measure). Considering Rudd's road course virtuosity, he may easily have finished the year in 7th. He finished ahead of seven drivers in the final 1979 point standings who had more starts—including Terry Labonte and Buddy Baker.

Just 22 years old, Rudd showed a knack for consistency. In an eight-race streak that started at Pocono in July and ended at Martinsville in September, he never finished worse than 9th in the final running order. The Pocono race, in which he finished 5th, marked the first time in Rudd's career that he finished on the lead lap. He followed with his best performance ever—3rd place—at Talladega. A month later at Richmond, he finished 3rd again. Rudd's run helped him climb from 16th to 12th in the point standings. Three more Top 10s in the final four races allowed him to leap-frog from 11th to 9th.

1979 Stats Chart

Category	Rudd's Total	Rudd's Rank	1979 Leader
Money	$146,302	10th	Richard Petty -- 561,934
Total Points	3,642	9th	Richard Petty -- 4,830
Avg. Start	11.5	12th	Buddy Baker -- 4.77
Avg. Finish	12.1	7th	Richard Petty -- 6.4
Wins	0	--	Darrell Waltrip -- 7
Top 5s	4	10th	Richard Petty -- 23
Top 10s	17	7th	Richard Petty -- 27
DNFs	6	23rd	Dick May -- 16
Poles	0	--	Buddy Baker -- 7
Front Row Starts	0	--	Buddy Baker -- 11
Laps Led	22	14th	Darrell Waltrip -- 2,128
Races Led	4	12th	Darrell Waltrip -- 26
Times Led	4	14th	Darrell Waltrip -- 119
Miles Led	30	15th	Darrell Waltrip -- 2,629
Times Led Most Laps	0	--	Darrell Waltrip -- 8
Bonus Points	20	12th	Darrell Waltrip -- 170
Laps Completed	8,836	9th	Darrell Waltrip -- 9,994
Miles Completed	9,917	11th	Darrell Waltrip -- 11,768
Points per Race	130.1	8th	Richard Petty -- 155.8
Lead-Lap Finishes	1	11th	Richard Petty -- 15

1979 Performance Chart

No. 90 Junie Donlavey Mercury

Career Race	Season Race	Date	Race	St.	Fin.	Total Laps	Laps Completed	Laps Led	Condition	Money	Pts.	Bonus Pts.	Point Standing	Behind Leader	Current Leader
47	2	Feb 18	Daytona -- Daytona 500	11	31	200	79	0	DNF - Engine	4,110	70	0	50	-290	D. Waltrip
48	3	Mar 4	Rockingham -- Carolina 500	6	34	492	9	0	DNF - Crash	1,030	61	0	33	-341	D. Waltrip
49	4	Mar 11	Richmond -- Richmond 400	15	11	400	390	0	Running	2,245	130	0	25	-376	D. Waltrip
50	5	Mar 18	Atlanta -- Atlanta 500	8	9	328	325	0	Running	5,720	138	0	23	-408	D. Waltrip
51	6	Mar 25	North Wilkesboro -- Northwestern Bank 400	9	14	400	392	0	Running	1,945	121	0	19	-451	B. Allison
52	7	Apr 1	Bristol -- Southeastern 500	15	10	500	485	0	Running	3,120	134	0	19	-492	B. Allison
53	8	Apr 8	Darlington -- CRC Chemicals Rebel 500	4	8	367	360	19	Running	5,950	147	5	19	-516	D. Waltrip
54	9	Apr 22	Martinsville -- Virginia 500	17	12	500	489	0	Running	2,470	127	0	19	-559	D. Waltrip
55	10	May 6	Talladega -- Winston 500	18	27	188	38	0	DNF - Steering	2,655	82	0	19	-652	D. Waltrip
56	11	May 12	Nashville -- Sun-Drop Music City 420	12	10	420	410	0	Running	1,850	134	0	17	-623	D. Waltrip
57	12	May 20	Dover -- Mason-Dixon 500	16	14	500	480	1	DNF - Crash	2,830	126	5	17	-641	B. Allison
58	13	May 27	Charlotte -- World 600	10	6	400	397	0	Running	14,845	150	0	16	-646	D. Waltrip
59	14	Jun 3	Texas World -- Texas 400	7	28	200	135	0	DNF - Engine	1,700	79	0	16	-752	D. Waltrip
60	16	Jun 17	Michigan -- Gabriel 400	8	8	200	199	0	Running	5,665	142	0	16	-914	D. Waltrip
61	17	Jul 4	Daytona -- Firecracker 400	19	13	160	155	0	Running	5,075	124	0	16	-955	D. Waltrip
62	19	Jul 30	Pocono -- Coca-Cola 500	6	5	200	200	0	Running	6,215	155	0	16	-1,141	D. Waltrip
63	20	Aug 5	Talladega -- Talladega 500	11	3	188	186	0	Running	13,920	165	0	16	-1,161	D. Waltrip
64	21	Aug 19	Michigan -- Champion Spark Plug 400	16	7	200	199	0	Running	5,320	146	0	15	-1,121	D. Waltrip
65	22	Aug 25	Bristol -- Volunteer 500	11	9	500	493	0	Running	3,030	138	0	14	-1,163	D. Waltrip
66	23	Sep 3	Darlington -- Southern 500[1]	14	8	367	361	0	Running	7,105	142	0	15	-1,161	D. Waltrip
67	24	Sep 9	Richmond -- Capital City 400	10	3	400	399	1	Running	5,650	170	5	13	-1,166	D. Waltrip
68	25	Sep 16	Dover -- CRC Chemicals 500	14	8	500	496	0	Running	4,400	142	0	13	-1,100	D. Waltrip
69	26	Sep 23	Martinsville -- Old Dominion 500	10	6	500	491	0	Running	4,700	150	0	12	-1,085	D. Waltrip
70	27	Oct 7	Charlotte -- NAPA National 500	21	11	334	327	0	Running	6,105	130	0	13	-1,125	D. Waltrip
71	28	Oct 14	North Wilkesboro -- Holly Farms 400	8	5	400	398	0	Running	3,325	155	0	11	-1,099	D. Waltrip
72	29	Oct 21	Rockingham -- American 500	13	20	492	420	0	DNF - Crash	2,480	103	0	10	-1,159	R. Petty
73	30	Nov 4	Atlanta -- Dixie 500	6	8	328	324	0	Running	6,285	142	0	9	-1,169	D. Waltrip
74	31	Nov 18	Ontario -- Los Angeles Times 500	8	10	200	199	1	Running	5,860	139	5	9	-1,188	R. Petty

[1] -- Relieved by Lennie Pond

1979 Breakout Chart

Donlavey Sandwich

After the 1978 season, car owner Junie Donlavey lost his driver, Dick Brooks. In 1980, he hired hotshot Jody Ridley. In between, Ricky Rudd drove Donlavey's Mercury. A comparison of their performances.

Driver	Year	Point Standing	Starts	Avg. Start	Avg. Finish	Top 5s	Top 10s	Money
Dick Brooks	1978	8th	27	12.4	13.4	5	17	132,350
Ricky Rudd	1979	9th	28	11.5	12.1	4	17	146,302
Jody Ridley	1980	7th	31	17.0	12.4	2	18	204,883

1980: To Those Who Wait

Ricky Rudd faced a depressingly familiar scenario when the 1980 season began. A solid performance one year was followed by an unceremonious benching the next. Junie Donlavey's decision to hand the reins to rookie Jody Ridley ousted Rudd from a car he had driven to a ninth-place finish in the final point standings. With no other opportunities available, Rudd was on his own for the 1980 season.

As usual, Rudd made the most of a tough situation. He hopped in and out of four different cars and started 13 of the season's 31 races. For the first time in four years, he didn't make the trip to Daytona in February—the last time in his career he would miss the Daytona 500. Starting in March, he raced for D.K. Ulrich, Nelson Malloch, and Bruce Hill. He even pulled the old No. 22 Al Rudd Chevrolet out of mothballs for three races.

In October of 1980, Rudd caught a much-needed break. It was a stroke of luck resulting in part from his own perseverance, and partly from another driver's. Rudd's perseverance was best illustrated in his constancy at Charlotte Motor Speedway. After 1977, regardless of whether he and his dad had the money, he had found a way to make both races at Charlotte. His persistence paid off when he qualified second for the National 500 in the fall of 1980—the first front-row start of his career. Driving the No. 22 Rudd machine, he led the second lap of the race, stayed on the lead lap throughout and finished fourth.

While not the best finish of his career, Rudd's effort caught the eye of Robert Yates, an engine builder with DiGard Racing, one of the Winston Cup Grand National series' strongest teams. That's where Rudd got an assist from the perseverance of another driver—Darrell Waltrip.

As the driver of the No. 88 DiGard Chevy since 1975, Waltrip had won 26 races and 18 poles. He had come within 11 points of winning the 1979 championship. And he wanted to leave. Unhappy with his contract, Waltrip had been angling to get out of his long-term contract with DiGard since 1977. Animosity between Waltrip and DiGard's management (particularly Jim and Bill Gardner) flared up for three years before they finally agreed to dissolve their relationship at Charlotte in October of 1980. Three weeks later, Waltrip was free to pursue the ride he really wanted: Junior Johnson's powerful No. 11 car.

Holding one of the series' best cars, DiGard Racing suddenly found itself without a driver. Rudd's Charlotte performance couldn't have been better timed. Prodded by an impressed Yates, DiGard signed Rudd to a five-year deal, though only the first year was guaranteed.

Rudd's good fortune was simply the latest in an illogical sequence of events. Good seasons yielded little or no opportunity, but the most disjointed season in his four-year career led to one of the best rides in NASCAR.

1980 Stats Chart

Category	Rudd's Total
Money	$50,500
Starts	13
Point Standing	32nd
Total Points	1,319
Avg. Start	14.0
Avg. Finish	21.1
Wins	0
Winning Pct.	0.0
Top 5s	1
Top 10s	3
DNFs	6
Poles	0
Front Row Starts	1
Laps Led	7
Races Led	2
Times Led	2
Bonus Points	10
Laps Completed	2,719
Pct. Laps Completed	68.4
Points per Race	101.5
Lead-Lap Finishes	1

1980 Performance Chart
Drove for Various Car Owners

Career Race	Season Race	Date	Race	St.	Fin.	Total Laps	Laps Completed	Laps Led	Condition	Money	Pts.	Bonus Pts.	Point Standing	Behind Leader	Current Leader
75	4	Mar 11	Rockingham -- Carolina 500[1]	11	12	492	472	0	Running	3,640	127	0	39	-533	Earnhardt
76	5	Mar 18	Atlanta -- Atlanta 500	5	31	328	147	6	DNF - Crash	1,420	75	5	37	-638	Earnhardt
77	7	Apr 1	Darlington -- CRC Chemicals Rebel 500	4	19	189	172	0	Running	2,965	106	0	33	-798	Earnhardt
78	13	May 27	Charlotte -- World 600[2]	13	9	400	394	0	Running	7,425	138	0	38	-1,506	Earnhardt
79	16	Jun 17	Michigan -- Gabriel 400	22	32	200	111	0	DNF - Engine	740	67	0	36	-1,874	Earnhardt
80	17	Jul 4	Daytona -- Firecracker 400[3]	28	13	160	155	0	Running	5,065	124	0	36	-1,920	Earnhardt
81	18	Jul 14	Nashville -- Busch Nashville 420	9	28	420	164	0	DNF - Engine	640	79	0	35	-2,021	Earnhardt
82	19	Jul 30	Pocono -- Coca-Cola 500	10	10	200	196	0	Running	4,890	134	0	33	-2,052	Earnhardt
83	20	Aug 5	Talladega -- Talladega 500[4]	28	20	188	150	0	Running	4,185	103	0	32	-2,119	Earnhardt
84	21	Aug 19	Michigan -- Champion Spark Plug 400	25	34	200	88	0	DNF - Transmission	1,220	61	0	32	-2,121	Earnhardt
85	22	Aug 25	Bristol -- Busch Volunteer 500	9	28	500	135	0	DNF - Mechanical	720	79	0	31	-2,217	Earnhardt
86	23	Sep 3	Darlington -- Southern 500	16	34	367	201	0	DNF - Steering	2,025	61	0	31	-2,307	Earnhardt
87	28	Oct 14	Charlotte -- National 500[5]	2	4	334	334	1	Running	15,350	165	5	32	-2,898	Earnhardt

[1] -- Drove No. 40 D.K. Ulrich Chevrolet

[2] -- Switched to No. 22 Al Rudd Chevrolet

[3] -- Switched to No. 7 Nelson Malloch Chevrolet

[4] -- Relieved by Bruce Hill

[5] -- Switched to No. 22 Al Rudd Chevrolet

Rudd exits pit road at Rockingham in 1991, with Alan Kulwicki, Dale Earnhardt, Ken Schrader, Sterling Marlin, and Bobby Hamilton in tow.

1981: Drivin' the No. 88 Gatorade Car

Given the best car in his career, Ricky Rudd responded with the best year of his career. In mediocre equipment, he had performed admirably. In the No. 88 DiGard powerhouse, he was a title contender. Taking over for the great—and grating—Darrell Waltrip, Rudd kept the No. 88 car up front.

On a personal level, Rudd reached many of the achievements that had eluded him during the early years of his career. Among the milestones Rudd achieved during the 1981 season:

• He won his first pole at Martinsville, then won two more at Nashville and Dover;

• He led the most laps in a race for the first time at Nashville, pacing the field for 210 of 420 laps;

• He started his first road course race at Riverside and immediately displayed his right-turn prowess. In the season-opening Winston Western 500 on the 2.6-mile course, he led 19 laps and raced among the Top 5 until engine trouble dropped him to 19th;

• He claimed his first Top 5 in the Daytona 500, finishing third—the best Daytona 500 finish of his career;

• For the first time, he strung together more than two consecutive Top 5 finishes, building a midseason streak of five straight Top 5s at Martinsville, Talladega, Nashville, Dover, and Charlotte.

Rudd started the season by finishing 10 of the first 15 races in sixth place or better. With his fourth place at Talladega, he pulled into second in the point standings behind Bobby Allison. He stayed in the runner-up position for six weeks before a DNF at Michigan knocked him back to third.

Unfortunately for Rudd, a career year wasn't enough.

The problem for Rudd in 1981 was the same problem he had in previous seasons: he didn't control his own destiny. DiGard Racing, one of the most powerful teams in NASCAR, held the position of strength over its 24-year-old driver. Worse yet, DiGard's management—particularly the volatile Gardner brothers—were mired in the intense rivalries and petty jealousies that afflicted the circuit's top teams during the late 1970s and early 1980s. Losses were taken personally. The championship was a matter of pride more than money. Every win by one team was met with charges of cheating by the others.

Still a relative newcomer, Rudd had almost no chance against the grudges and political forces that propelled his owners. Rudd finished in second-place three times in 1981—tying his career-best performance at Charlotte in 1980. He ended the year in sixth place in the final point standings. For the young driver, these were accomplishments to celebrate. For DiGard's hyper-talented and competitive team—with Yates building the engines and Gary Nelson leading the race-day crew—those second-place finishes were tainted: all three came when Darrell Waltrip, DiGard's former driver, won. And while Rudd was solid in the points all season, Waltrip was off winning the championship with Junior Johnson—something Waltrip couldn't accomplish in five seasons with DiGard.

Given Rudd's proven abilities in 118 races on the Winston Cup circuit, a second season with DiGard almost certainly would have been even better. Rudd may well have developed into the next big winner in NASCAR. But he never got that chance. The DiGard boys weren't interested in developing a driver. They needed to win a championship "today," if only to prevent the damnable Waltrip from winning another.

When Bobby Allison, coming off a bitterly disappointing season in 1980, left Harry Rainier's No. 28 team, DiGard chose not to exercise their option years with Rudd. They signed Allison, one of the greatest drivers in stock-car racing history, and let Rudd go. The 1981 season was one of the most uniquely exhilarating and frustrating years of his career. But it held true to the trend of Rudd's early career: Success must not go unpunished.

1981 Stats Chart

Category	Rudd's Total	Rudd's Rank	1981 Leader
Money	$381,968	4th	Darrell Waltrip -- 799,134
Total Points	3,988	6th	Darrell Waltrip -- 4,880
Avg. Start	7.6	4th	Darrell Waltrip -- 5.3
Avg. Finish	13.8	8th	Bobby Allison -- 6.8
Wins	0	--	Darrell Waltrip -- 12
Top 5s	14	3rd	B. Allison, D. Waltrip -- 21
Top 10s	17	5th	Bobby Allison -- 26
DNFs	9	12th	Kyle Petty -- 18
Poles	3	2nd	Darrell Waltrip -- 11
Front Row Starts	5	4th	Darrell Waltrip -- 15
Laps Led	443	9th	Darrell Waltrip -- 2,517
Races Led	12	9th	Darrell Waltrip -- 27
Times Led	20	12th	Bobby Allison -- 121
Miles Led	359	9th	Darrell Waltrip -- 2,330
Times Led Most Laps	1	6th	Darrell Waltrip -- 11
Bonus Points	65	9th	Darrell Waltrip -- 190
Laps Completed	8,942	7th	Bobby Allison -- 10,098
Miles Completed	9,879	8th	Bobby Allison -- 11,609
Points per Race	128.6	7th	Darrell Waltrip -- 157.4
Lead-Lap Finishes	7	5th	Darrell Waltrip -- 22

1981 Performance Chart
No. 88 DiGard Chevrolet

Career Race	Season Race	Date	Race	St.	Fin.	Total Laps	Laps Completed	Laps Led	Condition	Money	Pts.	Bonus Pts.	Point Standing	Behind Leader	Current Leader
88	1	Jan 11	Riverside -- Winston Western 500	3	19	119	98	19	DNF - Engine	$6,950	111	5	18	-74	B. Allison
89	2	Feb 15	Daytona -- Daytona 500	5	3	200	200	9	Running	53,115	170	5	5	-84	B. Allison
90	3	Feb 22	Richmond -- Richmond 400	8	2	400	400	7	Running	13,400	175	5	4	-54	R. Petty
91	4	Mar 1	Rockingham -- Carolina 500	5	31	492	224	1	DNF - Crash	6,045	75	5	7	-149	R. Petty
92	5	Mar 15	Atlanta -- Coca-Cola 500	16	22	328	280	0	Running	7,760	97	0	7	-151	B. Allison
93	6	Mar 29	Bristol -- Valleydale 500	5	2	500	500	0	Running	14,375	170	0	6	-146	B. Allison
94	7	Apr 5	North Wilkesboro -- Northwestern Bank 400	4	6	400	399	0	Running	6,550	150	0	5	-176	B. Allison
95	8	Apr 12	Darlington -- CRC Chemicals Rebel 500	10	11	367	359	0	Running	8,225	130	0	4	-184	B. Allison
96	9	Apr 26	Martinsville -- Virginia 500	1	3	500	499	24	Running	15,250	170	5	3	-138	B. Allison
97	10	May 3	Talladega -- Winston 500	10	4	188	188	8	Running	18,750	165	5	2	-153	B. Allison
98	11	May 9	Nashville -- Melling Tool 420	1	5	420	419	210	Running	7,375	165	10	2	-153	B. Allison
99	12	May 17	Dover -- Mason-Dixon 500	4	5	500	490	0	Running	9,450	155	0	2	-168	B. Allison
100	13	May 24	Charlotte -- World 600	13	4	400	397	0	Running	18,975	160	0	2	-193	B. Allison
101	14	Jun 7	Texas World -- Budweiser NASCAR 400	11	24	200	122	0	DNF - Engine	6,850	91	0	2	-272	B. Allison
102	15	Jun 14	Riverside -- Warner W. Hodgdon 400	6	5	95	95	0	Running	8,900	155	0	2	-193	B. Allison
103	16	Jun 21	Michigan -- Gabriel 400	15	30	200	172	1	DNF - Engine	6,215	78	5	3	-295	B. Allison
104	17	Jul 4	Daytona -- Firecracker 400	12	40	160	16	0	DNF - Crash	6,625	43	0	4	-336	B. Allison
105	18	Jul 11	Nashville -- Busch Nashville 420	2	4	420	419	0	Running	7,450	160	0	4	-351	B. Allison
106	19	Jun 26	Pocono -- Mountain Dew 500	7	6	200	199	0	Running	8,665	150	0	4	-294	B. Allison
107	20	Aug 2	Talladega -- Talladega 500	12	23	188	133	0	Running	7,575	94	0	4	-365	B. Allison
108	21	Aug 16	Michigan -- Champion Spark Plug 400	9	3	200	200	0	Running	15,150	165	0	4	-351	B. Allison
109	22	Aug 22	Bristol -- Busch 500	3	2	500	499	92	Running	12,375	175	5	4	-341	B. Alllison
110	23	Sep 7	Darlington -- Southern 500	7	23	367	343	0	DNF - Crash	7,850	94	0	4	-390	B. Allison
111	24	Sep 13	Richmond -- Wrangler Sanfor-Set 400	12	12	400	392	0	Running	5,550	127	0	4	-423	B. Allison
112	25	Sep 20	Dover -- CRC Chemicals 500	1	5	500	495	55	Running	11,375	160	5	4	-435	D. Waltrip
113	26	Sep 27	Martinsville -- Old Dominion 500	2	8	500	486	1	Running	7,950	147	5	4	-468	D. Waltrip
114	27	Oct 4	North Wilkesboro -- Holly Farms 400	15	25	400	112	0	DNF - Crash	5,085	88	0	4	-565	D. Waltrip
115	28	Oct 11	Charlotte -- National 500	8	3	334	334	0	Running	29,925	165	0	4	-580	D. Waltrip
116	29	Nov 1	Rockingham -- American 500	3	18	492	434	16	Running	7,000	114	5	4	-651	D. Waltrip
117	30	Nov 8	Atlanta -- Atlanta Journal 500	14	39	328	36	0	DNF - Engine	6,070	46	0	4	-780	D. Waltrip
118	31	Nov 22	Riverside -- Winston Western 500	13	40	119	2	0	DNF - Engine	6,150	43	0	6	-892	D. Waltrip

1981 Breakout Chart

DiGard Sandwich

In between two legends of stock-car racing, Ricky Rudd piloted the No. 88 DiGard Chevrolet for one season. A look at his performance in 1981 vs. those of Darrell Waltrip and Bobby Allison in 1980 and 1982.

Driver	Year	Point Standing	Avg. Start	Avg. Finish	Wins	Top 5s	Top 10s	Poles
Darrell Waltrip	1980	5th	5.1	12.8	5	16	17	5
Ricky Rudd	1981	6th	7.6	13.7	0	14	17	3
Bobby Allison	1982	2nd	7.7	9.3	8	14	20	1

1982: Drivin' for Childress

Pushed out of the powerful No. 88 car despite having the best season of his career, the 25-year-old Rudd hooked up with one of the newest owners on the Winston Cup circuit: Richard Childress. Childress retired as a driver 20 races into the 1981 season when he saw the opportunity to hire Dale Earnhardt to pilot his cars. Earnhardt was in the midst of a chaotic season in which his original owner, Rod Osterlund, sold his team without warning to J.D. Stacy. Earnhardt drove four races before deciding the financially unstable Stacy wasn't his ticket to a second championship.

Recognizing Earnhardt's unhappiness—and overwhelming talent—Childress retired from driving and handed his ride to the future Intimidator. Though he would become one of NASCAR's most successful car owners, Childress was remarkably unproductive as a driver. In an 11-season, 285-race career, he never won a race. In fact, he never finished second. He ended his career with just 6 Top 5 finishes and 76 Top 10s. He raced his own car for the last time at Talladega in July 1981. His last race as a driver came three months later, when he drove a Junior Johnson-owned car in the season-ending event at Atlanta.

The Childress-Earnhardt pairing in 1981 enjoyed mild success. In 11 races, they scored two Top 5s and four Top 10s. However, they also suffered three mechanically induced DNFs in the season's final five races. Given a chance to drive for long-time owner Bud Moore, Earnhardt left Childress and drove a Ford in 1982.

Deciding not to get back into the driver's seat, Childress hired Rudd to drive the No. 3 Chevrolet. While not as successful as he was in 1981, Rudd continue to develop rapidly in 1982. Most impressive was his improved qualifying performance. In 30 starts, he qualified eighth or better 22 times. His average start of 7.6 was the third best in the Winston Cup series, trailing only Darrell Waltrip (3.8) and Harry Gant (6.6). After winning the first three poles of his career in 1981, Rudd followed with two more—at Dover and Martinsville—in 1982.

Although they had qualifying figured out, Rudd and his Childress team had difficulty finishing races. Rudd had a career-high 13 DNFs in 1982, 12 of which were engine or mechanical in nature. He countered all of those Top-8 starts with 13 finishes outside of the Top 20. Not surprisingly, he completed just 7,753, or 76 percent, of the laps he attempted—a career low.

The inability to finish races wreaked havoc on Rudd's championship hopes. He started the year with six straight finishes of 15th or worse and dropped to 24th in the point standings. As the season—and his equipment—progressed, he was able to climb into 9th in the final point standings—the third Top 10 finish of his career.

1982 Stats Chart

Category	Rudd's Total	Rudd's Rank	1982 Leader
Money	$201,130	14th	Darrell Waltrip -- 923,151
Total Points	3,542	9th	Darrell Waltrip -- 4,489
Avg. Start	7.6	3rd	Darrell Waltrip -- 3.8
Avg. Finish	16.4	16th	Darrell Waltrip -- 9.1
Wins	0	--	Darrell Waltrip -- 12
Top 5s	6	12th	T. Labonte, D. Waltrip -- 17
Top 10s	13	8th	Terry Labonte -- 21
DNFs	13	8th	Lake Speed -- 19
Poles	2	4th	Darrell Waltrip -- 7
Front Row Starts	4	5th	Darrell Waltrip -- 14
Laps Led	140	15th	Darrell Waltrip -- 3,027
Races Led	8	14th	Darrell Waltrip -- 27
Times Led	10	16th	Bobby Allison -- 125
Miles Led	83	18	Bobby Allison -- 3,217
Times Led Most Laps	0	--	Bobby Allison -- 10
Bonus Points	40	15th	Darrell Waltrip -- 175
Laps Completed	7,753	11th	Darrell Waltrip -- 9,455
Miles Completed	8,680	10th	Bobby Allison -- 10,860
Points per Race	118.1	17th	Darrell Waltrip -- 149.6
Lead-Lap Finishes	5	10th	Darrell Waltrip -- 15

In his 700-plus race career, Rudd has 22 wins and 27 poles.

1982 Performance Chart
No. 3 Richard Childress Racing Pontiac

Career Race	Season Race	Date	Race	St.	Fin.	Total Laps	Laps Completed	Laps Led	Condition	Money	Pts.	Bonus Pts.	Point Standing	Behind Leader	Current Leader
119	1	Feb 14	Daytona -- Daytona 500	16	35	200	51	0	DNF - Engine	$6,050	58	0	36	-127	B. Allison
120	2	Feb 21	Richmond -- Richmond 400	14	22	250	242	0	Running	2,450	97	0	25	-172	B. Allison
121	3	Mar 14	Bristol -- Valleydale 500	7	27	500	217	0	DNF - Valve	1,110	82	0	23	-248	T. Labonte
122	4	Mar 21	Atlanta -- Coca-Cola 500	2	25	287	221	0	DNF - Engine	4,160	88	0	24	-302	T. Labonte
123	5	Mar 28	Rockingham -- Warner W. Hodgdon Carolina 500	10	15	492	437	0	Running	3,960	118	0	24	-359	T. Labonte
124	6	Apr 4	Darlington -- CRC Chemicals Rebel 500	7	29	367	133	0	DNF - Trans.	3,050	76	0	24	-433	T. Labonte
125	7	Apr 18	North Wilkesboro -- Northwestern Bank 400	7	9	400	398	0	Running	3,525	138	0	21	-470	T. Labonte
126	8	Apr 25	Martinsville -- Virginia National Bank 500	4	4	500	496	55	Running	8,520	165	5	16	-413	T. Labonte
127	9	May 2	Talladega -- Winston 500	3	24	188	116	1	Running	4,470	96	5	17	-492	T. Labonte
128	10	May 8	Nashville -- Cracker Barrel 420	8	19	420	393	0	DNF - Engine	1,885	106	0	18	-556	T. Labonte
129	11	May 16	Dover -- Mason-Dixon 500	4	22	500	271	0	DNF - Engine	2,620	97	0	18	-619	T. Labonte
130	12	May 30	Charlotte -- World 600	10	7	400	397	0	Running	11,130	146	0	16	-539	T. Labonte
131	13	Jun 6	Pocono -- Van Scoy Diamond Mine 500	15	6	200	199	0	Running	7,150	150	0	15	-549	T. Labonte
132	14	Jun 13	Riverside -- Budweiser 400	22	29	95	39	0	DNF - Oil Leak	1,785	76	0	17	-653	T. Labonte
133	15	Jun 20	Michigan -- Gabriel 400	8	5	200	200	1	Running	11,530	160	5	15	-577	T. Labonte
134	16	Jul 4	Daytona -- Firecracker 400	2	7	160	160	0	Running	10,420	146	0	14	-553	B. Allison
135	17	Jul 10	Nashville -- Busch Nashville 420	16	4	420	419	0	Running	5,360	160	0	12	-528	T. Labonte
136	18	Jul 25	Pocono -- Mountain Dew 500	3	31	200	62	0	DNF - Engine	2,050	70	0	11	-623	T. Labonte
137	19	Aug 1	Talladega -- Talladega 500	6	9	188	188	0	Running	8,250	138	0	11	-645	T. Labonte
138	20	Aug 22	Michigan -- Champion Spark Plug 400	3	14	200	195	0	Running	5,160	121	0	11	-674	B. Allison
139	21	Aug 28	Bristol -- Busch 500	6	7	500	498	0	Running	4,140	146	0	11	-708	B. Allison
140	22	Sep 6	Darlington -- Southern 500	6	31	367	168	1	DNF - Engine	4,175	75	5	11	-741	B. Allison
141	23	Sep 12	Richmond -- Wrangler Sanfor-Set 400	5	4	400	399	0	Running	7,930	160	0	10	-766	B. Allison
142	24	Sep 19	Dover -- CRC Chemicals 500	1	11	500	478	2	DNF - Crash	6,875	135	5	10	-770	B. Allison
143	25	Oct 3	North Wilkesboro -- Holly Farms 400	4	25	400	67	0	DNF - Engine	1,260	88	0	10	-781	B. Allison
144	26	Oct 10	Charlotte -- National 500	6	31	334	122	0	DNF - Engine	3,445	70	0	10	-859	B. Allison
145	27	Oct 17	Martinsville -- Old Dominion 500	1	2	500	500	77	Running	22,770	175	5	10	-832	D. Waltrip
146	28	Oct 31	Rockingham -- Warner W. Hodgdon American 500	6	28	492	242	0	DNF - Engine	2,610	79	0	10	-933	D. Waltrip
147	29	Nov 7	Atlanta -- Atlanta Journal 500	20	7	328	326	2	Running	7,255	151	5	9	-952	D. Waltrip
148	30	Nov 21	Riverside -- Winston Western 500	5	2	119	119	1	Running	16,980	175	5	9	-947	D. Waltrip

1982 Breakout Chart

Richard Childress Racing: The Major Drivers

A look at where Ricky Rudd stacks up in the storied history of Richard Childress Racing.

Driver	Seasons	Starts	Wins	Top 5s	Top 10s	Poles	DNFs	Money
Dale Earnhardt	1984-2001	529	67	227	348	17	47	$39,662,737
Mike Skinner	1997-2001	152	0	10	38	5	18	9,111,703
Ricky Rudd	1982-1983	60	2	13	27	6	21	458,715
Kevin Harvick	2001	35	2	6	16	0	1	4,302,202

1983: First Visit to Victory Lane

Ricky Rudd's second season in Richard Childress' No. 3 car was one of the best of his career. He picked up his first career victory, then his second. Nearly as impressive was his qualifying. Rudd won the first three poles of the season and finished the 1983 season with the best average starting position in the Winston Cup series.

Rudd's first win came on the road course at Riverside. The victory capped a steady progression in his road-course development and initiated his reputation as one of the Winston Cup series' best right turners. (He had two Top 5s in his previous five Riverside starts.) Rudd inadvertently helped secure his win by sliding off the road and kicking up dirt behind him. His accidental smoke screen created a wreck that collected Tim Richmond and Terry Labonte, two of the top contenders in the race. With his main competition sidelined, Rudd led the final 41 laps and cruised to a seven-second win over Bill Elliott.

Rudd needed 161 Winston Cup starts to get his first win. He needed just 12 more to get his second. At Martinsville, in another dominating performance, he led the final 330 laps—380 overall—and won by 4.5 seconds over Bobby Allison and Rudd's former DiGard team. The win was especially sweet because it came in Rudd's home state of Virginia. Martinsville is 205 miles west of his hometown of Chesapeake.

Throughout the season, Rudd displayed an unfailing ability to start up front. He won four poles and started on the front row nine times—totals exceeded in 1983 only by Darrell Waltrip. Of the season's 30 races, he started 24 of them in the top 10. Bolstering Rudd's qualifying effort was a record-setting run to open the year. He became the first and, so far, only driver in the Modern Era to win the pole for the first three races of a season.

Rudd's run started, naturally, at Daytona, where his qualifying lap of 198.864 miles per hour was second-fastest—but still won the pole. Cale Yarborough actually turned in a much faster lap (at 200.503 miles per hour), but lost control and crashed his car on his second qualifying lap. Under NASCAR rules at the time, Yarborough had to throw both laps out when his team was forced to pull out a back-up car. Because Yarborough would not be starting the Daytona 500 in the car he qualified, the rules stated, he could not hold on to his fast qualifying lap.

The pole fell to Rudd, the second-fastest qualifier. It remains Rudd's only Daytona pole. He finished the 1983 Daytona 500 in 24th, after experiencing mechanical problems.

Rudd's next two poles were not aided by NASCAR. At Richmond and Rockingham, he outpaced the competition with laps of 93.439 miles per hour at Richmond and 143.413 miles per hour at Rockingham. His pole streak ended in the season's fourth weekend at Atlanta, where he struggled to his worst qualifying effort (20th) of the year. He added a fourth pole a month later at Martinsville, setting his career-high for number of poles in a season. (He also won four in 1984.)

The 1983 season wasn't all wins and poles, however. For the first time in his career, Rudd ran afoul of NASCAR. At Martinsville—where he started from the pole—a late-race scuffle with Joe Ruttman cost Rudd $1,500 and placed him on a 10-race probation. The trouble started with the race's final restart with just nine laps to go. Rudd lined up behind race-leader Darrell Waltrip. When the checkered flag waved, however, Rudd had been bumped back to fifth. On the cool-down lap, an angry Rudd smashed up his car by repeatedly banging into Ruttman and then giving him a final shove on pit road. Members of Ruttman's crew threw punches at Rudd. Two days later, NASCAR penalized Rudd.

Not surprisingly, another breakthrough season by Rudd led to . . . the unemployment line. Similar to Donlavey and DiGard, Childress searched for a new driver after Rudd's solid campaign. Leaps in improvement and multiple wins couldn't help. Childress decided to reunite with Dale Earnhardt following the 1983 season. Childress and Earnhardt had teamed for 11 races in 1981, but parted ways during the off-season. Starting in 1984, they joined to form one of the most successful teams in NASCAR history.

1983 Stats Chart

Category	Rudd's Total	Rudd's Rank	1983 Leader*
Money	$257,585	11th	Bobby Allison -- 883,010
Total Points	3,693	9th	Bobby Allison -- 4,667
Avg. Start	6.6	1st	(Geoffrey Bodine -- 7.0)
Avg. Finish	15.3	9th	Bobby Allison -- 7.0
Wins	2	5th	B. Allison, D. Waltrip -- 6
Top 5s	7	10th	Darrell Waltrip -- 22
Top 10s	14	9th	B. Allison, D. Waltrip -- 25
DNFs	8	16th	G. Bodine, T. Gale -- 15
Poles	4	2nd	Darrell Waltrip -- 7
Front Row Starts	9	2nd	Darrell Waltrip -- 10
Laps Led	871	4th	Darrell Waltrip -- 2,363
Races Led	13	8th	Bobby Allison -- 25
Times Led	28	12th	Bobby Allison -- 88
Miles Led	707	7th	Bobby Allison -- 2,093
Times Led Most Laps	2	4th	Bobby Allison -- 8
Bonus Points	75	7th	Bobby Allison -- 165
Laps Completed	8,581	8th	Bobby Allison -- 10,038
Miles Completed	9,907	8th	Bobby Allison -- 11,526
Points per Race	123.1	10th	Bobby Allison -- 155.6
Lead-Lap Finishes	7	10th	Darrell Waltrip -- 20

* -- Second-place driver(s) in parentheses if Rudd is category leader

1983 Performance Chart
No. 3 Richard Childress Chevrolet

Career Race	Season Race	Date	Race	St.	Fin.	Total Laps	Laps Completed	Laps Led	Condition	Money	Pts.	Bonus Pts.	Point Standing	Behind Leader	Current Leader
149	1	Feb 20	Daytona -- Daytona 500	1	24	200	182	1	DNF - Mechanical	$16,515	96	5	23	-84	Yarborough
150	2	Feb 27	Richmond -- Richmond 400	1	28	400	177	26	DNF - Engine	3,615	84	5	21	-146	Ruttman
151	3	Mar 13	Rockingham -- Warner W. Hodgdon Carolina 500	1	6	492	489	30	Running	8,465	155	5	12	-165	Elliott
152	4	Mar 27	Atlanta -- Coca-Cola 500	20	10	328	326	0	Running	6,805	134	0	11	-117	Brooks
153	5	Apr 10	Darlington -- TranSouth 500	8	4	367	366	0	Running	9,905	160	0	8	-106	Bonnett
154	6	Apr 17	North Wilkesboro -- Northwestern Bank 400	7	27	400	59	0	DNF - Crash	1,875	82	0	7	-189	Bonnett
155	7	Apr 24	Martinsville -- Virginia National Bank 500	1	5	500	500	100	Running	9,670	160	5	8	-166	B. Allison
156	8	May 1	Talladega -- Winston 500	4	8	188	187	0	Running	10,865	142	0	7	-174	Gant
157	9	May 7	Nashville -- Marty Robbins 420	3	14	420	410	0	Running	2,540	121	0	8	-218	Gant
158	10	May 15	Dover -- Mason-Dixon 500	2	24	500	277	0	DNF - Engine	3,140	91	0	9	-306	B. Allison
159	11	May 21	Bristol -- Valleydale 500	3	26	500	393	0	DNF - Engine	1,120	85	0	11	-396	B. Allison
160	12	May 29	Charlotte -- World 600	9	32	400	245	0	Running	3,425	67	0	11	-504	B. Allison
161	13	Jun 5	Riverside -- Budweiser 400	4	1	95	95	57	Running	24,530	185	10	9	-416	B. Allison
162	14	Jun 12	Pocono -- Van Scoy Diamond Mine 500	2	31	200	100	8	DNF - Engine	2,550	75	5	9	-526	B. Allison
163	15	Jun 19	Michigan -- Gabriel 400	14	6	200	200	0	Running	10,075	150	0	9	-551	B. Allison
164	16	Jul 4	Daytona -- Firecracker 400	6	21	160	149	0	Running	4,315	100	0	9	-577	B. Allison
165	17	Jul 16	Nashville -- Busch Nashville 420	6	5	420	417	0	Running	4,770	155	0	10	-587	B. Allison
166	18	Jul 24	Pocono -- Like Cola 500	6	7	200	200	0	Running	7,460	146	0	9	-616	B. Allison
167	19	Jul 31	Talladega -- Talladega 500	17	16	188	182	0	Running	5,750	115	0	9	-644	B. Allison
168	20	Aug 21	Michigan -- Champion Spark Plug 400	9	27	200	188	0	Running	3,165	82	0	10	-628	B. Allison
169	21	Aug 27	Bristol -- Busch 500	4	14	419	396	0	Running	3,110	121	0	10	-672	B. Allison
170	22	Sep 5	Darlington -- Southern 500	8	25	367	272	76	DNF - Engine	7,415	93	5	9	-764	B. Allison
171	23	Sep 11	Richmond -- Wrangler Sanfor-Set 400	13	2	400	400	133	Running	19,025	175	5	9	-774	B. Allison
172	24	Sep 18	Dover -- Budweiser 500	2	13	500	467	0	Running	4,855	124	0	9	-835	B. Allison
173	25	Sep 25	Martinsville -- Goody's 500	2	1	500	500	380	Running	31,395	185	10	8	-825	B. Allison
174	26	Oct 2	North Wilkesboro -- Holly Farms 400	3	6	400	399	1	Running	4,675	155	5	9	-840	B. Allison
175	27	Oct 9	Charlotte -- Miller High Life 500	13	9	334	334	1	Running	8,265	143	5	8	-848	B. Allison
176	28	Oct 30	Rockingham -- Warner W. Hodgdon American 500	8	3	492	491	57	Running	11,370	170	5	8	-798	B. Allison
177	29	Nov 6	Atlanta -- Atlanta Journal 500	18	26	328	148	0	DNF - Engine	3,000	85	0	8	-888	B. Allison
178	30	Nov 20	Riverside -- Winston Western 500	2	37	119	32	1	Running	1,900	57	5	9	-974	B. Allison

1984: Surviving Daytona

Following his successful 1983 campaign, Ricky Rudd spent the off-season shopping for a job. After a brief flirtation with the RahMoc Racing team, owned by Bob Rahilly and Butch Mock, Rudd signed with Bud Moore to pilot his No. 15 Fords. Weighing in favor of Moore in Rudd's mind was his long history in NASCAR and, most importantly, his established sponsorship deal with Wrangler Jeans.

Like Bill Champion and Junie Donlavey, two of Rudd's previous car owners, Moore's association with NASCAR stretched back to the beginning. Moore first entered a car in a NASCAR event in 1950. Since 1961, he had been a more-or-less full-time competitor in the series. His drivers included a who's-who of stock-car greats, including Joe Weatherly, Darrell Waltrip, Bobby Isaac, Buddy Baker, Bobby Allison, and Dale Earnhardt. Earnhardt drove for Moore during the two seasons preceding Rudd's tenure.

Though Rudd and Moore's relationship started tentatively—with Rudd accepting Moore's offer after appearing committed to Rahilly and Mock—they raced together for four seasons between 1984 and 1987. No other driver stayed with Moore as long as Rudd. Similarly, only when Rudd owned his own team for six seasons from 1994–1999, did he stick with the same team longer than he did with Moore. (Rudd also raced for Rick Hendrick for four years from 1990 to 1993.)

If their off-track partnership was calm, their on-track start was anything but. In his first race for Moore—the 1984 Busch Clash—Rudd suffered the worst wreck of his career. On the 16th of 20 laps, he lost control of his car coming out of Turn 4 and began a violent, tumbling one-car accident that left him bruised and battered. During the ordeal, Rudd's No. 15 Ford rolled end over end seven times.

During the early part of his career, Rudd displayed mental toughness annually as his struggles to gain a solid ride rarely detracted from his solid on-track performance. After his Daytona wreck, Rudd demonstrated an uncommon physical toughness. With a face so swollen he could barely open his eyes, he nevertheless competed and finished well in the Twin 125s and Daytona 500 just days later. In a move that created a legend, Rudd used duct tape on his forehead and cheeks to help keep his eyes open as he drove. Three days after the crash, he turned a lap of 194.696 in his backup Ford Thunderbird during practice. The following day, he finished his Twin 125 qualifying event in seventh. In the Daytona 500, he finished seventh again.

In one of the season's best moments, Rudd won the Miller High Life 400 at Richmond just 14 days after his accident. Before a friendly crowd in his home state of Virginia, he took the lead from Darrell Waltrip with 20 laps to go and cruised to a three-second win. The victory gave Rudd wins at both Virginia tracks (he won at Martinsville in 1983) and pushed him to second in the point standings, just 24 points behind Waltrip.

Rudd maintained a strong position in the point standings throughout the first half of the season. With 10 Top 10 finishes in the first 13 races, he was just 44 points behind Waltrip at the midpoint of the year. A summer slump doomed any title hopes, however. He finished eight straight races outside of the Top 12 and saw his 44-point deficit balloon to 476 by the time the series went to Darlington for the Southern 500.

The poor finishes masked another solid season of qualifying for Rudd. For the fourth season in a row, his average starting position was in the Top 10. His four poles—at Bristol, North Wilkesboro, Dover, and Nashville—tied him with Bill Elliott, Cale Yarborough, and Waltrip for the most pole starts in 1984.

1984 Stats Chart

Category	Rudd's Total	Rudd's Rank	1984 Leader*
Money	$476,602	7th	Terry Labonte -- 713,010
Total Points	3,918	7th	Terry Labonte -- 4,508
Avg. Start	8.7	7th	Bill Elliott -- 5.2
Avg. Finish	12.5	8th	Cale Yarborough -- 7.4
Wins	1	10th	Darrell Waltrip -- 7
Top 5s	7	8th	Terry Labonte -- 17
Top 10s	16	7th	B. Elliott, T. Labonte -- 24
DNFs	6	27th	J. Ruttman, G. Sacks -- 14
Poles	4	T-1st	(B. Elliott, D. Waltrip, C. Yarborough -- 4)
Front Row Starts	6	2nd	Bill Elliott -- 11
Laps Led	566	9th	Darrell Waltrip -- 2,030
Races Led	8	10th	Terry Labonte -- 26
Times Led	19	13th	Cale Yarborough -- 77
Miles Led	338	12th	Darrell Waltrip -- 1,577
Times Led Most Laps	1	8th	Darrell Waltrip -- 7
Bonus Points	45	10th	T. Labonte, D. Waltrip -- 145
Laps Completed	9,271	7th	Harry Gant -- 9,899
Miles Completed	10,584	5th	Harry Gant -- 11,395
Points per Race	130.6	9th	Cale Yarborough -- 153.0
Lead-Lap Finishes	7	8th	H. Gant, T. Labonte, D. Waltrip -- 15

* -- Second-place driver(s) listed in parentheses if Rudd is category leader.

1984 Performance Chart

No. 15 Bud Moore Ford

Career Race	Season Race	Date	Race	St.	Fin.	Total Laps	Laps Completed	Laps Led	Condition	Money	Pts.	Bonus Pts.	Point Standing	Behind Leader	Current Leader
179	1	Feb 19	Daytona -- Daytona 500	14	7	200	199	0	Running	$38,700	146	0	7	-39	Yarborough
180	2	Feb 26	Richmond -- Miller High Life 400	4	1	400	400	36	Running	31,775	180	5	2	-24	D. Waltrip
181	3	Mar 3	Rockingham -- Warner W. Hodgdon Carolina 500	3	7	492	488	0	Running	11,415	146	0	3	-12	D. Waltrip
182	4	Mar 18	Atlanta -- Coca-Cola 500	2	8	328	326	0	Running	12,825	142	0	4	-9	T. Labonte
183	5	Apr 1	Bristol -- Valleydale 500	1	6	500	498	0	Running	10,630	150	0	4	-39	D. Waltrip
184	6	Apr 8	North Wilkesboro -- Northwestern Bank 400	1	3	400	400	290	Running	22,190	175	10	3	-24	T. Labonte
185	7	Apr 15	Darlington -- TranSouth 500	3	9	367	358	1	Running	11,400	143	5	3	-56	D. Waltrip
186	8	Apr 29	Martinsville -- Sovran Bank 500	9	18	500	487	121	Running	7,950	114	5	4	-112	D. Waltrip
187	9	May 6	Talladega -- Winston 500	10	22	188	165	0	DNF - Valve	11,000	97	0	5	-64	D. Waltrip
188	10	May 12	Nashville -- Coors 420	2	4	420	420	0	Running	10,450	160	0	3	-84	D. Waltrip
189	11	May 20	Dover -- Budweiser 500	1	8	500	497	13	Running	14,200	147	5	3	-87	D. Waltrip
190	12	May 27	Charlotte -- World 600	10	11	400	395	0	Running	14,025	130	0	3	-47	D. Waltrip
191	13	Jun 3	Riverside -- Budweiser 400	7	9	95	94	0	Running	10,100	138	0	4	-44	D. Waltrip
192	14	Jun 10	Pocono -- Van Scoy Diamond Mine 500	14	18	200	197	0	Running	10,490	109	0	4	-90	D. Waltrip
193	15	Jun 17	Michigan -- Miller High Life 400	14	40	200	41	0	DNF - Engine	9,250	43	0	7	-217	D. Waltrip
194	16	Jul 4	Daytona -- Pepsi Firecracker 400	22	15	160	156	0	Running	11,950	118	0	7	-216	Earnhardt
195	17	Jul 14	Nashville -- Pepsi 420	1	16	420	413	36	Running	9,575	120	5	7	-266	Earnhardt
196	18	Jul 22	Pocono -- Like Cola 500	21	39	200	23	0	DNF - Engine	9,675	46	0	9	-359	Earnhardt
197	19	Jul 29	Talladega -- Talladega 500	24	14	188	188	0	Running	11,870	121	0	9	-418	Earnhardt
198	20	Aug 12	Michigan -- Champion Spark Plug 400	10	12	200	198	0	Running	11,950	127	0	8	-437	Earnhardt
199	21	Aug 25	Bristol -- Busch 500	7	16	500	442	0	DNF - Rear End	7,850	115	0	8	-476	T. Labonte
200	22	Sep 2	Darlington -- Southern 500	11	5	367	364	0	Running	17,050	155	0	7	-468	T. Labonte
201	23	Sep 9	Richmond -- Wrangler Sanfor-Set 400	4	2	400	400	68	Running	22,325	175	5	7	-440	T. Labonte
202	24	Sep 16	Dover -- Delaware 500	7	3	500	498	1	Running	17,200	170	5	7	-445	T. Labonte
203	25	Sep 23	Martinsville -- Goody's 500	5	27	500	58	0	DNF - Engine	8,030	82	0	7	-538	T. Labonte
204	26	Oct 7	Charlotte -- Miller High Life 500	7	8	334	332	0	Running	14,225	142	0	7	-556	T. Labonte
205	27	Oct 14	North Wilkesboro -- Holly Farms 400	8	6	400	400	0	Running	9,475	150	0	7	-549	T. Labonte
206	28	Oct 21	Rockingham -- Warner W. Hodgdon American 500	21	23	492	389	0	DNF - Engine	9,950	94	0	7	-625	T. Labonte
207	29	Nov 11	Atlanta -- Atlanta Journal 500	13	3	328	328	0	Running	19,350	165	0	7	-538	T. Labonte
208	30	Nov 18	Riverside -- Winston Western 500	6	15	119	117	0	Running	11,000	118	0	7	-590	T. Labonte

1985: Saving the Streak at Riverside

In Ricky Rudd's second season with Bud Moore, the winning streak he would later become best known for nearly died. Starting in 1983, Rudd embarked on a 16-year streak in which he won at least one race (the streak ended with a winless 1999). In 12 of those 16 years, he won just one time. In 1995, he waited until the next-to-last race before winning. In 1996, he waited until the third-to-last race.

In 1985, however, Rudd procrastinated until the very last race of the season before picking up his annual victory. At Riverside, after starting fourth and overcoming a cut tire that required an unscheduled pit stop, he passed Terry Labonte and led the final 24 laps to secure the win. The last-minute triumph was Rudd's second victory at Riverside, and it ended a 56-race winless streak dating back to his inspiring Richmond win in the second race of 1984.

Though finding Victory Lane was a difficult task all season long, Rudd nevertheless enjoyed one of the best seasons of his career. For the fifth straight year, he was among the series' best qualifiers. He started 22 of 28 races inside the Top 10—though, curiously, he failed to win a pole after winning four in each of the previous two seasons. More importantly, his ability to finish races improved to a career-best level. He enjoyed a career-low five DNFs, and his average finish (10.5) is still the second-best in his career.

Unfortunately, his improvement coincided with amazing seasons recorded by Bill Elliott and Darrell Waltrip. Elliott won 11 races and the Winston Million, while Waltrip won his third Winston Cup championship through consistent finishes. Waltrip's 18 Top 5s and 21 Top 10s led the series. Rudd was second in Top 10s with 19.

Mixed into Rudd's successful season was a moment of controversy at Dover. In the 1-mile oval's second race in September, Rudd appeared to finish second, but was placed third in the finishing order by NASCAR's scoring officials. NASCAR later acknowledged that Waltrip was mistakenly credited with a second place finish. However, the sanctioning body refused to correct the problem, saying that the event was completed and the results set in stone.

Though he has yet to win a Winston Cup championship, Rudd has developed a loyal following among race fans.

1985 Stats Chart

Category	Rudd's Total	Rudd's Rank	1985 Leader
Money	$512,441	8th	Bill Elliott -- 2,433,187
Total Points	3,857	6th	Darrell Waltrip -- 4,292
Avg. Start	7.9	4th	Bill Elliott -- 4.9
Avg. Finish	10.5	4th	Darrell Waltrip -- 7.3
Wins	1	7th	Bill Elliott -- 11
Top 5s	13	4th	Darrell Waltrip -- 18
Top 10s	19	2nd	Darrell Waltrip -- 21
DNFs	5	28th	J.D. McDuffie -- 15
Poles	0	--	Bill Elliott -- 11
Front Row Starts	1	10th	Bill Elliott -- 12
Laps Led	329	11th	Bill Elliott -- 1,920
Races Led	6	12th	Darrell Waltrip -- 21
Times Led	12	11th	Bill Elliott -- 80
Miles Led	288	11th	Bill Elliott -- 3,188
Times Led Most Laps	0	--	Bill Elliott -- 7
Bonus Points	30	12th	Bill Elliott -- 130
Laps Completed	8,475	9th	Darrell Waltrip -- 8,932
Miles Completed	10,281	6th	Darrell Waltrip -- 10,910
Points per Race	137.8	6th	Darrell Waltrip -- 153.3
Lead-Lap Finishes	8	6th	Darrell Waltrip -- 17

1985 Performance Chart

No. 15 Bud Moore Ford

Career Race	Season Race	Date	Race	St.	Fin.	Total Laps	Laps Completed	Laps Led	Condition	Money	Pts.	Bonus Pts.	Point Standing	Behind Leader	Current Leader
209	1	Feb 17	Daytona -- Daytona 500	9	5	200	199	0	Running	$52,900	155	0	6	-30	Elliott
210	2	Feb 24	Richmond -- Miller High Life 400	21	25	400	108	0	DNF - Engine	7,155	88	0	9	-97	D. Waltrip
211	3	Mar 3	Rockingham -- Carolina 500	3	32	492	162	0	DNF - Engine	7,975	67	0	16	-159	Speed
212	4	Mar 17	Atlanta -- Coca-Cola 500	5	4	328	327	30	Running	15,825	165	5	11	-143	G. Bodine
213	5	Apr 6	Bristol -- Valleydale 500	6	2	500	500	163	Running	18,050	175	5	8	-88	T. Labonte
214	6	Apr 14	Darlington -- TranSouth 500	9	25	367	249	0	DNF - Crash	8,200	88	0	11	-165	T. Labonte
215	7	Apr 21	North Wilkesboro -- Northwestern Bank 400	13	4	400	400	0	Running	9,870	160	0	8	-151	T. Labonte
216	8	Apr 28	Martinsville -- Sovran Bank 500	7	2	500	500	1	Running	22,450	175	5	7	-140	G. Bodine
217	9	May 5	Talladega -- Winston 500	15	5	188	187	0	Running	21,025	155	0	5	-127	T. Labonte
218	10	May 19	Dover -- Budweiser 500	5	4	500	498	0	Running	15,375	160	0	5	-109	Elliott
219	11	May 26	Charlotte -- Coca-Cola World 600	17	13	400	391	0	Running	13,255	124	0	6	-118	T. Labonte
220	12	Jun 2	Riverside -- Budweiser 400	5	4	95	95	0	Running	11,825	160	0	5	-143	T. Labonte
221	13	Jun 9	Pocono -- Van Scoy Diamond Mine 500	9	7	200	198	0	Running	12,130	146	0	5	-128	Elliott
222	14	Jun 16	Michigan -- Miller 400	5	7	200	199	0	Running	13,900	146	0	5	-162	Elliott
223	15	Jul 4	Daytona -- Pepsi Firecracker 400	3	7	160	160	0	Running	14,500	146	0	5	-196	Elliott
224	16	Jul 21	Pocono -- Summer 500	10	14	200	197	0	Running	9,765	121	0	5	-255	Elliott
225	17	Jul 28	Talladega -- Talladega 500	12	18	188	180	0	Running	11,050	109	0	5	-316	Elliott
226	18	Aug 11	Michigan -- Champion Spark Plug 400	4	31	200	128	0	DNF - Oil Leak	8,035	70	0	7	-426	Elliott
227	19	Aug 24	Bristol -- Busch 500	6	9	500	495	0	Running	7,450	138	0	7	-448	Elliott
228	20	Sep 1	Darlington -- Southern 500	11	6	367	366	0	Running	13,450	150	0	7	-478	Elliott
229	21	Sep 8	Richmond -- Wrangler Sanfor-Set 400	3	5	400	400	53	Running	9,900	160	5	6	-445	Elliott
230	22	Sep 15	Dover -- Delaware 500	7	3	500	499	55	Running	31,450	170	5	5	-383	Elliott
231	23	Sep 22	Martinsville -- Goody's 500	5	4	500	499	0	Running	12,350	160	0	5	-335	Elliott
232	24	Sep 29	North Wilkesboro -- Holly Farms 400	2	5	400	399	0	Running	9,500	155	0	5	-283	D. Waltrip
233	25	Oct 6	Charlotte -- Miller High Life 500	8	15	334	320	0	Running	11,350	118	0	5	-330	D. Waltrip
234	26	Oct 20	Rockingham -- Nationwise 500	9	7	492	492	0	Running	11,150	146	0	4	-364	D. Waltrip
235	27	Nov 3	Atlanta -- Atlanta Journal 500	7	31	328	208	0	DNF - Piston	7,650	70	0	6	-464	D. Waltrip
236	28	Nov 17	Riverside -- Winston Western 500	4	1	119	119	27	Running	37,875	180	5	6	-435	D. Waltrip

1985 Breakout Chart

Close Calls

At several points during his career, Ricky Rudd nearly lost one of his signature accomplishments—his 16-year winning streak. A look at his close calls

Season	Victory	Race No.	No. of Races that Season
1985	Riverside—Winston Western 500	28	28
1995	Phoenix—Dura-Lube 400	30	31
1996	Rockingham—AC Delco 400	29	31
1992	Dover—Peak AntiFreeze 500	23	29
1998	Martinsville—NAPA Autocare 500	27	33

1986: Lapping the Field at Martinsville

At Martinsville in 1986, Ricky Rudd became one of the last Winston Cup drivers to win a race by a full lap. A regular phenomenon in NASCAR's earlier history, only 85 races have been won by one or more laps in the Modern Era. Most of those lopsided wins occurred during the 1970s, when the distribution of sponsorship dollars and mechanical expertise was disproportionately weighted toward fewer well-financed, high-powered teams. The obvious result was huge numbers of races in which only a handful of cars remained on the lead lap at the end.

As NASCAR's popularity increased and sponsors poured money into the sport in hopes of gaining Victory Lane exposure, the number of competitive teams increased markedly. In each decade, the number of races in which the winner lapped the field fell precipitously. In the 1970s, 67 races were decided by at least a lap. In the 1990s, only two races featured lapped fields. The last driver to win by a lap was Geoffrey Bodine in 1994 in the fall race at North Wilkesboro.

Rudd accomplished the feat in the Sovran Bank 500 at Martinsville in April of 1986. Thanks to a solid car and a little luck—more precisely, bad luck for other drivers—he crossed the finish line a full lap ahead of second-place Joe Ruttman. Rudd started the race in the fourth position, but didn't take the lead until lap 292, after race leader Harry Gant exited with a blown engine. Seven of the event's Top 10 starters were forced out of the race early. Only 19 of the 31 starters were running at the end of the race.

Rudd took advantage of the others' misfortune, grabbing the lead for good on lap 352, when race leader Bodine's engine failed. He paced the final 149 laps, including the final 100 with a full-lap lead on Ruttman.

The victory—Rudd's second at Martinsville—was the first of two wins for the No. 15 Ford in 1986. At Dover in September, he recovered from losing a lap to the leaders early in the race due to a NASCAR penalty and powered his way to the win. He was penalized a lap for passing the pace car during a caution on lap 130. He got back on the lead lap 70 laps later and cruised to a five-second win over Neil Bonnett. It was Rudd's first victory on a track measuring a mile or greater. All of his previous wins had come on short tracks or the road course at Riverside.

Dover was the second straight race in which Rudd led the most laps, and the third time in 1986 when he dominated a race. As he had with every team willing to hire him, Rudd showed continued improvement in his third season with Moore. He finished the season fifth in the final point standings, his best finish to that point in his career. The march to his first Top 5 championship effort began slowly. Rudd finished 26th or worse in four of the season's first six races. He followed his slow start with 11 Top 10s in the next 12 races, however. The run pushed him into 5th in the standings.

Lapped Fields

The number of races won by a least a lap, by decade

1970s	67
1980s	16
1990s	2
2000s	0

1986 Stats Chart

Category	Rudd's Total	Rudd's Rank	1986 Leader
Money	$671,548	6th	Dale Earnhardt -- 1,783,880
Total Points	3,823	5th	Dale Earnhardt -- 4,468
Avg. Start	12.7	13th	Geoffrey Bodine -- 4.2
Avg. Finish	12.7	6th	Dale Earnhardt -- 7.4
Wins	2	4th	Tim Richmond -- 7
Top 5s	11	4th	Darrell Waltrip -- 21
Top 10s	17	3rd	Dale Earnhardt -- 23
DNFs	7	22nd	Morgan Shepherd -- 15
Poles	1	5th	Geoffrey Bodine -- 9
Front Row Starts	1	9th	G. Bodine, T. Richmond -- 15
Laps Led	525	7th	Dale Earnhardt -- 2,127
Races Led	7	13th	Dale Earnhardt -- 26
Times Led	13	13th	Dale Earnhardt -- 103
Miles Led	366	10th	Dale Earnhardt -- 2,439
Times Led Most Laps	3	4th	Dale Earnhardt -- 7
Bonus Points	50	12th	Dale Earnhardt -- 165
Laps Completed	8,120	11th	Dale Earnhardt -- 9,212
Miles Completed	10,193	6th	Dale Earnhardt -- 11,164
Points per Race	131.8	5th	Dale Earnhardt -- 154.1
Lead-Lap Finishes	13	3rd	Darrell Waltrip -- 17

1986 Performance Chart
No. 15 Bud Moore Ford

Career Race	Season Race	Date	Race	St.	Fin.	Total Laps	Laps Completed	Laps Led	Condition	Money	Pts.	Bonus Pts.	Point Standing	Behind Leader	Current Leader
237	1	Feb 16	Daytona -- Daytona 500	22	11	200	198	0	Running	$32,690	130	0	11	-55	G. Bodine
238	2	Feb 23	Richmond -- Miller High Life 400	8	30	400	17	0	DNF - Crash	7,715	73	0	16	-129	G. Bodine
239	3	Mar 2	Rockingham -- Goodwrench 500	14	28	492	315	0	DNF - Engine	9,715	79	0	19	-208	D. Waltrip
240	4	Mar 16	Atlanta -- Motorcraft 500	23	26	328	301	0	Running	9,695	85	0	19	-288	D. Waltrip
241	5	Apr 6	Bristol -- Valleydale 500	8	2	500	500	0	Running	20,125	170	0	15	-288	D. Waltrip
242	6	Apr 13	Darlington -- TranSouth 500	8	26	367	207	1	DNF - Crash	9,605	90	5	14	-373	D. Waltrip
243	7	Apr 20	North Wilkesboro -- First Union 400	14	2	400	400	102	Running	20,075	175	5	12	-358	D. Waltrip
244	8	Apr 27	Martinsville -- Sovran Bank 500	4	1	500	500	163	Running	40,850	185	10	10	-260	D. Waltrip
245	9	May 4	Talladega -- Winston 500	20	36	188	85	0	DNF - Engine	10,500	55	0	12	-375	Earnhardt
246	10	May 18	Dover -- Budweiser 500	1	4	500	498	0	Running	18,875	160	0	10	-385	Earnhardt
247	11	May 25	Charlotte -- Coca-Cola 600	13	8	400	399	0	Running	18,200	142	0	10	-423	Earnhardt
248	12	Jun 1	Riverside -- Budweiser 400	8	3	95	95	0	Running	18,650	165	0	9	-413	Earnhardt
249	13	Jun 8	Pocono -- Miller High Life 500	14	4	200	200	3	Running	18,375	165	5	7	-423	Earnhardt
250	14	Jun 15	Michigan -- Miller American 400	18	10	200	200	0	Running	15,150	134	0	7	-444	Earnhardt
251	15	Jul 4	Daytona -- Firecracker 400	33	6	160	160	0	Running	17,200	150	0	7	-386	Earnhardt
252	16	Jul 20	Pocono -- Summer 500	13	2	150	150	0	Running	29,500	170	0	5	-362	Earnhardt
253	17	Jul 27	Talladega -- Talladega 500[1]	20	3	188	188	0	Running	29,255	165	0	5	-292	Earnhardt
254	18	Aug 10	Watkins Glen -- The Bud at the Glen	7	7	90	90	0	Running	14,090	146	0	5	-311	Earnhardt
255	19	Aug 17	Michigan -- Champion Spark Plug 400	18	21	200	191	0	Running	10,195	100	0	5	-371	Earnhardt
256	20	Aug 23	Bristol -- Busch 500	4	23	500	250	0	DNF - Crash	7,910	94	0	6	-442	Earnhardt
257	21	Aug 31	Darlington -- Southern 500	15	6	367	367	0	Running	15,735	150	0	6	-435	Earnhardt
258	22	Sep 7	Richmond -- Wrangler Jeans Indigo 400	8	24	400	350	113	DNF - Crash	8,235	101	10	6	-509	Earnhardt
259	23	Sep 14	Dover -- Delaware 500	11	1	500	500	141	Running	51,500	185	10	5	-429	Earnhardt
260	24	Sep 21	Martinsville -- Goody's 500	10	28	500	319	0	DNF - Crash	8,345	79	0	6	-482	Earnhardt
261	25	Sep 28	North Wilkesboro -- Holly Farms 400	7	7	400	399	0	Running	9,300	146	0	5	-479	Earnhardt
262	26	Oct 5	Charlotte -- Oakwood Homes 500	16	4	334	333	0	Running	25,700	160	0	4	-499	Earnhardt
263	27	Oct 19	Rockingham -- Nationwise 500	4	2	492	492	0	Running	26,550	170	0	4	-484	Earnhardt
264	28	Nov 2	Atlanta -- Atlanta Journal 500	25	25	328	301	0	Running	9,435	88	0	5	-581	Earnhardt
265	29	Nov 16	Riverside -- Winston Western 500	3	19	119	115	2	Running	9,855	111	5	5	-645	Earnhardt

[1] -- Relieved by Rusty Wallace

A Dying Trend
A look at the most recent Winston Cup races in which the winner lapped the field

Year	Track	Winner	2nd Place
1994	North Wilkesboro (Fall race)	Geoffrey Bodine	Terry Labonte
1991	Dover (Fall race)	Harry Gant	Geoffrey Bodine
1987	Charlotte (Coca-Cola 600)	Kyle Petty	Morgan Shepherd
1986	Martinsville (Spring race)	Ricky Rudd	Joe Ruttman

1987: Leaving Bud Moore

The luster started to wear off as Ricky Rudd entered his fourth season in Bud Moore's No. 15 Ford. With the longest tenure of any driver in Moore's long NASCAR career, Rudd could point to a record of success. In his 116-race partnership with Moore, he won 6 times, bagged 5 poles, scored 41 Top 5s and 65 Top 10s, and finished in the Top 10 among the point leaders in each of his four seasons.

In 1987, however, the team's performance slipped. Rudd's starting average (13.8) was his worst in seven years; his average finish (13.5) was his worst since joining Moore. His DNFs crept up to nine, his worst since 1982. The number of Rudd's finishes outside of the Top 10 (16) was the most he suffered with Moore.

Though the 1987 season wasn't a complete loss—Rudd won twice at Atlanta and Dover, and managed a seventh straight Top-10 finish in the final point standings—Rudd listened when Kenny Bernstein, owner of the King Motorsports Buick, came calling. Bernstein, in his second season as a Winston Cup owner, was hungry to establish his team among the series' elite. Rudd's record with Moore made him an attractive driver who could bring stability to the young outfit. Joe Ruttman and Morgan Shepherd had driven the No. 26 Buick in Bernstein's first two seasons. Neither had been able to win a race in a combined 58 starts. Nor had either threatened to contend for a championship; Ruttman finished 15th in 1986, while Shepherd ended the 1987 campaign in 17th.

Rudd accepted an offer from Bernstein late in the season. Just before the second Dover race, Rudd told Moore that he intended to leave the No. 15 team following the season. Rudd then went out and dominated the Delaware 500 en route to his eighth career victory. Starting 13th, he climbed into the lead by lap 49 and fronted the field for 373 of the race's 500 laps. He took the lead for the final time with 29 to go and beat Davey Allison to the finish line by 20 car lengths.

The 373 laps led at Dover marked the second-highest total in a victory for Rudd, next to the 380 laps he led to win at Martinsville in 1983. Earlier in 1987, he won at Atlanta with the exact opposite effect, leading just seven laps to win the Motorcraft 500. The win on Atlanta's 1.5-mile track was Rudd's first-ever on a track longer than a mile. After starting sixth, he didn't lead the race until the final laps. Only at Watkins Glen in 1988 would Rudd get a win with fewer laps led.

The Tide logo is one of the most recognizable on the Winston Cup circuit.

1987 Stats Chart

Category	Rudd's Total	Rudd's Rank	1987 Leader
Money	$653,508	5th	Dale Earnhardt -- 2,099,243
Total Points	3,742	6th	Dale Earnhardt -- 4,696
Avg. Start	13.8	14th	Bill Elliott -- 6.1
Avg. Finish	13.5	10th	Dale Earnhardt -- 5.9
Wins	2	3rd	Dale Earnhardt -- 11
Top 5s	10	4th	Dale Earnhardt -- 21
Top 10s	13	9th	Dale Earnhardt -- 24
DNFs	9	13th	Harry Gant -- 21
Poles	0	--	Bill Elliott -- 8
Front Row Starts	1	14th	Bill Elliott -- 11
Laps Led	505	5th	Dale Earnhardt -- 3,358
Races Led	12	7th	Dale Earnhardt -- 27
Times Led	21	7th	Dale Earnhardt -- 116
Miles Led	553	6th	Dale Earnhardt -- 3,339
Times Led Most Laps	1	5th	Dale Earnhardt -- 13
Bonus Points	65	8th	Dale Earnhardt -- 200
Laps Completed	8,206	10th	Dale Earnhardt -- 9,043
Miles Completed	9,891	9th	Darrell Waltrip -- 11,034
Points per Race	129.0	7th	Dale Earnhardt -- 161.9
Lead-Lap Finishes	12	4th	Dale Earnhardt -- 23

1987 Performance Chart
No. 15 Bud Moore Ford

Career Race	Season Race	Date	Race	St.	Fin.	Total Laps	Laps Completed	Laps Led	Condition	Money	Pts.	Bonus Pts.	Point Standing	Behind Leader	Current Leader
266	1	Feb 15	Daytona -- Daytona 500	31	9	200	200	0	Running	$38,425	138	0	9	-47	Elliott
267	2	Mar 1	Rockingham -- Goodwrench 500	5	2	492	492	70	Running	28,135	175	5	3	-32	Elliott
268	3	Mar 8	Richmond -- Miller High Life 400	8	28	400	143	0	DNF - Crash	8,215	79	0	8	-138	Earnhardt
269	4	Mar 15	Atlanta -- Motorcraft Quality Parts 500	6	1	328	328	7	Running	62,400	180	5	4	-83	Earnhardt
270	5	Mar 29	Darlington -- TranSouth 500	10	30	367	144	12	DNF - Crash	9,885	78	5	7	-190	Earnhardt
271	6	Apr 5	North Wilkesboro -- First Union 400	11	5	400	399	0	Running	14,890	155	0	5	-220	Earnhardt
272	7	Apr 12	Bristol -- Valleydale Meats 500	15	3	500	500	0	Running	17,175	165	0	5	-235	Earnhardt
273	8	Apr 26	Martinsville -- Sovran Bank 500	15	16	500	440	0	DNF - Rear End	9,050	115	0	5	-305	Earnhardt
274	9	May 3	Talladega -- Winston 500	17	30	178	89	0	DNF - Crash	11,745	73	0	9	-397	Earnhardt
275	10	May 24	Charlotte -- Coca-Cola 600	25	25	400	254	0	DNF - Crash	11,950	88	0	10	-412	Earnhardt
276	11	May 31	Dover -- Budweiser 500	11	12	500	490	1	Running	11,300	132	5	10	-445	Earnhardt
277	12	Jun 14	Pocono -- Miller High Life 500	23	7	200	200	5	Running	14,825	151	5	7	-454	Earnhardt
278	13	Jun 21	Riverside -- Budweiser 400	4	2	95	95	5	Running	28,450	175	5	6	-425	Earnhardt
279	14	Jun 28	Michigan -- Miller American 400	17	14	200	199	0	Running	12,950	121	0	6	-489	Earnhardt
280	15	Jul 4	Daytona -- Pepsi Firecracker 400	17	14	160	159	0	Running	12,855	121	0	8	-523	Earnhardt
281	16	Jul 19	Pocono -- Summer 500	8	26	200	142	4	DNF - Engine	10,620	90	5	8	-618	Earnhardt
282	17	Jul 26	Talladega -- Talladega 500	27	15	188	187	0	Running	12,975	118	0	8	-670	Earnhardt
283	18	Aug 10	Watkins Glen -- The Bud at the Glen	7	4	90	90	0	Running	20,135	160	0	8	-657	Earnhardt
284	19	Aug 16	Michigan -- Champion Spark Plug 400	27	25	200	180	0	Running	11,485	88	0	8	-749	Earnhardt
285	20	Aug 22	Bristol -- Busch 500	7	3	500	500	0	Running	20,275	165	0	7	-769	Earnhardt
286	21	Sep 6	Darlington -- Southern 500	12	7	202	202	0	Running	15,055	146	0	6	-808	Earnhardt
287	22	Sep 13	Richmond -- Wrangler Jeans Indigo 400	6	3	400	400	0	Running	20,050	165	0	6	-828	Earnhardt
288	23	Sep 20	Dover -- Delaware 500	13	1	500	500	373	Running	54,550	185	10	5	-718	Earnhardt
289	24	Sep 27	Martinsville -- Goody's 500	15	21	500	387	1	DNF - Overheating	8,800	105	5	5	-793	Earnhardt
290	25	Oct 4	North Wilkesboro -- Holly Farms 400	12	13	400	397	0	Running	8,720	124	0	6	-844	Earnhardt
291	26	Oct 11	Charlotte -- Oakwood Homes 500	27	11	334	329	0	Running	15,190	130	0	5	-846	Earnhardt
292	27	Oct 25	Rockingham -- AC Delco 500	7	31	492	342	3	DNF - Engine	9,985	75	5	6	-946	Earnhardt
293	28	Nov 8	Riverside -- Winston Western 500	2	31	119	90	5	DNF - Engine	9,600	75	5	8	-949	Earnhardt
294	29	Nov 22	Atlanta -- Atlanta Journal 500	14	3	328	328	19	Running	22,585	170	5	6	-954	Earnhardt

1988: Losing Ground in the No. 26

Ricky Rudd's gamble that a change of scenery might produce improved championship chances in 1988 failed to return the wished-for results. For the first time since 1980, when he ran a limited 13-race schedule, he finished outside the Top 10 in the final point standings. Driving the green Quaker State No. 26 King Motorsports Buick, he finished 11th, 941 points behind Winston Cup champion Bill Elliott.

Unreliable equipment hurt Rudd most. On 11 separate occasions, he was forced out of action due to a failed engine. He finished the season with 12 DNFs, three more than during his disappointing 1987 season. The engine situation wasn't completely unexpected, as the two previous King Motorsports drivers—Joe Ruttman and Morgan Shepherd—had suffered similar fates. Shepherd had 13 DNFs in 1987, while Ruttman had 9 in 1986. The maddening part of Rudd's constant woes for: two sure victories were stolen by late engine failures.

At Martinsville in September, Rudd led 237 of the first 423 laps, despite starting 14th on the tight half-mile track. He had built a comfortable lead when his engine gave out with just 40 laps to go. Darrell Waltrip took advantage of his misfortune and won. A month later, Rudd dominated the inaugural Winston Cup race at Phoenix when, while leading the race, his engine failed with just 16 laps to go. Alan Kulwicki waltzed to victory in Rudd's stead.

The engine problems had a predictable effect on Rudd's title chase. He was sitting in 7th after the first three races, but fell to 16th before the midpoint of the season. Until his struggles as an owner in the late 1990s, the 1988 season saw Rudd finish outside of the Top 10 more times (18) than at any other point in his career. His Top 5 and Top 10 finishes fell to pre-Bud Moore levels. If it was any consolation for Rudd, Moore also struggled with his new driver, Brett Bodine, who finished 20th in the final point standings.

On the positive side for Rudd, he regained his pole-winning qualifying ability. Overall, however, his average start in 1988 was the worst of his career since joining the series full time. He won poles at Martinsville, his fourth at the track, and at Riverside, his first road course pole. His pole at Riverside set a track record that will remain permanent forever; the event was the final Winston Cup race at Riverside, which closed and was torn down shortly afterward. Rudd's lap of 118.484 miles per hour topped the previous record of 118.247 miles per hour set by Tim Richmond.

Once again proving his toughness, Rudd won the Riverside pole despite wearing a bulky cast on his left leg. He injured his leg in a hard crash in Turn 1 at Charlotte during the Winston all-star race three weeks earlier. The wreck, which resulted from a cut right front tire, caused significant ligament damage in his left knee. He was relieved by Mike Alexander in the Coca-Cola 600 the following week due to the injury. To aid their driver's effort, Rudd's team removed his clutch pedal and installed a hand-lever clutch. They also began using a Jerico transmission, which doesn't require a clutch to shift gears once the car has started rolling.

Three months after his injury, Rudd found Victory Lane for the sixth straight season on another road course, Watkins Glen. The win was his third on a road course, but didn't come easily. In the race's opening laps, he was forced to visit the pits to replace a bad set of tires. The extra stop put him a lap down in 38th. Thanks to a race-record eight cautions, Rudd was able to regain his place on the lead lap. With just four laps to go, he passed a faltering Darrell Waltrip and then held off a furious attack from road-course master Rusty Wallace.

Another interesting feature of the 1988 season was Rudd's budding on-track quarrel with Dale Earnhardt. At North Wilkesboro, the two got into a scrape during the track's fall event. Rudd led the most laps in the race, but was sitting in second place behind Earnhardt with less than 50 laps to go. To make the pass for the lead, Rudd nudged Earnhardt and turned him sideways. Rudd held the lead for exactly one lap when Earnhardt recovered and nailed Rudd, who got spun around by the contact. NASCAR flagged both drivers, dropping them to the back of the field. They continued their tête-à-tête in the closing laps, with Earnhardt emerging ahead in sixth place. Rudd finished seventh. NASCAR fined Rudd $6,000 for the incidents. It would not be the last battle between the two hard-nosed drivers.

1988 Stats Chart

Category	Rudd's Total	Rudd's Rank	1988 Leader
Money	$410,954	14th	Bill Elliott -- 1,574,639
Total Points	3,547	11th	Bill Elliott -- 4,488
Avg. Start	14.9	13th	Geoffrey Bodine -- 6.8
Avg. Finish	15.7	15th	Bill Elliott -- 6.6
Wins	1	7th	B. Elliott, R. Wallace -- 6
Top 5s	6	9th	Rusty Wallace -- 19
Top 10s	11	11th	Rusty Wallace -- 23
DNFs	12	6th	Derrike Cope -- 16
Poles	2	5th	Bill Elliott -- 6
Front Row Starts	2	10th	Bill Elliott -- 10
Laps Led	695	4th	Dale Earnhardt -- 1,808
Races Led	16	6th	B. Elliott, D. Earnhardt -- 20
Times Led	32	6th	Dale Earnhardt -- 63
Miles Led	564	7th	Bill Elliott -- 1,851
Times Led Most Laps	3	4th	Dale Earnhardt -- 7
Bonus Points	95	4th	Dale Earnhardt -- 135
Laps Completed	8,867	10th	Bill Elliott -- 9,647
Miles Completed	10,428	10th	Bill Elliott -- 11,521
Points per Race	122.3	12th	Bill Elliott -- 154.8
Lead-Lap Finishes	10	9th	Rusty Wallace -- 21

1988 Performance Chart
No. 26 King Motorsports Buick

Career Race	Season Race	Date	Race	St.	Fin.	Total Laps	Laps Completed	Laps Led	Condition	Money	Pts.	Bonus Pts.	Point Standing	Behind Leader	Current Leader
295	1	Feb 14	Daytona -- Daytona 500	27	17	200	200	0	Running	$20,125	112	0	17	-73	B. Allison
296	2	Feb 21	Richmond -- Pontiac Excitement 400	22	2	400	400	0	Running	25,660	170	0	8	-63	Bonnett
297	3	Mar 6	Rockingham -- Goodwrench 500	3	17	492	487	0	Running	7,120	112	0	7	-136	Bonnett
298	4	Mar 20	Atlanta -- Motorcraft Quality Parts 500	28	24	328	253	0	DNF - Engine	5,430	91	0	12	-147	Bonnett
299	5	Mar 27	Darlington -- TranSouth 500	10	30	367	208	0	DNF - Engine	4,635	73	0	15	-200	Earnhardt
300	6	Apr 10	Bristol -- Valleydale Meats 500	10	20	500	378	1	DNF - Crash	4,800	108	5	16	-218	Earnhardt
301	7	Apr 17	North Wilkesboro -- First Union 400	7	2	400	400	3	Running	21,025	175	5	12	-218	Earnhardt
302	8	Apr 24	Martinsville -- Pannill Sweatshirts 500	1	18	500	446	37	DNF - Engine	8,555	114	5	14	-289	Earnhardt
303	9	May 1	Talladega -- Winston 500	14	29	188	177	0	DNF - Engine	6,345	76	0	16	-351	Earnhardt
304	10	May 29	Charlotte -- Coca-Cola 600[1]	34	7	400	399	0	Running	17,050	146	0	15	-329	Earnhardt
305	11	Jun 5	Dover -- Budweiser 500	20	19	500	493	0	Running	5,200	106	0	16	-338	Earnhardt
306	12	Jun 12	Riverside -- Budweiser 400	1	3	95	95	30	Running	20,950	170	5	11	-337	R. Wallace
307	13	Jun 19	Pocono -- Miller High Life 500	10	30	200	105	0	DNF - Engine	4,935	73	0	15	-434	R. Wallace
308	14	Jun 26	Michigan -- Miller High Life 400	31	11	200	199	0	Running	10,425	130	0	13	-489	R. Wallace
309	15	Jul 2	Daytona -- Pepsi Firecracker 400	12	22	160	158	2	Running	6,230	102	5	13	-514	R. Wallace
310	16	Jul 24	Pocono -- AC Spark Plug 500	25	12	200	200	2	Running	7,875	132	5	12	-473	R. Wallace
311	17	Jul 31	Talladega -- Talladega DieHard 500	9	41	188	45	0	DNF - Engine	5,135	40	0	13	-588	R. Wallace
312	18	Aug 14	Watkins Glen -- The Bud at the Glen	6	1	90	90	4	Running	49,625	180	5	11	-583	R. Wallace
313	19	Aug 21	Michigan -- Champion Spark Plug 400	10	16	200	198	3	DNF - Engine	7,895	120	5	11	-643	R. Wallace
314	20	Aug 27	Bristol -- Busch 500	19	16	500	451	10	DNF - Engine	4,850	120	5	12	-677	Elliott
315	21	Sep 4	Darlington -- Southern 500	29	10	367	366	6	Running	13,130	139	5	11	-723	Elliott
316	22	Sep 11	Richmond -- Miller High Life 400	12	26	400	349	14	DNF - Engine	5,010	90	5	11	-784	Elliott
317	23	Sep 18	Dover -- Delaware 500	19	10	500	497	0	Running	10,650	134	0	11	-835	Elliott
318	24	Sep 25	Martinsville -- Goody's 500	14	24	500	423	237	DNF - Engine	6,025	101	10	11	-889	Elliott
319	25	Oct 9	Charlotte -- Oakwood Homes 500	36	8	334	334	0	Running	13,825	142	0	11	-912	Elliott
320	26	Oct 16	North Wilkesboro -- Holly Farms 400	4	7	400	400	154	Running	10,025	156	10	11	-916	Elliott
321	27	Oct 23	Rockingham -- AC Delco 500	9	2	492	492	8	Running	26,985	175	5	11	-911	Elliott
322	28	Nov 6	Phoenix -- Checker 500	4	26	312	296	183	DNF - Engine	17,350	95	10	11	-976	Elliott
323	29	Nov 20	Atlanta -- Atlanta Journal 500	5	4	328	328	1	Running	14,725	165	5	11	-941	Elliott

[1] -- Relieved by Mike Alexander

1989: Battling Earnhardt

In his second—and final—season with King Motorsports, Ricky Rudd again was not a factor in the championship chase. But to say Rudd had no effect on the title race would be false. At North Wilkesboro in October 1989, the continuation of his on-track animosities with Dale Earnhardt reached new heights—and may have cost Earnhardt the championship.

As the season wound down, Earnhardt and Rusty Wallace battled closely for the championship. Earnhardt led the points for much of the season before Wallace took over with five races to go. Earnhardt trailed by 35 points as the series went to North Wilkesboro for the Holly Farms 400. Looking to regain his points lead, Earnhardt dominated the race, leading 343 of the first 399 laps. A late crash set up a two-lap dash to the finish with Earnhardt in the lead and Rudd in second place. On the race's final lap, Rudd got underneath Earnhardt as they headed into Turn 1. Earnhardt came down on Rudd—or Rudd bumped into Earnhardt, depending on your point of view—and the two cars slid out of the racing groove.

The remaining eight cars on the lead lap passed Earnhardt and Rudd. One of those cars belonged to Wallace, who finished seventh. Rudd recovered to finish in ninth, while Earnhardt limped to 10th. The effect on the point situation was dramatic. If the spin never happened, Wallace probably would have finished ninth. Had Earnhardt won, he would have taken a 12-point lead into the final four races. Instead, he fell 37 points behind Wallace—a 49-point swing that appeared decisive when Earnhardt ended up losing the championship by 12 points.

Not surprisingly, Earnhardt was livid with Rudd. The two hard-headed drivers—whose quarrel had intensified a year earlier at North Wilkesboro—also tangled in the season's second race at Rockingham. In that race, Rudd was in the lead and trying to put Earnhardt a lap down when the fireworks started. Earnhardt, who had repeatedly ignored NASCAR's order to move over and allow the leader to pass, came down on Rudd as the two cars exited Turn 2. The contact turned Rudd around and into the inside wall. He was then tagged by Harry Gant, who was following closely behind. Rudd ended up 42 laps down in 32nd place. Earnhardt, meanwhile, never went a lap down and recovered to finish third.

When not trading paint with Earnhardt, Rudd enjoyed an improved season over 1988. Thanks to car owner Kenny Bernstein's hiring of engine specialist Lou LaRosa and the work of crew chief Larry McReynolds, the team's equipment failures decreased, allowing Rudd to complete more miles than any other driver. He failed to finish five races (much improved over his 12 DNFs in 1988). Also, his final points position improved to 8th place (from 12th).

Most significantly, Rudd won the inaugural race at Sears Point, making him the first driver to score victories at all three of NASCAR's Modern Era road courses—Riverside, Watkins Glen, and Sears Point. Rudd was dominant throughout the race—he led 61 of 74 laps—but needed mistake-free, late-race defensive driving to hold off Wallace in the closing laps. The win solidified Rudd's standing as one of the best road warriors in NASCAR history. Only two other drivers (Rusty Wallace and Geoffrey Bodine) have won on all three Modern Era road courses.

1989 Stats Chart

Category	Rudd's Total	Rudd's Rank	1989 Leader*
Money	$534,824	12th	Rusty Wallace -- 2,247,950
Total Points	3,608	8th	Rusty Wallace -- 4,176
Avg. Start	16.3	16th	Mark Martin -- 5.3
Avg. Finish	14.4	7th	Dale Earnhardt -- 10.28
Wins	1	7th	R. Wallace, D. Waltrip -- 6
Top 5s	7	10th	D. Earnhardt, M. Martin, D. Waltrip -- 14
Top 10s	15	5th	Rusty Wallace -- 20
DNFs	5	27th	G. Sacks, J. Means -- 13
Poles	0	--	A. Kulwicki, M. Martin -- 6
Front Row Starts	0	--	Mark Martin -- 9
Laps Led	247	11th	Dale Earnhardt -- 2,735
Races Led	7	13th	Rusty Wallacec23
Times Led	14	13th	Dale Earnhardt -- 88
Miles Led	363	11th	Dale Earnhardt -- 2,624
Times Led Most Laps	1	7th	Rusty Wallace -- 9
Bonus Points	40	12th	Rusty Wallace -- 160
Laps Completed	9,326	2nd	Darrell Waltrip -- 9,333
Miles Completed	11,075	1st	(Darrell Waltrip -- 10,984)
Points per Race	124.4	8th	Rusty Wallace -- 144.0
Lead-Lap Finishes	11	8th	Dale Earnhardt -- 19

* -- Second-place driver list in parentheses if Rudd is category leader.

1989 Performance Chart
No. 26 King Motorsports Buick

Career Race	Season Race	Date	Race	St.	Fin.	Total Laps	Laps Completed	Laps Led	Condition	Money	Pts.	Bonus Pts.	Point Standing	Behind Leader	Current Leader
324	1	Feb 19	Daytona -- Daytona 500	36	19	200	197	2	Running	$19,120	111	5	17	-69	D. Waltrip
325	2	Mar 5	Rockingham -- Goodwrench 500	11	32	492	450	104	Running	5,825	72	5	24	-152	Earnhardt
326	3	Mar 19	Atlanta -- Motorcraft Quality Parts 500	15	24	328	270	0	DNF - Engine	5,730	91	0	27	-236	Earnhardt
327	4	Mar 26	Richmond -- Pontiac Excitement 400	18	4	400	400	0	Running	13,600	160	0	15	-246	Earnhardt
328	5	Apr 2	Darlington -- TranSouth 500	25	12	367	365	0	Running	7,425	127	0	15	-206	Kulwicki
329	6	Apr 9	Bristol -- Valleydale Meats 500	18	8	500	500	0	Running	7,325	142	0	13	-197	G. Bodine
330	7	Apr 16	North Wilkesboro -- First Union 400	8	6	400	400	0	Running	7,475	150	0	9	-201	Earnhardt
331	8	Apr 23	Martinsville -- Pannill Sweatshirts 500	25	23	500	433	0	Running	3,945	94	0	11	-282	Earnhardt
332	9	May 7	Talladega -- Winston 500	32	31	188	169	0	DNF - Crash	6,445	70	0	15	-359	Earnhardt
333	10	May 28	Charlotte -- Coca-Cola 600	9	10	400	397	0	Running	16,925	134	0	13	-328	D. Waltrip
334	11	Jun 4	Dover -- Budweiser 500	7	6	500	500	0	Running	11,675	150	0	11	-316	D. Waltrip
335	12	Jun 11	Sears Point -- Banquet Frozen Foods 300	4	1	74	74	61	Running	62,350	185	10	10	-289	Earnhardt
336	13	Jun 18	Pocono -- Miller High Life 500	13	20	200	197	0	Running	11,225	103	0	10	-356	Earnhardt
337	14	Jun 25	Michigan -- Miller High Life 400	33	4	200	200	0	Running	24,575	160	0	9	-308	Earnhardt
338	15	Jul 1	Daytona -- Pepsi 400	38	9	160	160	0	Running	16,842	138	0	7	-284	Earnhardt
339	16	Jul 23	Pocono -- AC Spark Plug 500	18	31	200	111	0	DNF - Engine	9,575	70	0	11	-357	Earnhardt
340	17	Jul 30	Talladega -- Talladega DieHard 500	24	17	188	187	0	Running	12,220	112	0	10	-375	Earnhardt
341	18	Aug 13	Watkins Glen -- The Bud at the Glen	8	29	90	69	12	DNF - Engine	9,145	81	5	11	-464	Earnhardt
342	19	Aug 20	Michigan -- Champion Spark Plug 400	16	8	200	200	0	Running	15,050	142	0	10	-434	Earnhardt
343	20	Aug 26	Bristol -- Busch 500	6	3	500	500	0	Running	19,200	165	0	9	-395	Earnhardt
344	21	Sep 3	Darlington -- Heinz Southern 500	8	3	367	367	0	Running	26,865	165	0	8	-415	Earnhardt
345	22	Sep 10	Richmond -- Miller High Life 400	7	4	400	399	0	Running	16,450	160	0	7	-430	Earnhardt
346	23	Sep 17	Dover -- Peak Performance 500	14	5	500	498	0	Running	18,375	155	0	6	-460	Earnhardt
347	24	Sep 24	Martinsville -- Goody's 500	7	8	500	499	0	Running	10,900	142	0	5	-461	Earnhardt
348	25	Oct 8	Charlotte -- All Pro Auto Parts 500	16	21	334	331	0	Running	10,480	100	0	7	-433	R. Wallace
349	26	Oct 15	North Wilkesboro -- Holly Farms 400	5	9	400	400	0	Running	8,630	138	0	7	-441	R. Wallace
350	27	Oct 22	Rockingham -- AC Delco 500	8	28	492	456	66	Running	10,700	84	5	7	-537	R. Wallace
351	28	Nov 5	Phoenix -- Autoworks 500	11	29	312	272	1	DNF - Radiator	10,930	81	5	9	-576	R. Wallace
352	29	Nov 19	Atlanta -- Atlanta Journal 500	33	14	328	325	1	Running	10,350	126	5	8	-568	R. Wallace

1989 Breakout Charts

Road Warriors

Only three drivers have won on each of NASCAR's three road courses.

Driver	No. of road course Victories	Victories by Track
Geoffrey Bodine	3	Riverside—1984 Sears Point—1993 Watkins Glen—1996
Ricky Rudd	5	Riverside—1983, 1985 Sears Point—1989 Watkins Glen—1988, 1990
Rusty Wallace	6	Riverside—1987, 1988 Sears Point—1990, 1996 Watkins Glen—1987, 1989

1990: Joining Hendrick's Juggernaut, Pit-Road Tragedy

Terry Labonte's decision to return to his former owner Billy Hagan for the 1990 season shook up the Winston Cup world, and introduced major change into Ricky Rudd's career. Labonte's departure from Junior Johnson's vaunted No. 11 car freed up one of the series' most coveted rides. Given Johnson's history—over 100 wins and six championships—he had no shortage of aspiring wheelmen.

Johnson eventually settled on Geoffrey Bodine to fill the No. 11's driver seat, which in turn opened another strong ride: Rick Hendrick's No. 5 Levi Garrett Chevrolet. Hendrick, one of the few multicar owners competing on the Winston Cup circuit at the time, chose Rudd to fill his vacated seat.

For Rudd, the change was massive. Long an employee of independents, novices and make-do specialists, he joined a well-financed corporation for the first time. The only previous comparable situation in his career was his successful season with DiGard Racing in 1981—an opportunity that lasted less than 12 months. Also, for the first time, Rudd was part of a team. Darrell Waltrip, in the No. 17 Tide ride, and Ken Schrader, in the No. 25 Kodiak car, were veteran Hendrick drivers who shared resources and the owner's attention.

Though a different and seemingly better world, nothing was certain. While Hendrick had enjoyed tremendous success since joining the series as an owner in 1984, he was often Exhibit A in the argument that shared equipment could not produce a champion. Hendrick drivers had 27 wins and 39 poles in the six seasons prior to Rudd's arrival, but had yet to win a title. Not until Jeff Gordon's 1995 championship did Hendrick finally quell the theory that multicar teams are not well-positioned to win the single biggest prize in NASCAR.

In 1990, joining Hendrick helped Rudd become competitive again. He finished seventh in the final point standings, his best showing since his Bud Moore days in 1987. He finished fourth in the Daytona 500, his best season-opener in 10 years. In August, he snagged his fifth road course victory at Watkins Glen. Due to Darrell Waltrip's season-interrupting injury at Daytona in July, Rudd emerged as the lead Hendrick driver. His 7th-place points finish easily outpaced Schrader, who ended in 10th place, and Waltrip, who dropped to 20th.

Unfortunately, Rudd's new prosperity was overshadowed by tragedy. In the season's final race at Atlanta, he lost control of his car as he entered pit road and spun into Bill Elliott's car, which was being tended to by his over-the-wall crew. Elliott's rear tire changer, Mike Rich, was crushed in the collision. Rich was rushed to a nearby hospital, where he died of a heart attack a short time later. Also injured were Tommy Cole, the team's jackman, and Dan Elliott, the front tire changer and Bill Elliott's brother. Each survived the incident. The tragedy inspired NASCAR to experiment with its pit-road rules. Chief among the regulations that emerged from the accident was a pit-road speed limit.

Rudd's season was also marked by increased on-track antagonism toward his fellow drivers. He was involved in five high-profile incidents that often cost him strong finishes. Among the confrontations:

At Sears Point, Rusty Wallace roughed up Rudd with 17 laps to go and went on to win. Rudd fell to third. The incident was a continuation of a road-course rivalry that had been marked by intense paint trading.

At Bristol, Rudd took out Sterling Marlin on the final lap of the spring race. Marlin confronted Rudd at his trailer after the race, while the two teams nearly came to blows.

While a lap down at Bristol in the fall, Rudd banged against leader Dale Earnhardt on a restart, cutting Earnhardt's left rear tire. Earnhardt had led 350 of the first 410 laps, but dropped to eighth after being forced to pit road.

In the fall race at Martinsville, Rudd was leading when he and teammate Schrader turned each other around. Schrader was passing for the lead when he broke loose and hit Rudd. Each blamed the other for racing too hard.

At North Wilkesboro in the fall, Rudd picked a fight with Derrike Cope, who was three laps down. Cope, who had clashed periodically with Rudd, retaliated and sent Rudd into the wall. Instead of an apparent strong finish, Rudd ended the race in 11th.

Rudd's run-ins weren't limited to the track. Off the track, he was the victim of mistaken identity in a story that appeared in one of the largest newspapers in the south, the Charlotte Observer. The paper reported that Rudd was convicted of drunk driving and had his driver's license revoked in December of 1987. The Ricky Rudd in question was a 50-year-old from Graham, N.C., not the 32-year-old Winston Cup star from Chesapeake, Va.

Rudd in 1990

Category	Rudd's Total	Rudd's Rank	1990 Leader
Money	$573,650	10th	Dale Earnhardt—3,083,056
Total Points	3,601	7th	Dale Earnhardt -- 4,430
Avg. Start	14.1	12th	Mark Martin -- 5.4
Avg. Finish	14.6	8th	Mark Martin -- 6.6
Wins	1	7th	Dale Earnhardt -- 9
Top 5s	8	6th	Dale Earnhardt -- 18
Top 10s	15	7th	Earnhardt, Martin -- 23
DNFs	5	19th	Rick Wilson, Rob Moroso -- 15
Poles	2	5th	Dale Earnhardt -- 4
Front Row Starts	2	8th	Mark Martin -- 11
Laps Led	180	14th	Dale Earnhardt -- 2,438
Races Led	7	14th	Dale Earnhardt -- 22
Times Led	14	11th	Dale Earnhardt -- 84
Miles Led	182	14th	Dale Earnhardt -- 3,203
Times Led Most Laps	1	6th	Dale Earnhardt -- 10
Bonus Points	40	12th	Dale Earnhardt -- 160
Laps Completed	8,664	11th	Mark Martin -- 9,636
Miles Completed	10,392	12th	Mark Martin -- 11,487
Points per Race	124.2	8th	Dale Earnhardt -- 152.8
Lead-Lap Finishes	12	9th	Mark Martin -- 22

1990 Performance Chart
No. 5 Hendrick Motorsports Chevrolet

Career Race	Season Race	Date	Race	St.	Fin.	Total Laps	Laps Completed	Laps Led	Condition	Money	Pts.	Bonus Pts.	Point Standing	Behind Leader	Current Leader
353	1	Feb 18	Daytona -- Daytona 500	19	4	200	200	1	Running	$77,050	165	5	5	-15	Cope
354	2	Feb 25	Richmond -- Pontiac Excitement 400	1	3	400	400	40	Running	25,050	170	5	2	-5	Earnhardt
355	3	Mar 4	Rockingham -- Goodwrench 500	25	31	492	302	15	DNF - Oil Pan	6,600	75	5	4	-64	Earnhardt
356	4	Mar 18	Atlanta -- Motorcraft Quality Parts 500	4	27	328	307	0	Running	6,545	82	0	11	-167	Earnhardt
357	5	Apr 1	Darlington -- TranSouth 500	10	24	367	294	0	Running	6,480	91	0	15	-256	Earnhardt
358	6	Apr 8	Bristol -- Valleydale Meats 500	13	3	500	500	0	Running	19,775	165	0	11	-197	Earnhardt
359	7	Apr 22	North Wilkesboro -- First Union 400	8	4	400	400	0	Running	12,775	160	0	7	-207	Earnhardt
360	8	Apr 29	Martinsville -- Hanes Activewear 500	11	23	500	417	0	Running	5,100	94	0	11	-273	Earnhardt
361	9	May 6	Talladega -- Winston 500	14	33	188	104	0	DNF - Crash	7,285	64	0	11	-394	Earnhardt
362	10	May 27	Charlotte -- Coca-Cola 600	34	28	400	320	0	DNF - Camshaft	7,450	79	0	15	-388	Earnhardt
363	11	Jun 3	Dover -- Budweiser 500	20	11	500	499	0	Running	9,025	130	0	15	-387	Shepherd
364	12	Jun 10	Sears Point -- Banquet Frozen Foods 300	1	3	74	74	13	Running	28,675	170	5	11	-355	Martin
365	13	Jun 17	Pocono -- Miller Genuine Draft 500	15	32	200	169	0	Running	6,275	67	0	13	-414	Martin
366	14	Jun 24	Michigan -- Miller Genuine Draft 400	13	9	200	200	0	Running	13,800	138	0	12	-441	Martin
367	15	Jul 7	Daytona -- Pepsi 400	9	13	160	158	0	Running	10,135	124	0	11	-447	Martin
368	16	Jul 19	Pocono -- AC Spark Plug 500	13	7	200	200	0	Running	12,650	146	0	10	-451	Martin
369	17	Jul 26	Talladega -- DieHard 500	25	5	188	188	0	Running	22,050	155	0	10	-434	Martin
370	18	Aug 12	Watkins Glen -- The Bud at the Glen	12	1	90	90	20	Running	55,000	180	5	9	-414	Martin
371	19	Aug 19	Michigan -- Champion Spark Plug 400	39	5	200	200	0	Running	20,670	155	0	8	-444	Martin
372	20	Aug 25	Bristol -- Busch 500	7	10	500	499	0	Running	10,100	134	0	7	-475	Martin
373	21	Sep 2	Darlington -- Heinz Southern 500	5	7	367	367	6	Running	12,755	151	5	6	-474	Martin
374	22	Sep 9	Richmond -- Miller Genuine Draft 400	14	8	400	399	0	Running	8,350	142	0	6	-507	Martin
375	23	Sep 16	Dover -- Peak AntiFreeze 500	20	32	500	246	0	DNF - Mechanical	5,600	67	0	7	-615	Martin
376	24	Sep 23	Martinsville -- Goody's 500	16	28	500	289	85	DNF - Crash	6,200	89	10	7	-696	Martin
377	25	Sep 30	North Wilkesboro -- Tyson/Holly Farms 400	15	11	400	399	0	Running	6,650	130	0	7	-746	Martin
378	26	Oct 7	Charlotte -- Mello Yello 500	16	6	334	334	0	Running	18,425	150	0	7	-717	Martin
379	27	Oct 21	Rockingham -- AC Delco 500	11	7	492	491	0	Running	10,925	146	0	7	-701	Martin
380	28	Nov 4	Phoenix -- Checker 500	9	32	312	293	0	Running	5,780	67	0	7	-774	Earnhardt
381	29	Nov 18	Atlanta -- Atlanta Journal 500	10	16	328	325	0	Running	7,550	115	0	7	-829	Earnhardt

1991: Chasing Earnhardt for the Championship

When Ricky Rudd pulled into Victory Lane at Darlington in April of 1991, he celebrated more than his first victory on an oval in four years. For the first—and only—time in his career, Rudd also sat atop the Winston Cup point standings. Sixteen years and 386 races into his career, he could finally claim to be the Winston Cup points leader.

Rudd kept his points lead for a month before losing it to Dale Earnhardt. He chased Earnhardt the rest of the season, twice closing to within 36 points. An end-of-season slump dashed any remaining hopes of a Winston Cup title, however. Rudd finished the season with five consecutive finishes outside of the Top 10 for second place overall, 195 points behind Earnhardt.

Only in 1981 and 2001 has Rudd ever gotten close to NASCAR's ultimate prize. In 1981, with DiGard Racing, he spent more than a month in second place early in the year before ending in fourth. In 2001, with Robert Yates Racing, he pursued Jeff Gordon for most of the second half of the season before settling for fourth in the final standings.

Besides his career-best run for the championship, Rudd was also involved in one of the most controversial race finishes in NASCAR history. At Sears Point in June, he crossed the finish line first, but was awarded second place after Winston Cup officials determined that Rudd had been "unnecessarily rough" while passing Davey Allison. With two laps to go in the Banquet Frozen Foods 300, Rudd bumped race-leader Allison in the track's tight Turn 11. Rudd's shot knocked Allison out of shape and allowed Rudd's No. 5 Tide Chevy to pass. Rudd took the lead as the white flag flew, but when he came around to the finish line, he was presented with the black flag instead of the checkered. Allison recovered and followed four seconds behind Rudd and was shown the checkered flag.

In an unprecedented move, NASCAR penalized Rudd five seconds—essentially giving the win to Allison and installing Rudd in the second position. Rudd claimed a simple misjudgment of speed and bad brakes going into the fateful 11th turn as reasons for the contact. After years of rough driving from Earnhardt, Rudd argued, how could the quintessential Earnhardt move incur such a heavy fine?

Ironically, Rudd had another opportunity to pull an "Earnhardt" on Earnhardt himself at Richmond. In the season's second race, the two on-track rivals dominated the race—leading a combined 304 of 400 laps—and were running 1–2 when the final restart occurred with just three laps to go. Earnhardt held the lead, but Rudd quickly moved to the inside. Debating whether to poke the No. 3 and remove it from the lead, Rudd instead steered clear of Earnhardt—and watched as Earnhardt pulled away on the outside and won the race.

The Richmond race symbolized Rudd's season. Close, but not quite enough. Rudd had his best chance at a title, but couldn't keep Earnhardt from pulling ahead. It was Earnhardt's fifth Winston Cup championship. Among the milestones knocked over by Rudd during his career year:

For the first and only time, he ended the season with an average finish inside of the Top 10 (9.5). Rudd's previous best was 10.5 in 1985.

He topped the $1 million mark in earnings; he reached 4,000 championship points.

Another important aspect of 1991 was Rudd's association with Tide. Thanks to Darrell Waltrip's decision to leave Hendrick Motorsports to form his own team, Rudd gained the sponsorship that would finance his racing efforts for nine years. Witnessing Waltrip's excursion into self-ownership also made an impression on Rudd. After starting his career with his family, he was starting to build the finances and the knowledge necessary to break away from the Hendrick's multicar team. Within two years, Rudd would return to directing his own career.

1991 Stats Chart

Category	Rudd's Total	Rudd's Rank	1991 Leader*
Money	$1,093,765	4th	Dale Earnhardt -- 2,416,685
Total Points	4,092	2nd	Dale Earnhardt -- 4,287
Avg. Start	12.0	11th	Alan Kulwicki -- 6.8
Avg. Finish	9.5	2nd	Dale Earnhardt -- 8.6
Wins	1	8th	D. Allison, H. Gant -- 5
Top 5s	9	7th	Harry Gant -- 15
Top 10s	17	4th	Dale Earnhardt -- 21
DNFs	1	54th	D. Cope, J. Spencer -- 14
Poles	1	10th	Mark Martin -- 5
Front Row Starts	1	15th	A. Kulwicki, M. Martin -- 8
Laps Led	425	9th	Harry Gant -- 1,684
Races Led	13	8th	Davey Allison -- 23
Times Led	34	8th	Davey Allison -- 72
Miles Led	421	9th	Davey Allison -- 1,879
Times Led Most Laps	2	5th	D. Allison, H. Gant -- 5
Bonus Points	75	7th	Davey Allison -- 140
Laps Completed	9,561	1st	(Dale Earnhardt -- 9,541)
Miles Completed	11,427	2nd	Dale Earnhardt -- 11,435
Points per Race	141.1	2nd	Dale Earnhardt -- 147.8
Lead-Lap Finishes	11	8th	Dale Earnhardt -- 17

* -- Second place driver listed in parentheses if Rudd is category leader

1991 Performance Chart

No. 5 Hendrick Motorsports Chevrolet

Career Race	Season Race	Date	Race	St.	Fin.	Total Laps	Laps Completed	Laps Led	Condition	Money	Pts.	Bonus Pts.	Point Standing	Behind Leader	Current Leader
382	1	Feb 17	Daytona -- Daytona 500 by STP	9	9	200	199	0	Running	$52,600	138	0	9	-42	Irvan
383	2	Feb 24	Richmond -- Pontiac Excitement 400	4	2	400	400	154	Running	45,675	180	10	2	-22	Earnhardt
384	3	Mar 3	Rockingham -- GM Goodwrench 500	5	4	492	491	0	Running	20,250	160	0	2	-4	Earnhardt
385	4	Mar 18	Atlanta -- Motorcraft Quality Parts 500	11	6	328	328	0	Running	17,750	150	0	2	-24	Earnhardt
386	5	Apr 7	Darlington -- TranSouth 500	13	1	367	367	69	Running	62,185	180	5	1	+80	(Earnhardt)
387	6	Apr 17	Bristol -- Valleydale Meats 500	4	5	500	500	145	Running	37,950	165	10	1	+119	(Irvan)
388	7	Apr 21	North Wilkesboro -- First Union 400	11	11	400	399	0	Running	10,175	130	0	1	+97	(Earnhardt)
389	8	Apr 28	Martinsville -- Hanes 500	22	11	500	496	0	Running	10,985	130	0	1	+42	(Earnhardt)
390	9	May 6	Talladega -- Winston 500	6	13	188	186	2	Running	15,860	129	5	2	-4	Earnhardt
391	10	May 26	Charlotte -- Coca-Cola 600	17	9	400	399	0	Running	21,500	138	0	2	-36	Earnhardt
392	11	Jun 2	Dover -- Budweiser 500	13	10	500	497	0	Running	18,000	134	0	2	-82	Earnhardt
393	12	Jun 9	Sears Point -- Banquet Frozen Foods 300	1	2	74	74	13	Running	41,975	175	5	2	-53	Earnhardt
394	13	Jun 16	Pocono -- Champion Spark Plug 500	4	20	200	199	16	Running	13,025	108	5	2	-120	Earnhardt
395	14	Jun 23	Michigan -- Miller Genuine Draft 400	7	8	200	200	1	Running	18,600	147	5	2	-138	Earnhardt
396	15	Jul 6	Daytona -- Pepsi 400	13	9	160	160	8	Running	16,500	143	5	2	-146	Earnhardt
397	16	Jul 21	Pocono -- Miller Genuine Draft 500	7	20	179	177	0	Running	12,725	103	5	2	-140	Earnhardt
398	17	Jul 28	Talladega -- DieHard 500	18	4	188	188	2	Running	29,400	165	5	2	-160	Earnhardt
399	18	Aug 11	Watkins Glen -- The Bud at the Glen	22	2	90	90	11	Running	37,325	175	5	2	-108	Earnhardt
400	19	Aug 18	Michigan -- Champion Spark Plug 400	12	11	200	199	0	Running	15,850	130	0	2	-69	Earnhardt
401	20	Aug 24	Bristol -- Bud 500	17	5	500	499	0	Running	16,450	155	0	2	-60	Earnhardt
402	21	Sep 1	Darlington -- Heinz Southern 500	18	15	367	363	0	Running	14,100	118	0	2	-89	Earnhardt
403	22	Sep 7	Richmond -- Miller Genuine Draft 400	7	5	400	400	1	Running	18,125	160	5	2	-64	Earnhardt
404	23	Sep 15	Dover -- Peak AntiFreeze 500	24	7	500	493	1	Running	15,800	151	5	2	-36	Earnhardt
405	24	Sep 22	Martinsville -- Goody's 500	4	8	500	500	2	Running	15,300	147	5	2	-59	Earnhardt
406	25	Sep 29	North Wilkesboro -- Tyson/Holly Farms 400	22	12	400	399	0	Running	9,950	127	0	2	-112	Earnhardt
407	26	Oct 6	Charlotte -- Mello Yello 500	10	32	334	232	0	DNF - Crash	10,550	67	0	2	-138	Earnhardt
408	27	Oct 20	Rockingham -- AC Delco 500	5	12	492	489	0	Running	13,800	127	0	2	-157	Earnhardt
409	28	Nov 3	Phoenix -- Pyroil 500	14	11	312	311	0	Running	13,250	130	0	3	-165	Earnhardt
410	29	Nov 17	Atlanta -- Hardee's 500	29	11	328	326	0	Running	12,800	130	0	2	-195	Earnhardt

Rudd battles Harry Gant at Rockingham in 1991. Rudd finished the season second in the final point standing to Dale Earnhardt.

Rudd awaits the start of the AC Delco 500 at Rockingham in 1991.

Rudd surveys Bristol Motor Speedway in 1992.

1992: Best Chevy in a Ford Season, IROC Champ

A year after the best championship run in his career, Ricky Rudd joined the other Chevy drivers on the Winston Cup circuit in taking a figurative year off. The 1992 season was the Year of the Ford. Led by Alan Kulwicki, Bill Elliott, and Davey Allison, the Ford team won the first 9 races of the year and 16 of the season's 29 events. Chevy drivers posted half as many wins, while Pontiacs accounted for three wins, and Oldsmobiles took two victories.

In the final point standings, Ford's dominance was even more pronounced. Four of the Top 6 finishers were Ford drivers. Rudd was the top-finishing Chevy, in 7th place. Ken Schrader, his Hendrick Motorsports teammate, plummeted to 17th in the standings. For the third straight season, Rudd was Hendrick's best driver, a stretch bettered only by Jeff Gordon, who paced Hendrick Motorsports for five seasons from 1997 to 2001.

Indicating how strange Winston Cup racing can be, Rudd's 1992 effort equaled or exceeded his title-contending 1991 season in many ways. In each season he finished with a single victory and nine Top 5s. In 1992, he earned one more Top 10 finish and enjoyed a much-improved starting average thanks to stronger qualifying (9.5 in 1992 vs. 12.0 in 1991). Rudd led the series in Top 10s in 1992 and was tied for the lead with six front row starts. Despite the apparent improvement, the end result was a significantly lower position in the final standings.

The difference was Rudd's performance in "off races"—that is, those races where racin' luck or missed setups resulted in poor finishes. In 1991, he finished just one race outside of the Top 20 and had an average finish of 14.9 in races in which he finished outside of the Top 10. In 1992, those numbers swelled. He had eight finishes outside of the Top 20 and a 25.8 average finish in non-Top 10 races.

Rudd's consecutive winning season streak reached its 10th year when he used pit strategy to win at Dover in September. Elliott dominated the event, leading 261 of 500 laps, and appeared headed to his fifth victory of the season when he stopped for fuel and two tires. When it was his turn to pit, Rudd followed the advice of his crew chief, Gary DeHart, and took fuel only. The time saved gave Rudd a straightaway lead over Elliott. Though Elliott quickly closed the gap, Rudd survived to claim his 13th career win and his third victory at Dover.

An extra pit stop for fuel prevented a Rudd win earlier at Bristol. In the first race on the track's new concrete surface, he led 139 laps before dropping to eighth. At Talladega, he led the first 50 laps after starting second, before making his first pit stop. He eventually dropped a lap down and finished in fourth place.

If the Winston Cup season was disappointing, Rudd made the most of his first opportunity to race in the International Race of Champions (IROC) series. He was invited to participate in the four-race series after finishing second in the Winston Cup point standings in 1991. Though he didn't win an IROC race, his two second-place and two third-place finishes were enough to beat Dale Earnhardt for the title. Rudd became just the fifth driver to win the IROC trophy in his first season. It was the first, and only, major championship in Rudd's career.

Rudd drove Tide-sponsored cars for nine seasons, three with Hendrick Motorsports and six with his self-owned Rudd Performance Motorsports.

1992 Stats Chart

Category	Rudd's Total	Rudd's Rank	1992 Leader*
Money	$793,903	10th	Alan Kulwicki -- 2,322,561
Total Points	3,735	7th	Alan Kulwicki -- 4,078
Avg. Start	9.5	4th	Ernie Irvan -- 7.1
Avg. Finish	13.3	8th	Alan Kulwicki -- 10.6
Wins	1	10th	D. Allison, B. Elliott -- 5
Top 5s	9	7th	Davey Allison -- 15
Top 10s	18	1st	(Five Tied with 17 Top 5s)
DNFs	4	27th	D. Marcis, J. Means -- 14
Poles	1	7th	Alan Kulwicki -- 6
Front Row Starts	6	T-1st	(A. Kulwicki, S. Marlin, M. Martin -- 6)
Laps Led	331	12th	Davey Allison -- 1,377
Races Led	9	10th	Alan Kulwicki -- 20
Times Led	16	12th	Alan Kulwicki -- 51
Miles Led	390	12th	Davey Allison -- 2,315
Times Led Most Laps	1	8th	Davey Allison -- 6
Bonus Points	50	11th	Alan Kulwicki -- 125
Laps Completed	8,968	9th	Ted Musgrave -- 9,253
Miles Completed	10,269	15th	Harry Gant -- 11,220
Points per Race	128.8	7th	Alan Kulwicki -- 140.6
Lead-Lap Finishes	11	7th	Alan Kulwicki -- 17

* -- Second-place driver(s) listed in parentheses if Rudd is category leader.

1992 Performance Chart

No. 5 Hendrick Motorsports Chevrolet

Career Race	Season Race	Date	Race	St.	Fin.	Total Laps	Laps Completed	Laps Led	Condition	Money	Pts.	Bonus Pts.	Point Standing	Behind Leader	Current Leader
411	1	Feb 16	Daytona -- Daytona 500 by STP	8	40	200	79	0	DNF - Engine	$34,350	43	0	40	-142	D. Allison
412	2	Mar 1	Rockingham -- GM Goodwrench 500	23	28	492	437	0	Running	12,950	79	0	33	-238	D. Allison
413	3	Mar 8	Richmond -- Pontiac Excitement 400	27	6	400	400	0	Running	16,050	150	0	23	-253	D. Allison
414	4	Mar 15	Atlanta -- Motorcraft Quality Parts 500	24	12	328	328	0	Running	15,425	127	0	20	-296	D. Allison
415	5	Mar 29	Darlington -- TranSouth 500	18	5	367	366	0	Running	21,020	155	0	14	-311	D. Allison
416	6	Apr 5	Bristol -- Food City 500	17	6	500	497	0	Running	16,485	150	0	11	-245	D. Allison
417	7	Apr 12	North Wilkesboro -- First Union 400	2	3	400	400	0	Running	23,465	165	0	10	-260	D. Allison
418	8	Apr 26	Martinsville -- Hanes 500	5	23	500	426	0	Running	11,850	94	0	11	-251	D. Allison
419	9	May 3	Talladega -- Winston 500	4	26	188	186	0	Running	16,005	85	0	12	-351	D. Allison
420	10	May 24	Charlotte -- Coca-Cola 600	3	9	400	398	33	Running	30,100	143	5	11	-373	D. Allison
421	11	May 31	Dover -- Budweiser 500	13	6	500	498	58	Running	21,215	155	5	10	-348	D. Allison
422	12	Jun 7	Sears Point -- SaveMart 300K	1	4	74	74	9	Running	25,710	165	5	8	-262	D. Allison
423	13	Jun 14	Pocono -- Champion Spark Plug 500	9	36	200	22	0	DNF - Engine	12,515	55	0	11	-367	D. Allison
424	14	Jun 21	Michigan -- Miller Genuine Draft 400	12	5	200	200	0	Running	25,760	155	0	10	-397	D. Allison
425	15	Jul 4	Daytona -- Pepsi 400	5	7	160	160	2	Running	20,875	151	5	9	-385	D. Allison
426	16	Jul 19	Pocono -- Miller Genuine Draft 500	2	4	200	200	0	Running	24,695	160	0	8	-308	Elliott
427	17	Jul 26	Talladega -- DieHard 500	2	4	188	187	54	Running	32,195	170	10	6	-299	D. Allison
428	18	Aug 9	Watkins Glen -- The Bud at the Glen	4	13	51	51	0	Running	14,400	124	0	6	-295	Elliott
429	19	Aug 16	Michigan -- Champion Spark Plug 400	11	36	200	55	0	DNF - Crash	13,765	55	0	11	-415	Elliott
430	20	Aug 29	Bristol -- Bud 500	2	8	500	499	139	Running	16,875	147	5	9	-418	Elliott
431	21	Sep 6	Darlington -- Mountain Dew Southern 500	18	10	298	297	3	Running	18,470	139	5	8	-449	Elliott
432	22	Sep 12	Richmond -- Miller Genuine Draft 400	2	6	400	400	1	Running	18,205	155	5	8	-415	Elliott
433	23	Sep 20	Dover -- Peak AntiFreeze 500	6	1	500	500	32	Running	64,965	180	5	7	-415	Elliott
434	24	Sep 28	Martinsville -- Goody's 500	21	10	500	499	0	Running	17,200	134	0	7	-354	Elliott
435	25	Oct 5	North Wilkesboro -- Tyson/Holly Farms 400	5	15	400	396	0	Running	12,275	118	0	7	-321	Elliott
436	26	Oct 11	Charlotte -- Mello Yello 500	5	5	334	334	0	Running	35,550	155	0	7	-244	Elliott
437	27	Oct 25	Rockingham -- AC Delco 500	7	3	492	491	0	Running	31,225	165	0	7	-244	Elliott
438	28	Nov 1	Phoenix -- Pyroil 500	4	30	312	288	0	Running	12,885	73	0	7	-281	D. Allison
439	29	Nov 15	Atlanta -- Hooters 500	16	25	328	300	0	DNF - Engine	12,735	88	0	7	-343	Kulwicki

1992 Breakout Chart

Fine Line

Though his season statistics were comparable, Rudd's championship performance in 1991 and 1992 differed drastically.

Year	Point Standing	Wins	Top 5s	Top 10s	Average Fin in Non Top 10s	Total Points
1991	2nd	1	9	17	14.9	4,092
1992	7th	1	9	18	25.8	3,735

1993: Saying Farewell to GM and Hendrick Motorsports

On June 19, 1993, Ricky Rudd announced his intention to create his own team and drive self-owned cars in 1994. The next day, he won the Miller Genuine Draft 400 while driving the No. 5 Hendrick Motorsports Chevy Lumina. The rapid-fire set of events mirrored Rudd's 1987 announcement that he would leave his four-year ride with Bud Moore and jump to the No. 26 King Motorsports team. The day after he told Moore of his decision, he won the Delaware 500 at Dover.

Career-altering decisions, apparently, excite the laid-back Virginian.

Alan Kulwicki's death in 1992—in a plane crash on his way to Bristol, Tennessee—prompted thoughts of team ownership in Rudd. After Kulwicki's untimely passing, rumors of Rudd's interest in buying the deceased driver-owner's team and equipment began to spread through the Winston Cup world. Though Rudd wasn't interested, a funny thing happened: sponsors and potential crew chiefs approached Rudd and expressed their desire to form partnerships. Geoffrey Bodine eventually bought Kulwicki's team, but Rudd started organizing a race team in his head.

One of the most important pieces of a team—a trustworthy sponsor—fell into place when Tide committed to join Rudd in his venture. Tide had been Rudd's primary sponsor since 1991. The rest of the organization—fabricators, mechanics, shop space, engines—also began to fall into place. The two remaining key components, namely a crew chief and a car manufacturer, were left for later consideration.

Another aspect that may have aided Rudd's departure was the changing dynamics at Hendrick Motorsports. Rudd—the lead driver for the team in each of his first three HMS seasons—watched owner Rick Hendrick pluck heralded Busch series driver Jeff Gordon from Bill Davis and the Ford camp. Gordon's sensational start in 1993 made the new world evident to Rudd: he was no longer the top driver on the team.

A woeful start to the season also helped solidify Rudd's decision. He finished 9 of the first 12 races outside of the Top 10—including 6 finishes of 26th or worse—and fell to 22nd in the points race. Combining positive financial and personnel conditions, a loss of influence with Hendrick and poor on-track performance, the choice to move on was an easy one.

To Rudd's credit, his effort for Hendrick never wavered despite obvious distractions. In fact, he stormed back with 11 Top 10s in the season's final 18 races to claim 10th in the final standings (four spots ahead of Gordon, who took the Rookie-of-the-Year Award). His victory at Michigan was due, once again, to fuel luck. Mark Martin drove away from the field and led 141 of 200 laps. He had to pull down pit road with 9 laps to go for fuel, however. That gave the lead to Rudd, whose team had switched carburetors prior to the race to stretch the No. 5 car's mileage. The 2-mile Michigan International Speedway became the longest track on which Rudd had won a race. It was his 14th career win and stretched his consecutive winning season streak to 11.

Rudd looked poised to win the second Michigan race, leading 86 of the first 104 laps, until an overheated engine forced him behind the wall on lap 125. He finished 35th. In the season-ending race at Atlanta, his second-place finish secured the manufacturer's championship for Chevrolet. The honor was bittersweet for Rudd, who by then had decided his new team would join the Ford contingent in 1994.

Rudd battles Brett Bodine at Atlanta in 1993. Rudd drove the No. 26 car for two seasons in the late 1980s.

1993 Stats Chart

Category	Rudd's Total	Rudd's Rank	1993 Leader
Money	$752,562	13th	Dale Earnhardt -- 3,353,789
Total Points	3,644	10th	Dale Earnhardt -- 4,526
Avg. Start	10.9	5th	Ernie Irvan -- 7.7
Avg. Finish	15.5	11th	Dale Earnhardt -- 8.2
Wins	1	5th	Rusty Wallace -- 10
Top 5s	9	6th	Rusty Wallace -- 19
Top 10s	14	9th	D. Earnhardt, R. Wallace -- 21
DNFs	6	14th	Jeff Gordon -- 11
Poles	0	--	Ken Schrader -- 6
Front Row Starts	3	8th	Ernie Irvan -- 9
Laps Led	136	13th	Rusty Wallace -- 2,860
Races Led	7	14th	Dale Earnhardt -- 21
Times Led	13	13th	Dale Earnhardt -- 81
Miles Led	240	12th	Dale Earnhardt -- 2,485
Times Led Most Laps	1	7th	D. Earnhardt, R. Wallace -- 9
Bonus Points	40	14th	Dale Earnhardt -- 150
Laps Completed	8,637	17th	Dale Earnhardt -- 9,787
Miles Completed	10,265	19th	Dale Earnhardt -- 11,808
Points per Race	121.5	11th	Dale Earnhardt -- 150.9
Lead-Lap Finishes	11	8th	Rusty Wallace -- 23

1993 Performance Chart

No. 5 Hendrick Motorsports Chevrolet

Career Race	Season Race	Date	Race	St.	Fin.	Total Laps	Laps Completed	Laps Led	Condition	Money	Pts.	Bonus Pts.	Point Standing	Behind Leader	Current Leader
440	1	Feb 14	Daytona -- Daytona 500	12	30	200	177	0	Running	$31,285	73	0	31	-107	Jarrett
441	2	Feb 28	Rockingham -- GM Goodwrench 500	12	12	492	490	0	Running	15,735	127	0	21	-155	Earnhardt
442	3	Mar 7	Richmond -- Pontiac Excitement 400	15	15	400	398	0	Running	13,035	118	0	19	-172	Jarrett
443	4	Mar 20	Atlanta -- Motorcraft Quality Parts 500	14	5	328	327	0	Running	26,550	155	0	13	-146	Earnhardt
444	5	Mar 28	Darlington -- TranSouth 500	13	19	367	353	0	Running	12,100	106	0	14	-225	Earnhardt
445	6	Apr 4	Bristol -- Food City 500	9	26	500	369	0	DNF - Crash	12,500	85	0	15	-315	Earnhardt
446	7	Apr 18	North Wilkesboro -- First Union 400	10	7	400	400	0	Running	14,960	146	0	14	-302	R. Wallace
447	8	Apr 25	Martinsville -- Hanes 500	14	29	500	310	0	Running	9,025	76	0	16	-411	R. Wallace
448	9	May 2	Talladega -- Winston 500	26	41	188	12	0	DNF - Camshaft	12,120	40	0	21	-526	R. Wallace
449	10	May 16	Sears Point -- SaveMart Supermarket 300K	2	3	74	74	0	Running	29,590	165	0	17	-435	Earnhardt
450	11	May 30	Charlotte -- Coca-Cola 600	20	37	400	164	0	Engine	11,310	52	0	20	-568	Earnhardt
451	12	Jun 6	Dover -- Budweiser 500	15	35	500	121	0	DNF - Crash	12,115	58	0	22	-695	Earnhardt
452	13	Jun 13	Pocono -- Champion Spark Plug 500	12	9	200	200	1	Running	15,765	143	5	21	-687	Earnhardt
453	14	Jun 20	Michigan -- Miller Genuine Draft 400	2	1	200	200	19	Running	77,890	180	5	17	-633	Earnhardt
454	15	Jul 3	Daytona -- Pepsi 400	10	4	160	160	1	Running	28,250	165	5	14	-653	Earnhardt
455	16	Jul 11	New Hampshire -- Slick 50 300	10	5	300	300	0	Running	25,375	155	0	14	-583	Earnhardt
456	17	Jul 18	Pocono -- Miller Genuine Draft 500	3	11	200	200	0	Running	15,615	130	0	14	-638	Earnhardt
457	18	Jul 25	Talladega -- DieHard 500	5	24	188	186	1	Running	14,155	96	5	14	-727	Earnhardt
458	19	Aug 8	Watkins Glen -- Bud at the Glen	9	24	90	87	0	Running	10,910	91	0	14	-750	Earnhardt
459	20	Aug 15	Michigan -- Champion Spark Plug 400	3	35	200	125	86	DNF - Engine	14,590	68	10	14	-820	Earnhardt
460	21	Aug 28	Bristol -- Bud 500	3	22	500	414	0	Running	13,900	97	0	15	-888	Earnhardt
461	22	Sep 5	Darlington -- Mountain Dew Southern 500	16	6	351	350	0	Running	16,940	150	0	16	-903	Earnhardt
462	23	Sep 11	Richmond -- Miller Genuine Draft 400	17	4	400	400	0	Running	26,505	160	0	13	-908	Earnhardt
463	24	Sep 19	Dover -- SplitFire Spark Plug 500	22	21	500	458	0	DNF - Flagged	13,205	100	0	15	-890	Earnhardt
464	25	Sep 26	Martinsville -- Goody's 500	20	4	500	500	0	Running	25,250	160	0	13	-806	Earnhardt
465	26	Oct 3	North Wilkesboro -- Tyson/Holly Farms 400	2	5	400	399	23	Running	21,235	160	5	10	-821	Earnhardt
466	27	Oct 10	Charlotte -- Mello Yello 500	8	8	334	333	0	Running	24,500	142	0	11	-849	Earnhardt
467	28	Oct 24	Rockingham -- AC Delco 500	5	14	492	490	0	Running	15,350	121	0	10	-903	Earnhardt
468	29	Oct 31	Phoenix -- Slick 50 500	4	6	312	312	0	Running	21,120	150	0	10	-918	Earnhardt
469	30	Nov 14	Atlanta -- Hooters 500	13	2	328	328	5	Running	57,225	175	5	10	-882	Earnhardt

1993 Breakout Chart

Hendrick Motorsport: The Drivers

A look at where Ricky Rudd stacks up in the storied history of Hendrick Motorsports

Driver	Years	Starts	Wins	Top 5s	Top 10s	Poles	Front Row Starts	DNFs	Money
Jeff Gordon	1992-2001	293	58	147	190	39	68	45	45,748,580
Ken Schrader	1988-96	267	4	58	126	17	31	43	7,953,016
Terry Labonte	1994-2001	260	11	59	105	6	12	34	18,766,517
Geoffrey Bodine	1984-89	174	7	49	79	22	44	46	3,414,680
Ricky Rudd	**1990-1993**	**117**	**4**	**35**	**64**	**4**	**12**	**16**	**3,213,880**
Darrell Waltrip	1987-1990	110	9	35	59	2	11	9	3,076,326
Jerry Nadeau	2000-01	70	1	7	15	0	2	17	4,672,605
Wally Dallenbach Jr.	1998-99	50	0	1	9	0	0	8	2,241,176
Ricky Craven	1997-98	38	0	4	8	1	3	7	1,659,550
Tim Richmond	1986-87	37	9	16	21	9	16	4	1,125,680
All-Time Totals*	**1984-2001**	**1,478**	**103**	**419**	**692**	**101**	**203**	**254**	**93,456,877**

* -- Includes stats from drivers not listed above

1994: First-Year Success

For the first time since 1978, when he raced his dad's No. 22 Chevy, Ricky Rudd was at the controls of his race team. He drove for six teams of varying size and strength between 1979 and 1993. In 1994, Rudd was the owner and driver of the No. 10 Rudd Performance Motorsports Ford.

Looked at from nearly any perspective, Rudd's season was a resounding success. From a purely career-minded point of view, his 1994 performance was the second-best in his 15-plus seasons. He finished fifth in the final point standings, a mark he bettered only in 1991 and 1986. For only the second time, he exceeded the 4,000-point mark. And, perhaps most impressive for a new team, he had the most reliable car on the track. He drove 12,046 miles, more than any driver in 1994.

Rudd looked even more successful when compared to other drivers of his generation who chose to create their own teams. Darrell Waltrip, Geoffrey Bodine, and Bill Elliott—three other drivers who started their driving careers during the 1970s—launched teams in the 1990s. As an owner, none of the three had a better first-season championship effort than Rudd. Waltrip and Elliott finished 8th in their first years, while Bodine finished 17th.

Like Bodine, Rudd won a race and a pole as a rookie owner. Rudd set a track record (since broken) while winning the pole at Rockingham in the fall. At New Hampshire, he won for the 12th consecutive season by using brains and brawn. Thanks to the smarts of crew chief Bill Ingle, Rudd took on just two tires on his final pit stop with 25 to go. The quick stop gave him the track position he needed to make a charge. With six laps left, he made that charge on Dale Earnhardt. The two long-time combatants put on a bumping, banging side-by-side battle down the straights and through the corners over the final laps of the race. Rudd was strong enough to hold off Earnhardt, however, giving him his 15th career win.

Rudd almost scored two more wins, but was done in by bad luck. At the Coca-Cola 600, he was in the lead with 10 laps to go, only to lose on fuel mileage. He dipped into the pits on lap 391 of 400, giving the lead to eventual winner Jeff Gordon. He ended the race in sixth. At Phoenix, a strong effort was nullified by a broken air wrench in the pits. The problem resulted in a 30-second stop under green that knocked him down a lap. He finished seventh.

Bristol holds Rudd's strongest memories from the 1994 season. In the spring event, he drilled the wall head-on, trashing his car and forcing him to make a visit to an area hospital. On August 26, he left the track to make another trip to the hospital—this time for the birth of his son, Landon Lee.

Rudd also got into trouble in 1994. At Charlotte in the fall, with less than 10 laps remaining, he badgered and wrecked Gordon going into Turn 1. Rudd claimed Gordon pushed him up the track just before the incident, though replays showing the veteran bullying and taking out the young driver got all of the attention. NASCAR nailed Rudd with a $10,000 fine and a three-race probation. Oddly, Rudd blamed the wreck on . . . Gordon's lack of talent. He theorized that had he raced similarly with a better, more experienced driver, the accident never would have occurred. Among other things, Rudd's explanation was certainly far-fetched: Gordon would go on to win more races in a single season (13 in 1998) than Rudd did in his first 13 Winston Cup seasons.

On a more positive note, Rudd reached an important milestone in the season's final race at Atlanta. Starting on the front row, he competed in the 500th race of his career. In NASCAR history, only 22 drivers have reached 500 starts (barring unforeseen circumstances, Michael Waltrip and Mark Martin will start their 500th races in 2002.)

1994 Stats Chart

Category	Rudd's Total	Rudd's Rank	1994 Leader*
Money	$1,044,441	11th	Dale Earnhardt -- 3,400,733
Total Points	4,050	5th	Dale Earnhardt -- 4,694
Avg. Start	17.1	13th	Ernie Irvan -- 6.6
Avg. Finish	12.3	4th	Dale Earnhardt -- 8.0
Wins	1	9th	Rusty Wallace -- 8
Top 5s	6	9th	Dale Earnhardt -- 20
Top 10s	15	6th	Dale Earnhardt -- 25
DNFs	2	44th	Geoffrey Bodine -- 15
Poles	1	7th	G. Bodine, Irvan -- 5
Front Row Starts	2	9th	Geoffrey Bodine -- 10
Laps Led	192	9th	Rusty Wallace -- 2,141
Races Led	10	8th	Dale Earnhardt -- 23
Times Led	16	10th	Ernie Irvan -- 79
Miles Led	226	10th	Ernie Irvan -- 2,419
Times Led Most Laps	0	--	Ernie Irvan -- 10
Bonus Points	50	8th	Ernie Irvan -- 135
Laps Completed	9,728	3rd	Darrell Waltrip -- 9,905
Miles Completed	12,046	1st	(Darrell Waltrip -- 12,026)
Points per Race	130.6	6th	Dale Earnhardt -- 151.4
Lead-Lap Finishes	14	6th	Dale Earnhardt -- 22

* -- Second-place driver(s) listed in parentheses if Rudd is category leader.

Rudd's crew tends to the No. 10 Tide Ford. In 1994, Rudd became a car owner.

1994 Performance Chart
No. 10 Rudd Performance Motorsports Ford

Career Race	Season Race	Date	Race	St.	Fin.	Total Laps	Laps Completed	Laps Led	Condition	Money	Pts.	Bonus Pts.	Point Standing	Behind Leader	Current Leader
470	1	Feb 20	Daytona -- Daytona 500	20	8	200	200	0	Running	$56,465	142	0	8	-38	Marlin
471	2	Feb 27	Rockingham -- Goodwrench Service 500	34	11	492	489	0	Running	12,885	130	0	7	-83	Marlin
472	3	Mar 6	Richmond -- Pontiac Excitement 400	34	18	400	398	0	Running	7,250	109	0	11	-139	Irvan
473	4	Mar 13	Atlanta -- Purolator 500	22	9	328	326	0	Running	12,350	138	0	8	-186	Irvan
474	5	Mar 27	Darlington -- TranSouth Financial 400	25	9	293	292	0	Running	9,260	138	0	5	-203	Irvan
475	6	Apr 10	Bristol -- Food City 500	11	32	500	187	0	DNF - Crash	6,625	67	0	8	-240	Earnhardt
476	7	Apr 17	North Wilkesboro -- First Union 400	25	6	400	400	5	Running	8,390	155	5	8	-240	Earnhardt
477	8	Apr 24	Martinsville -- Hanes 500	19	12	500	498	0	Running	6,825	127	0	7	-268	Irvan
478	9	May 1	Talladega -- Winston Select 500	33	25	188	180	0	Running	9,045	88	0	9	-360	Irvan
479	10	May 15	Sears Point -- Save Mart Supermarkets 300	3	14	74	74	0	Running	9,155	121	0	8	-424	Irvan
480	11	May 29	Charlotte -- Coca-Cola 600	13	6	400	400	10	Running	28,700	155	5	7	-429	Irvan
481	12	Jun 5	Dover -- Budweiser 500	18	19	500	489	0	Running	11,465	106	0	6	-503	Irvan
482	13	Jun 12	Pocono -- UAW-GM Teamwork 500	2	21	200	198	11	Running	10,850	105	5	7	-549	Irvan
483	14	Jun 19	Michigan -- Miller Genuine Draft 400	6	4	200	200	0	Running	31,430	160	0	7	-503	Irvan
484	15	Jul 2	Daytona -- Pepsi 400	31	17	160	160	3	Running	13,985	117	5	7	-566	Irvan
485	16	Jul 10	New Hampshire -- Slick 50 300	3	1	300	300	55	Running	91,875	180	5	7	-473	Earnhardt
486	17	Jul 17	Pocono -- Miller Genuine Draft 500	6	6	200	200	0	Running	17,260	150	0	7	-469	Earnhardt
487	18	Jul 24	Talladega -- DieHard 500	28	7	188	188	1	Running	19,350	151	5	7	-400	Irvan
488	19	Aug 6	Indy -- Brickyard 400	8	11	160	160	0	Running	57,100	130	0	7	-414	Earnhardt
489	20	Aug 14	Watkins Glen -- The Bud at the Glen	7	5	90	90	3	Running	20,875	160	5	6	-424	Earnhardt
490	21	Aug 21	Michigan -- GM Goodwrench Dealer 400	15	10	200	199	0	Running	17,940	134	0	6	-342	Earnhardt
491	22	Aug 27	Bristol -- Goody's 500	33	12	500	499	0	Running	16,540	127	0	6	-385	Earnhardt
492	23	Sep 4	Darlington -- Mountain Dew Southern 500	18	4	367	367	3	Running	24,715	165	5	4	-395	Earnhardt
493	24	Sep 10	Richmond -- Miller Genuine Draft 400	32	5	400	400	0	Running	26,705	155	0	4	-410	Earnhardt
494	25	Sep 18	Dover -- SplitFire Spark Plug 500	16	18	500	496	0	Running	15,450	109	0	4	-476	Earnhardt
495	26	Sep 25	Martinsville -- Goody's 500	13	25	500	490	0	Running	10,975	88	0	5	-563	Earnhardt
496	27	Oct 2	North Wilkesboro -- Tyson Holly Farms 400	26	11	400	397	0	Running	13,550	130	0	5	-584	Earnhardt
497	28	Oct 9	Charlotte -- Mello Yello 500	16	29	334	324	0	DNF - Crash	10,420	76	0	5	-678	Earnhardt
498	29	Oct 23	Rockingham -- AC Delco 500	1	4	492	492	2	Running	28,076	165	5	5	-698	Earnhardt
499	30	Oct 30	Phoenix -- Slick 50 300	4	7	312	311	99	Running	20,220	151	5	5	-590	Earnhardt
500	31	Nov 13	Atlanta -- Hooters 500	8	14	328	324	0	Running	17,200	121	0	5	-644	Earnhardt

1994 Breakout Chart

First-Year Owners

Long-time drivers Darrell Waltrip, Geoffrey Bodine, Bill Elliott, and Ricky Rudd ventured into NASCAR ownership in the same five-year period. A look at how they fared in their first seasons as driver/owners.

Driver/Owner	First Year	Point Standing	Wins	Top 5s	Top 10s	Poles	Money
Ricky Rudd	1994	5th	1	6	15	1	$1,044,441
Bill Elliott	1995	8th	0	4	11	2	996,816
Darrell Waltrip	1991	8th	2	5	17	0	604,854
Geoffrey Bodine	1994	17th	3	7	10	5	1,287,626

1995: Can't Fight City Hall

The 1995 season was one of the strangest and most eventful in Ricky Rudd's career. From off-track run-ins with NASCAR to a top-level personnel change to an on-track run-in with NASCAR to a last-minute, streak-saving victory at Phoenix, Rudd never lacked for excitement in his second year as a Winston Cup owner.

Early in the year, Rudd and his crew chief Bill Ingle couldn't escape NASCAR's all-seeing eye. At Bristol, Ingle was fined $1,000 by the sport's governing body for an illegal A-frame offset. Three weeks later, Ingle was fined $250 for punching Ted Musgrave in a postrace altercation. Then, a week later at Talladega, Rudd and Ingle were slapped with the largest monetary fine ever levied by NASCAR—a combined $50,000.

Rudd was fined $45,000 as driver and team owner, while Ingle was assessed a $5,000 penalty. NASCAR imposed the fine after discovering an ingenious hydraulic device designed to help the No. 10 Ford skirt height requirements during the race, but not before or after. The device turned the clutch pedal into a pump that allowed Rudd to control the height of his car's rear end. Had Rudd and Ingle's scheme worked, their car would have passed prerace inspection, during which the height of the rear end is measured. During the race, gravity and G-forces would have lowered the Ford's rear by as much as an inch, helping Rudd get through Talladega's turbulent air more quickly. Then, on the cool-down lap, Rudd could have used his clutch pedal to lift the rear of his car back to regulation height, thus allowing it to pass postrace inspection.

NASCAR officials noticed the device during inspection before practice. A similar device had been installed by two other teams at Daytona in February. Caught red-handed, Rudd had to accept the fine. NASCAR stayed attentive to Rudd's every move on the track, too. At North Wilkesboro, with Rudd in position to win with just 30 laps to go, Winston Cup officials called the Tide car back down pit road to replace a missing lug nut. The penalty occurred under caution, but still cost Rudd any chance he had of winning. He ended the race in fifth place. Livid, Rudd asserted that NASCAR didn't want him to win.

When not "searching for gray areas" in NASCAR's rule book, Rudd's crew chief was planning his next career move. In September at Darlington, just before the Southern 500, Ingle announced his intention to leave Rudd's team after the season to take over the crew chief job at Diamond Ridge Motorsports. In addition to leading DRM, Ingle hoped to revive his driving career in the Busch series. He had last raced in 1988.

Despite their imminent separation, Ingle and Rudd finished the 1995 season with a flourish. Rudd won the pole and led the most laps at Charlotte in October. Later that month, they extended Rudd's consecutive winning-season streak to 13 years with a victory at Phoenix. He used a strong finish to win on the 1-mile track. In sixth on a restart with 31 laps to go, Rudd needed just 8 laps to move into the lead. He led the remaining 23 laps en route to victory. Only in 1985, when he won the season's final race at Riverside, did Rudd procrastinate longer before getting a win. The victory gave him 10 Top 5 finishes, the first time he reached double-digits in that category in 8 years.

The strong finish—he had seven Top 10s in the final eight races—also helped Rudd creep back into the Top 10 in the final point standings. He had fallen to 18th in the standings after the season's eighth race. He climbed as high at 8th after his Phoenix win.

Among the other memorable moments for Rudd in 1995 was his pole at Sears Point—his fourth in the track's first seven Winston Cup races. He was less fond of his experience at Michigan in June. He started the race second—one of six front row starts during the season—and appeared to have one of the race's best cars. A hard-hitting wreck in Turn 1, however, ended any thoughts of winning. Instead, a woozy Rudd was transported to a local hospital and treated for amnesia, a sore ribcage and tender right foot.

Rudd starts on the outside pole next to Darrell Waltrip in the fall Atlanta in 1995. It was one of seven front row starts for Rudd during the year.

1995 Stats Chart

Category	Rudd's Total	Rudd's Rank	1995 Leader
Money	$1,337,703	9th	Jeff Gordon -- 4,347,343
Total Points	3,734	9th	Jeff Gordon -- 4,614
Avg. Start	11.2	3rd	Jeff Gordon -- 5.0
Avg. Finish	16.0	9th	Dale Earnhardt -- 9.2
Wins	1	8th	Jeff Gordon -- 7
Top 5s	10	6th	Dale Earnhardt -- 19
Top 10s	16	7th	Earnhardt, Gordon -- 23
DNFs	6	13th	G. Sacks, D. Waltrip -- 11
Poles	2	4th	Jeff Gordon -- 9
Front Row Starts	7	2nd	Jeff Gordon -- 12
Laps Led	368	7th	Jeff Gordon -- 2,600
Races Led	11	7th	Jeff Gordon -- 29
Times Led	23	7th	Jeff Gordon -- 94
Miles Led	511	6th	Jeff Gordon -- 3,458
Times Led Most Laps	1	6th	Jeff Gordon -- 11
Bonus Points	60	7th	Jeff Gordon -- 200
Laps Completed	8,813	18th	Sterling Marlin -- 9,728
Miles Completed	10,834	19th	Sterling Marlin -- 11,936
Points per Race	120.5	9th	Jeff Gordon -- 148.8
Lead-Lap Finishes	13	9th	Jeff Gordon -- 23

1995 Performance Chart
No. 10 Rudd Performance Motorsports Ford

Career Race	Season Race	Date	Race	St.	Fin.	Total Laps	Laps Completed	Laps Led	Condition	Money	Pts.	Bonus Pts.	Point Standing	Behind Leader	Current Leader
501	1	Feb 19	Daytona -- Daytona 500	18	13	200	200	0	Running	$60,620	124	0	13	-61	Marlin
502	2	Feb 26	Rockingham -- Goodwrench 500	2	4	492	492	3	Running	33,480	165	5	6	-56	Earnhardt
503	3	Mar 5	Richmond -- Pontiac Excitement 400	30	21	400	395	0	Running	23,150	100	0	6	-131	Earnhardt
504	4	Mar 12	Atlanta -- Purolator 500	6	8	328	327	0	Running	26,200	142	0	7	-154	Earnhardt
505	5	Mar 26	Darlington -- TranSouth Financial 400	4	41	293	74	0	DNF - Crash	21,409	40	0	12	-289	Earnhardt
506	6	Apr 2	Bristol -- Food City 500	13	5	500	500	0	Running	32,260	155	0	10	-222	Earnhardt
507	7	Apr 9	North Wilkesboro -- First Union 400	12	29	400	392	0	Running	19,215	76	0	14	-331	Earnhardt
508	8	Apr 23	Martinsville -- Hanes 500	8	30	356	313	0	DNF - Trans.	19,465	73	0	18	-334	Earnhardt
509	9	Apr 30	Talladega -- Winston 500	26	22	188	187	0	Running	25,115	97	0	17	-342	Gordon
510	10	May 7	Sears Point -- SaveMart Supermarkets 300	1	4	74	74	4	Running	39,870	165	5	13	-357	Earnhardt
511	11	May 28	Charlotte -- Coca-Cola 600	18	5	400	399	3	Running	49,000	160	5	13	-352	Earnhardt
512	12	Jun 4	Dover -- Miller 500	29	31	500	436	0	Running	25,665	70	0	12	-442	Earnhardt
513	13	Jun 11	Pocono -- UAW/GM 500	4	13	200	200	0	Running	23,655	124	0	13	-460	Earnhardt
514	14	Jun 18	Michigan -- Miller 400	2	38	200	70	31	DNF - Crash	24,780	54	5	15	-475	Marlin
515	15	Jul 1	Daytona -- Pepsi 400	14	8	160	160	5	Running	31,775	147	5	13	-508	Marlin
516	16	Jul 9	New Hampshire -- Slick 50 300	7	5	300	300	0	Running	35,125	155	0	12	-531	Gordon
517	17	Jul 16	Pocono -- Miller 500	13	3	200	200	0	Running	41,010	165	0	11	-541	Gordon
518	18	Jul 23	Talladega -- DieHard 500	6	41	188	68	0	DNF - Engine	24,175	40	0	12	-653	Gordon
519	19	Aug 5	Indy -- Brickyard 400	22	20	160	159	0	Running	73,450	103	0	14	-705	Gordon
520	20	Aug 13	Watkins Glen -- Bud at the Glen	7	4	90	90	0	Running	34,320	160	0	12	-715	Gordon
521	21	Aug 20	Michigan -- Goodwrench Service 400	2	30	200	160	46	DNF - Engine	23,615	78	5	12	-812	Gordon
522	22	Aug 26	Bristol -- Goody's 500	8	36	500	138	0	DNF - Crash	23,510	55	0	14	-912	Gordon
523	23	Sep 3	Darlington -- Mountain Dew Southern 500	2	6	367	367	37	Running	34,865	155	5	13	-937	Gordon
524	24	Sep 9	Richmond -- Miller 400	12	8	400	399	0	Running	25,455	142	0	14	-950	Gordon
525	25	Sep 17	Dover -- MBNA 500	6	10	500	498	0	Running	33,665	134	0	13	-1,001	Gordon
526	26	Sep 24	Martinsville -- Goody's 500	13	27	500	450	0	Running	19,700	82	0	14	-1,070	Gordon
527	27	Oct 1	North Wilkesboro -- Tyson 400	24	5	400	400	58	Running	31,640	160	5	14	-1,080	Gordon
528	28	Oct 8	Charlotte -- UAW-GM Quality 500	1	4	334	334	107	Running	90,200	170	10	12	-988	Gordon
529	29	Oct 22	Rockingham -- AC Delco 400	7	13	393	392	0	Running	21,950	124	0	10	-972	Gordon
530	30	Oct 29	Phoenix -- Dura-Lube 500K	29	1	312	312	63	Running	78,260	180	5	8	-947	Gordon
531	31	Nov 12	Atlanta -- NAPA 500	2	10	328	327	11	Running	29,775	139	5	9	-880	Gordon

Rudd's victory at Phoenix—the next-to-last race of the 1995 season—extended his consecutive winning season streak to 15.

1996: A Great Run Ends

The 1996 season marked the end of a remarkable run in Ricky Rudd's career. Though he had no way of knowing it at the time, he was about to enter the "dark years" of his Winston Cup existence. During the 1997, 1998, and 1999 seasons, his performance plummeted to depths to which he had never fallen before. He finished 17th in the final 1997 points standings. He dropped to 22nd in 1998, then bottomed out at 31st in 1999.

Such a future could not have been foreseen in 1996. Rudd broke out to one of the best starts of his career, finishing the first five races in the Top 10. He jumped to third in the points and never fell outside of the series' Top 10. Though he never seriously contended for the championship, he finished a strong sixth in the final standings.

With his solid 1996 effort, Rudd completed a 16-year stretch in which he finished among the points leaders 15 times. Since joining the series as a true full-time driver in 1981, no driver—not Earnhardt, Waltrip, Elliott, nor Wallace—could boast as consistent a record as Rudd. Unlike the others, Rudd couldn't point to a championship. Neither, however, could he point to a steady, strong ride like the others. During his successful 16-year streak, Rudd had provided quality performances for five different owners.

To help direct his team, Rudd hired a new crew chief—Richard Broome—to replace the departed Bill Ingle. Broome had guided Ken Schrader and Hendrick Motorsports to a winning season in 1991. (More recently, Broome directed Jimmy Spencer's team.)

The highlight of Rudd and Broome's 1996 adventure was their victory at Rockingham in the fall. The race was notable for the fact that it was a top-down mutiny. The ship's captains—that is, Rudd and Broome—revolted against the crew. Rudd suffered repeated poor pit stops that threatened to ruin what looked to be his best race of the season. Twice, he brought the No. 10 Tide car to the pits in second place, only to exit well back in the field. After one particularly bad stop, instead of mashing the gas when the jack came down, Rudd sat and stared angrily at his crew.

Exasperated, Rudd and Broome ordered their crew to take a hike while Broome scoured the garage area searching for over-the-wall crew members from other teams that had already been knocked out of the race. He found several of Derrike Cope's crew, but they, too, proved to be inadequate. When the yellow flag came out on lap 315, Rudd chose not to pit, fearing another loss of track position. Miraculously, on old tires (at Rockingham, of all places), he led the final 74 laps and beat Dale Jarrett to the finish line by over three seconds.

The victory extended Rudd's consecutive winning season streak to 14 years, topping the 13-year Modern Era run put together by the great Cale Yarborough.

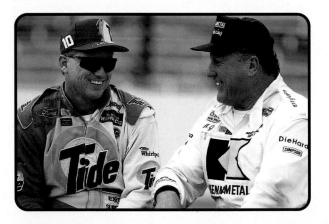

1996 Stats Chart

Category	Rudd's Total	Rudd's Rank	1996 Leader
Money	$1,503,025	9th	Terry Labonte -- 4,030,648
Total Points	3,845	6th	Terry Labonte -- 4,657
Avg. Start	20.5	17th	Jeff Gordon -- 6.3
Avg. Finish	14.6	6th	Terry Labonte -- 8.2
Wins	1	8th	Jeff Gordon -- 10
Top 5s	5	9th	J. Gordon, T. Labonte -- 21
Top 10s	16	7th	J. Gordon, T. Labonte -- 24
DNFs	1	48th	Andretti, Cope, D. Waltrip -- 11
Poles	0	--	Jeff Gordon -- 5
Front Row Starts	2	8th	Jeff Gordon -- 15
Laps Led	150	14th	Jeff Gordon -- 2,314
Races Led	12	9th	Jeff Gordon -- 25
Times Led	17	11th	Jeff Gordon -- 97
Miles Led	186	13th	Jeff Gordon -- 2,386
Times Led Most Laps	0	--	Jeff Gordon -- 10
Bonus Points	60	10th	Jeff Gordon -- 175
Laps Completed	9,281	7th	Dale Earnhardt -- 9,530
Miles Completed	11,400	4th	Dale Earnhardt -- 11,523
Points per Race	124.0	6th	Terry Labonte -- 150.2
Lead-Lap Finishes	13	8th	J. Gordon, T. Labonte -- 24

1996 Performance Chart

No. 10 Rudd Performance Motorsports Ford

Career Race	Season Race	Date	Race	St.	Fin.	Total Laps	Laps Completed	Laps Led	Condition	Money	Pts.	Bonus Pts.	Point Standing	Behind Leader	Current Leader
532	1	Feb 18	Daytona -- Daytona 500	10	9	200	200	0	Running	$79,987	138	0	10	-42	Jarrett
533	2	Feb 25	Rockingham -- Goodwrench Service 400	25	4	393	393	3	Running	35,810	165	5	3	-52	Earnhardt
534	3	Mar 3	Richmond -- Pontiac Excitement 400	34	9	400	400	0	Running	27,875	138	0	3	-89	Jarrett
535	4	Mar 10	Atlanta -- Purolator 500	20	8	328	327	1	Running	29,650	147	5	3	-72	Jarrett
536	5	Mar 24	Darlington -- TranSouth Financial 400	24	9	293	292	0	Running	27,560	138	0	3	-57	Jarrett
537	6	Mar 31	Bristol -- Food City 500	9	14	342	340	8	Running	26,115	126	5	3	-81	Jarrett
538	7	Apr 14	North Wilkesboro -- First Union 400	33	15	400	397	0	Running	24,140	118	0	5	-93	Jarrett
539	8	Apr 21	Martinsville -- Goody's Headache Powder 500	30	23	500	490	0	Running	24,615	94	0	6	-157	Earnhardt
540	9	Apr 28	Talladega -- Winston Select 500	18	28	188	175	0	Running	27,480	79	0	7	-248	Earnhardt
541	10	May 5	Sears Point -- SaveMart Supermarkets 300	2	7	74	74	0	Running	31,195	146	0	6	-267	Earnhardt
542	11	May 26	Charlotte -- Coca-Cola 600	30	15	400	396	0	Running	30,620	118	0	6	-324	Earnhardt
543	12	Jun 2	Dover -- Miller 500	16	8	500	499	0	Running	32,765	142	0	5	-352	Earnhardt
544	13	Jun 16	Pocono -- UAW/GM Teamwork 500	9	2	200	200	11	Running	52,900	175	5	5	-244	Earnhardt
545	14	Jun 23	Michigan -- Miller Genuine Draft 400	14	31	200	195	5	Running	35,540	75	5	5	-307	Earnhardt
546	15	Jul 6	Daytona -- Pepsi 400	39	33	117	116	0	Running	28,255	64	0	7	-403	Earnhardt
547	16	Jul 14	New Hampshire -- Jiffy Lube 300	20	3	300	300	6	Running	49,825	170	5	6	-383	T. Labonte
548	17	Jul 21	Pocono -- Miller 500	7	2	200	200	9	Running	56,615	175	5	5	-323	T. Labonte
549	18	Jul 28	Talladega -- DieHard 500	28	37	129	113	0	Running	27,406	52	0	6	-371	Gordon
550	19	Aug 3	Indianapolis -- Brickyard 400	35	6	160	160	1	Running	118,385	155	5	5	-377	T. Labonte
551	20	Aug 11	Watkins Glen -- Bud at the Glen	3	34	90	69	0	Running	24,370	61	0	6	-491	T. Labonte
552	21	Aug 18	Michigan -- Goodwrench Service 400	23	8	200	200	6	Running	35,465	147	5	6	-514	T. Labonte
553	22	Aug 24	Bristol -- Goody's 500	13	9	500	500	0	Running	32,115	138	0	6	-531	T. Labonte
554	23	Sep 1	Darlington -- Mountain Dew Southern 500	18	16	367	365	2	Running	27,805	120	5	6	-501	T. Labonte
555	24	Sep 7	Richmond -- Miller 400	37	12	400	399	0	Running	29,405	127	0	6	-534	T. Labonte
556	25	Sep 15	Dover -- MBNA 500	14	34	500	433	0	Running	28,430	61	0	6	-654	Gordon
557	26	Sep 22	Martinsville -- Hanes 500	33	35	500	283	0	DNF - Rear End	24,050	58	0	8	-776	Gordon
558	27	Sep 29	North Wilkesboro -- Tyson/Holly Farms 400	21	7	400	400	17	Running	24,765	151	5	6	-810	Gordon
559	28	Oct 6	Charlotte -- UAW/GM Quality 500	39	13	334	333	0	Running	26,250	124	0	6	-761	Gordon
560	29	Oct 20	Rockingham -- AC Delco 400	2	1	393	393	81	Running	90,025	180	5	6	-745	T. Labonte
561	30	Oct 27	Phoenix -- Dura-Lube 500	3	14	312	311	0	Running	26,855	121	0	6	-794	T. Labonte
562	31	Nov 10	Atlanta -- NAPA 500	28	8	328	328	0	Running	34,100	142	0	6	-812	T. Labonte

1996 Breakout Chart

NASCAR's Most Consistent (1981-1996)

From 1981 (when he joined the Winston Cup Grand National series as a full-time driver) until 1996, no driver finished in the Top 10 in points more often than Ricky Rudd.

Driver	No. of Top 10 Finishes	Best Finish
Ricky Rudd	15	2nd (1990)
Dale Earnhardt	14	1st (1986-87, 1990-91, 1993-94)
Darrell Waltrip	12	1st (1981-82, 1985)
Bill Elliott	12	1st (1988)
Terry Labonte	12	1st (1984, 1996)
Rusty Wallace	10	1st (1989)

1997: Brickyard Champion

Back in the early 1970s, when he was a kid, Ricky Rudd traveled to Indianapolis, Indiana, from Chesapeake, Virginia, to race go-karts at the .686-mile track at Indianapolis Raceway Park. He won races and national titles, and on one of his trips, toured the Indianapolis Motor Speedway, perhaps the most famous race track in the world.

Thirty years later, Rudd returned to Victory Lane in Indianapolis when he won the 1997 Brickyard 400. In one of the biggest upsets in recent memory, he used fuel mileage to claim the richest victory in his career. Rudd's take from the Brickyard was $571,000—a single-race prize that exceeded his earnings from entire seasons earlier in his career. At the time, the check was the second largest prize ever handed out at a NASCAR event (Jeff Gordon's 1994 Brickyard prize of $613,000 was the largest).

Rudd nursed his gas tank over the last half of the Brickyard 400, knowing he could make the finish with just one stop while the rest of the leaders needed two stops. His final pit-road visit came with 46 laps to go. Thanks to a caution, the top cars—Gordon, Jeff Burton and Dale Jarrett—pitted with 13 to go. Rudd stayed on the track and took the lead. His commanding track position was all he needed. He beat second-place Bobby Labonte to the line by two car lengths.

Although the Indy win was the biggest of Rudd's career, it wasn't the victory that extended his consecutive winning season string to a record-tying 15. That had happened earlier in the season at Dover. As at Indianapolis, Rudd didn't have the best car, just the best luck. With 50 laps to go in the spring Dover event, he was riding in fourth place. Over the next 21 laps, each of the top three cars went out with engine woes or due to crashes. Gordon wrecked, Jarrett's engine seized up, and Ernie Irvan wrecked himself. With 29 laps remaining, Rudd assumed the lead and held off Mark Martin for the win. It marked the first time he had won two races in a season since 1987, when he won at Atlanta and Dover while driving the No. 15 Bud Moore Ford. The 1997 Dover win was his fourth on the 1-mile oval.

Despite the success, 1997 turned into a disappointment. After his Brickyard win, Rudd finished 13th or worse in 11 of the season's last 13 races. That dismal stretch included four finishes of 40th or worse. After finishing 29th at Michigan, Rudd dropped out of the Top 10 in the point standings for the first time in nearly two years—a streak of 54 races. After crashing and ending up 41st at Charlotte two months later, he began the opposite kind of run. He dropped to 12th in the points and would not get back into the Top 10 over the next two years—a depressing period that would last for 73 races.

Rudd ended the season 17th in the final standings, his worst showing since his rookie season in 1977.

1997 Breakout Chart

Brickyard Riches

Rudd's winnings from his 1997 Brickyard 400 victory exceeded his winnings from seven different seasons in which he raced full-time.

Season	No. of Starts	Total Winnings
1997 Brickyard 400	1	$571,000
1989	29	534,824
1985	28	512,441
1984	30	476,602
1988	29	410,954
1981	31	381,968
1983	30	257,585
1982	30	201,130

In 1997, Jim Long (right) was Ricky Rudd's crew chief.

1997 Stats Chart

Category	Rudd's Total	Rudd's Rank	1997 Leader
Money	$1,975,981	8th	Jeff Gordon -- 6,375,658
Total Points	3,330	17th	Jeff Gordon -- 4,710
Avg. Start	20.3	14th	Dale Jarrett -- 7.2
Avg. Finish	20.6	18th	Mark Martin -- 9.
Wins	2	5th	Jeff Gordon -- 10
Top 5s	6	9th	Jeff Gordon -- 22
Top 10s	11	11th	Mark Martin -- 24
DNFs	6	11th	Kenny Wallace -- 10
Poles	0	--	Bobby Labonte -- 3
Front Row Starts	0	--	Dale Jarrett -- 6
Laps Led	72	18th	Dale Jarrett -- 2,083
Races Led	3	26th	Jeff Gordon -- 24
Times Led	6	25th	Dale Jarrett -- 71
Miles Led	108	20th	Dale Jarrett -- 2,541
Times Led Most Laps	0	--	Dale Jarrett -- 8
Bonus Points	15	26th	Dale Jarrett -- 150
Laps Completed	9,094	17th	Dale Jarrett -- 9,769
Miles Completed	11,623	16th	Dale Jarrett -- 12,652
Points per Race	104.1	18th	Jeff Gordon -- 147.2
Lead-Lap Finishes	13	11th	Dale Jarrett -- 24

1997 Performance Chart
No. 10 Rudd Performance Motorsports Ford

Career Race	Season Race	Date	Race	St.	Fin.	Total Laps	Laps Completed	Laps Led	Condition	Money	Pts.	Bonus Pts.	Point Standing	Behind Leader	Current Leader
563	1	Feb 16	Daytona -- Daytona 500	13	9	200	200	0	Running	$88,590	138	0	9	-42	Gordon
564	2	Feb 23	Rockingham -- Goodwrench Service 400	10	4	393	393	0	Running	39,210	160	0	5	-62	Gordon
565	3	Mar 2	Richmond -- Pontiac Excitement 400	6	6	400	399	0	Running	30,770	150	0	4	-77	Gordon
566	4	Mar 9	Atlanta -- Primestar 500	25	30	328	293	0	Running	32,975	73	0	6	-113	Jarrett
567	5	Mar 23	Darlington -- TranSouth Financial 400[1]	16	23	293	291	0	Running	26,055	94	0	8	-204	Jarrett
568	6	Apr 6	Texas -- Interstate Batteries 500	8	5	334	334	26	Running	118,775	160	5	6	-219	Jarrett
569	7	Apr 13	Bristol -- Food City 500	22	27	500	483	0	Running	27,991	82	0	7	-297	Jarrett
570	8	Apr 20	Martinsville -- Goody's Headache Powder 500	5	13	500	500	0	Running	27,065	124	0	7	-288	Jarrett
571	9	May 5	Sears Point -- SaveMart Supermarkets 300	10	34	74	66	0	Running	45,890	61	0	10	-392	Jarrett
572	10	May 10	Talladega -- Winston 500	29	11	188	188	0	Running	34,295	130	0	8	-372	T. Labonte
573	11	May 25	Charlotte -- Coca-Cola 600	18	10	333	333	0	Running	70,550	134	0	8	-385	T. Labonte
574	12	Jun 1	Dover -- Miller 500	13	1	500	500	31	Running	95,255	180	5	8	-326	T. Labonte
575	13	Jun 8	Pocono -- Pocono 500	6	21	200	199	0	Running	26,505	100	0	8	-369	Gordon
576	14	Jun 15	Michigan -- Miller 400	34	13	200	200	0	Running	33,750	124	0	8	-400	Gordon
577	15	Jun 22	California -- California 500	39	3	250	250	0	Running	78,525	165	0	8	-420	Gordon
578	16	Jul 5	Daytona -- Pepsi 400	13	34	160	155	0	DNF - Crash	29,985	61	0	8	-464	Gordon
579	17	Jul 13	New Hampshire -- Jiffy Lube 300	18	9	300	300	0	Running	38,325	138	0	8	-423	T. Labonte
580	18	Jul 20	Pocono -- Pennsylvania 500	19	36	200	192	0	Running	25,640	55	0	8	-540	Gordon
581	19	Aug 3	Indy -- Brickyard 400	7	1	160	160	15	Running	571,000	180	5	8	-525	Gordon
582	20	Aug 10	Watkins Glen -- Bud at the Glen	31	40	90	24	0	DNF - Handling	27,865	43	0	9	-667	Gordon
583	21	Aug 17	Michigan -- DeVilbiss 400	27	29	200	198	0	Running	30,915	76	0	11	-766	Gordon
584	22	Aug 23	Bristol -- Goody's Headache Powder 500	39	19	500	496	0	Running	30,750	106	0	10	-736	Martin
685	23	Aug 31	Darlington -- Mountain Dew Southern 500	21	5	367	367	0	Running	39,345	155	0	9	-748	Gordon
586	24	Sep 6	Richmond -- Exide 400	35	28	400	395	0	Running	30,320	79	0	10	-834	Gordon
587	25	Sep 14	New Hampshire -- CMT 300	37	42	300	233	0	DNF - Crash	37,400	37	0	11	-982	Gordon
588	26	Sep 21	Dover -- MBNA 400	16	6	400	399	0	Running	34,440	150	0	10	-983	Gordon
589	27	Sep 28	Martinsville -- Hanes 500	5	13	500	500	0	Running	27,065	124	0	10	-1,024	Gordon
590	28	Oct 5	Charlotte -- UAW-GM Quality 500	22	41	334	102	0	DNF - Crash	28,880	40	0	12	-1,139	Gordon
591	29	Oct 12	Talladega -- DieHard 500	41	34	188	153	0	Running	36,745	61	0	15	-1,141	Gordon
592	30	Oct 27	Rockingham -- AC Delco 400	13	40	393	241	0	DNF - Crash	26,550	43	0	15	-1,263	Gordon
593	31	Nov 2	Phoenix -- Dura-Lube 500	39	36	312	308	0	Running	26,495	55	0	17	-1,320	Gordon
594	32	Nov 16	Atlanta -- NAPA 500	11	37	325	242	0	DNF - Handling	36,030	52	0	17	-1,380	Gordon

[1] -- Relieved by Elton Sawyer

After what was perhaps the greatest triumph of his career, Rudd celebrates his improbable win in the 1997 Brickyard 400.

1998: Single-Car Blues and Setting the Record

In his fifth season of self-ownership, Ricky Rudd began to lose his grip on his increasingly overwhelming organizational, technical, and driving responsibilities. Following the 1997 season, which ended poorly, his team was in disarray. Rudd Performance Motorsports missed preseason testing sessions at Rockingham and Atlanta simply because it couldn't get cars built in time.

Rudd took part in testing at Daytona, but his team's preparation was undone by a wreck in the Twin 125s. Three days later, a broken spring valve knocked the No. 10 Tide out of the Daytona 500 on lap 123. He finished the race in 42nd. A week later at Rockingham, a blown engine forced him out of the race after just 90 laps. Rudd finished dead last in 43rd and found himself in 43rd in the driver point standings. Since joining the Winston Cup circuit full-time in 1981, he had never fallen that low in the standings at any point.

Looking for help, Rudd talked his former crew chief Bill Ingle into rejoining the team after the Daytona 500. Ingle had led RPM during its first two seasons in 1994 and 1995, during which Rudd won twice and had 31 Top 10s. Ingle joined Rudd ostensibly as a "team manager," though he replaced Jim Long as crew chief within six weeks.

Though Ingle provided stability, he couldn't help Rudd overcome his true problem: single-car ownership. The 1998 season illustrated more than any other the advantages of multicar ownership. Of the season's 33 races, 29 were won by drivers from multicar operations. Only Bobby Labonte (two wins), Bobby Hamilton, and Rudd scored victories for the single-car contingent. Labonte's team—Joe Gibbs Racing—planned to add a second car in 1999 (driven by Tony Stewart).

Hindering Rudd was the long-term deal he entered into with Tide as his sponsor in 1994. In the first two seasons of the sponsorship, his funding was among the highest in the series and allowed RPM to become a successful team. In the contract's later seasons, however, escalating costs on the Winston Cup circuit made Tide's dollar commitment inadequate. Rudd looked to add a second team in 1998 or purchase an existing team, but couldn't for a simple reason: he didn't have the money.

Looking to combat the information- and resource-sharing advantages of the bigger teams, Rudd and Junie Donlavey entered into a loose partnership in which they agreed to search for ways to share costs and track data. Rudd drove for Donlavey in 1979 and had a successful season, finishing ninth in the standings with four Top 5s and 17 Top 10s. Their reunion in 1998 didn't yield the same results. Rudd ended the season in 22nd place, while Donlavey's driver, Dick Trickle, finished in 29th.

The bright spot of Rudd's season was his victory at Martinsville—though he had to pay a price for the glory. On a 100-degree, high-humidity Virginia day, he led the final 95 laps and set the Modern Era record for most consecutive seasons with at least one victory. Getting to Victory Lane almost didn't happen, however. By lap 100, Rudd's cooling systems had stopped working and his driver's seat was slowly, but relentlessly toasting his backside. When his crew attempted to cool him off by squirting water down his back from a hose, the move backfired: the hose had been baking in the sun. Instead of a cool stream, he got a scalding splash.

Rudd called for a back-up driver early on. Hut Stricklin volunteered and sat patiently in the Tide pit for nearly 400 laps, waiting his turn. Rudd never gave up his seat, however. Realizing that he had a winning car for the first time that season, he soldiered on. Despite a late caution, he reached the finish line by a comfortable five-car margin over second-place Jeff Gordon.

Rudd was so overcome by heat during the race that he needed 30 minutes of oxygen and cool-down treatments before he could join his team's celebration in Victory Lane. His 16-year winning streak topped the previous Modern Era record of 15 set by Darrell Waltrip and Dale Earnhardt. Earnhardt's streak had ended in 1997. In NASCAR history, only Richard Petty (18) and David Pearson (17) had longer winning streaks. In 2001, Rusty Wallace tied Rudd's mark.

Rudd reached another important milestone at Bristol in the spring. It was the 41-year-old driver's 600th Winston Cup start. In NASCAR history, only 12 other drivers have started 600 races.

1998 Stats Chart

Category	Rudd's Total	Rudd's Rank	1998 Leader
Money	$1,602,895	15th	Jeff Gordon -- 9,306,584
Total Points	3,131	22nd	Jeff Gordon -- 5,328
Avg. Start	20.2	17th	Jeff Gordon -- 7.0
Avg. Finish	23.2	23rd	Jeff Gordon -- 5.7
Wins	1	6th	Jeff Gordon -- 13
Top 5s	1	17th	Jeff Gordon -- 26
Top 10s	5	20th	Jeff Gordon -- 28
DNFs	7	9th	Kenny Wallace -- 13
Poles	0	--	Jeff Gordon -- 7
Front Row Starts	1	12th	Jeff Gordon -- 11
Laps Led	256	11th	Mark Martin -- 1,730
Races Led	4	23rd	Jeff Gordon -- 26
Times Led	8	19th	Jeff Gordon -- 76
Miles Led	155	17th	Jeff Gordon -- 2,765
Times Led Most Laps	0	--	J. Gordon, M. Martin -- 8
Bonus Points	20	23rd	Jeff Gordon -- 170
Laps Completed	9,127	17th	Bobby Hamilton -- 9,840
Miles Completed	11,590	21st	Jeff Gordon -- 12,785
Points per Race	94.9	23rd	Jeff Gordon -- 161.5
Lead-Lap Finishes	9	21st	Jeff Gordon -- 28

1998 Performance Chart
No. 10 Rudd Performance Motorsports Ford

Career Race	Season Race	Date	Race	St.	Fin.	Total Laps	Laps Completed	Laps Led	Condition	Money	Pts.	Bonus Pts.	Point Standing	Behind Leader	Current Leader
595	1	Feb 15	Daytona -- Daytona 500	40	42	200	117	0	DNF - Valve Spring	$86,480	37	0	42	-148	Earnhardt
596	2	Feb 22	Rockingham -- Goodwrench Service Plus 400	30	43	393	90	0	DNF - Engine	30,615	34	0	43	-264	R. Wallace
597	3	Mar 1	Las Vegas -- Las Vegas 400	19	12	267	266	0	Running	77,200	127	0	34	-307	R. Wallace
598	4	Mar 9	Atlanta -- Primestar 500	23	23	325	322	0	Running	38,555	94	0	32	-373	R. Wallace
599	5	Mar 22	Darlington -- TranSouth Financial 400	18	33	293	288	0	Running	32,745	64	0	34	-479	R. Wallace
600	6	Mar 29	Bristol -- Food City 500	35	30	500	482	0	Running	34,485	73	0	32	-480	R. Wallace
601	7	Apr 5	Texas -- Texas 500	20	27	334	315	0	DNF - Handling	65,900	82	0	32	-525	R. Wallace
602	8	Apr 19	Martinsville -- Goody's Headache Powder 500	4	14	500	499	0	Running	39,150	121	0	29	-559	R. Wallace
603	9	Apr 26	Talladega -- Diehard 500	13	24	188	179	0	Running	40,985	91	0	28	-595	R. Wallace
604	10	May 3	California -- California 500	23	11	250	250	0	Running	58,025	130	0	27	-604	Mayfield
605	11	May 24	Charlotte -- Coca-Cola 600	35	31	400	396	0	Running	59,025	70	0	27	-667	Gordon
606	12	May 31	Dover -- MBNA Platinum 400	5	6	400	399	1	Running	49,275	155	5	25	-687	Gordon
607	13	Jun 6	Richmond -- Pontiac Excitement 400	26	11	400	400	0	Running	41,900	130	0	24	-660	Mayfield
608	14	Jun 14	Michigan -- Miller Lite 400	9	37	200	195	0	Running	35,390	52	0	24	-763	Mayfield
609	15	Jun 21	Pocono -- Pocono 500	33	41	200	49	0	DNF - Engine	29,315	40	0	25	-908	Mayfield
610	16	Jun 28	Sears Point -- Save Mart/Kragen 350	15	28	112	112	14	Running	41,455	84	5	27	-973	Gordon
611	17	Jul 12	New Hampshire -- Jiffy Lube 300	33	19	300	299	0	Running	48,400	106	0	25	-1037	Gordon
612	18	Jul 26	Pocono -- Pennsylvania 500	13	42	200	136	0	DNF - Radiator	37,450	37	0	27	-1,185	Gordon
613	19	Aug 1	Indy -- Brickyard 400	27	31	160	155	0	DNF - Crash	85,685	70	0	28	-1,300	Gordon
614	20	Aug 9	Watkins Glen -- Bud at the Glen	3	14	90	90	0	Running	24,900	121	0	26	-1,364	Gordon
615	21	Aug 16	Michigan -- Pepsi 400	19	13	200	199	0	Running	39,490	124	0	26	-1,420	Gordon
616	22	Aug 22	Bristol -- Goody's Headache Powder 500	3	9	500	500	43	Running	45,540	143	5	24	-1,432	Gordon
617	23	Aug 30	New Hampshire -- Farm Aid on CMT 300	35	10	300	300	0	Running	59,500	134	0	23	-1,478	Gordon
618	24	Sep 6	Darlington -- Mountain Dew Southern 500	14	22	367	362	0	Running	38,095	97	0	21	-1,561	Gordon
619	25	Sep 12	Richmond -- Exide Batteries 400	25	34	400	383	0	Running	36,035	61	0	23	-1,675	Gordon
620	26	Sep 20	Dover -- MBNA Gold 400	11	13	400	399	0	Running	35,140	124	0	21	-1,726	Gordon
621	27	Sep 27	Martinsville -- NAPA Autocare 500	2	1	500	500	198	Running	102,575	180	5	20	-1,716	Gordon
622	28	Oct 4	Charlotte -- UAW-GM Quality 500	14	37	334	231	0	DNF - Crash	32,235	52	0	21	-1,824	Gordon
623	29	Oct 11	Talladega -- Winston 500	17	18	188	187	0	Running	44,155	109	0	21	-1,890	Gordon
624	30	Oct 17	Daytona -- Pepsi 400	41	27	160	159	0	Running	42,715	82	0	21	-1,993	Gordon
625	31	Oct 25	Phoenix -- Dura-Lube 500	21	27	257	254	0	Running	31,895	82	0	23	-2,057	Gordon
626	32	Nov 1	Rockingham -- AC Delco 400	7	10	393	393	0	Running	43,150	134	0	21	-2,103	Gordon
627	33	Nov 8	Atlanta -- NAPA 500	34	24	221	221	0	Running	44,225	91	0	22	-2,197	Gordon

1998 Breakout Chart

Consecutive Winning Seasons

Ricky Rudd set the record for number of consecutive winning seasons in the Modern Era in 1998. Rusty Wallace tied his mark in 2001.

Driver	Consecutive Seasons	Winning Years	No. of Wins during the streak
Ricky Rudd	16	1983-98	20
Rusty Wallace	16	1986-2001	54
Darrell Waltrip	15	1975-89	79
Dale Earnhardt	15	1982-96	64
Cale Yarborough	13	1973-85	69
Bill Elliott	10	1983-92	39

Looking for help, Rudd talked his former crew chief Bill Ingle into rejoining the team after the Daytona 500.

1999: Rudd Loses His Team

Ricky Rudd was a story throughout the season in 1999. Unfortunately for the 42-year-old driver, the headlines had nothing to do with his on-track performance. Looking to save his team and get it structured for NASCAR's new multicar reality, he endured a soap opera season that started with hopes of forming a two-car operation and ended with a massive auction that cleared out his team's shop.

Rudd entered the year looking to add a second car to his team, whether through an acquisition, a merger, or some sort of sponsor-partner relationship. The final, distant option in Rudd's mind was to sell off his team and begin driving for hire again. That last option of course, became the reality.

In September, Rudd and Robert Yates announced a three-year contract that put Rudd in the No. 28 Texaco-Havoline Ford. Though the car had an extremely troubling history, it remained one of the most coveted Winston Cup rides, due to Yates' racing success and his unstoppable horsepower. In 1999, Dale Jarrett steered Robert Yates Racing cars to the Winston Cup title, the first championship in Yates' three-decade NASCAR career.

Between the start of the season and his September announcement, Rudd was more of an owner than a driver. His off-track business consumed him. After months of searching and negotiating, he announced in early June that he was close to signing with a business partner who could help fund a second team and ease his overwhelming management responsibilities. Before the deal ever became reality, Rudd's sponsor dropped a bomb: Tide would no longer sponsor the No. 10 Ford. Instead, Procter & Gamble, the maker of Tide, would throw its sponsor weight behind a NASCAR unknown, Cal Wells. A successful owner in other racing series, including CART, Wells was looking to get into the Winston Cup series.

The Tide announcement took the NASCAR world by surprise. Larry McReynolds thought Tide would sign with his new team (he was unhappily working for Richard Childress at the time). Jack Roush thought he was about to land Tide as sponsor of one of his planned six teams. The rest of the garage area was stung because one of NASCAR's oldest, most reliable sponsors had chosen an "outsider." Two months earlier, McDonald's had pulled a similar move on Bill Elliott.

Rudd and other owners began calling on NASCAR to enact franchise protection measures that existed in other series, such as Formula One and CART. Essentially, franchising limits the number of teams allowed to compete, which makes a team's value greater than its people and equipment. Just as major league baseball teams cannot be formed and start competing without the blessing of the league's owners (who charge huge entry fees for startups), Rudd and others wanted greater power in preserving their interests.

As was the case with most others, Rudd's support of franchising was more than a little odd. If franchising had existed when he entered the NASCAR world in the mid-1970s, his opportunity to win the 1977 Rookie-of-the-Year Award in a family-owned car would not have existed. Entering Grand National racing would have been too expensive for the likes of Rudd and his father, Al.

Angered, but focused, Rudd continued his search for a sponsor and a partnership deal after the Tide announcement. On August 13, Yates announced his plans to release driver Kenny Irwin from the No. 28 team at the end of the 1999 season. Immediately, Rudd was pegged as the logical replacement by racing insiders. At Bristol in late August, he and Yates came to a tentative agreement for the 2000 season, though Rudd continued to meet with potential partners in early September. When he couldn't nail down a deal, Rudd called Yates and made a commitment to drive the No. 28 team.

Part of the new deal called for Yates to buy Rudd's shop in Mooresville, N.C., and move the No. 28 operation into Rudd's facilities. To make room, Rudd auctioned off his entire inventory—built up over six years of owning the No. 10 Tide ride. Also brought over in the deal was Rudd's new crew chief, Michael McSwain. Rudd hired McSwain away from Rick Mast's Burdette Motorsports team in May after a two-month search. Rudd had released his long-time crew chief, Bill Ingle, in March after a disappointing start.

Not surprisingly, the never-ending jockeying off the track ruined Rudd's on-track performance. He failed to win in 1999, ending his 16-year streak. He came close to wins at Talladega and Phoenix, thanks to engine power and chassis/aerodynamic expertise supplied by Yates. He finished third at Talladega and fifth at Phoenix. From a points perspective, however, the season was a disaster. Rudd never improved on the 30th-place position he assumed after the first race of the season. He ended the year 31st in the final point standings.

1999 Stats Chart

Category	Rudd's Total	Rudd's Rank	1999 Leader
Money	$1,632,011	23rd	Dale Jarrett -- 6,649,596
Total Points	2,922	31st	Dale Jarrett -- 5,262
Avg. Start	20.3	15th	Jeff Gordon -- 7.4
Avg. Finish	26.2	34th	Dale Jarrett -- 6.8
Wins	0	--	Jeff Gordon -- 7
Top 5s	3	12th	Dale Jarrett -- 24
Top 10s	5	19th	Dale Jarrett -- 29
DNFs	7	4th	John Andretti -- 10
Poles	1	8th	Jeff Gordon -- 7
Front Row Starts	3	8th	Jeff Gordon -- 9
Laps Led	21	22nd	Jeff Gordon -- 1,319
Races Led	3	23rd	Bobby Labonte -- 30
Times Led	3	26th	Jeff Gordon -- 86
Miles Led	49	20th	Jeff Gordon -- 1,923
Times Led Most Laps	0	--	Jeff Burton -- 6
Bonus Points	15	23rd	Bobby Labonte -- 165
Laps Completed	9,230	28th	Bobby Labonte -- 10,013
Miles Completed	12,033	26th	Bobby Labonte -- 13,135
Points per Race	85.9	34th	Dale Jarrett -- 154.8
Lead-Lap Finishes	8	23rd	Bobby Labonte -- 28

1999 Performance Chart
No. 10 Rudd Performance Motorsports Ford

Career Race	Season Race	Date	Race	St.	Fin.	Total Laps	Laps Completed	Laps Led	Condition	Money	Pts.	Bonus Pts.	Point Standing	Behind Leader	Current Leader
628	1	Feb 14	Daytona -- Daytona 500	29	30	200	168	0	Running	$102,226	73	0	30	-107	Gordon
629	2	Feb 21	Rockingham -- Dura-Lube/Big Kmart 400	1	30	393	389	3	Running	38,325	78	5	34	-164	Skinner
630	3	Mar 7	Las Vegas -- Las Vegas 400	34	43	267	115	0	DNF - Engine	51,975	34	0	37	-290	Skinner
631	4	Mar 14	Atlanta -- Cracker Barrel Old Country Store 500	41	25	325	322	0	Running	33,985	88	0	35	-357	Skinner
632	5	Mar 21	Darlington -- TranSouth Financial 400	41	27	164	163	0	Running	31,400	82	0	34	-408	J. Burton
633	6	Mar 28	Texas -- Primestar 500	34	19	334	333	0	Running	73,400	106	0	33	-448	J. Burton
634	7	Apr 11	Bristol -- Food City 500	5	38	500	410	0	DNF - Handling	32,250	49	0	35	-554	J. Burton
635	8	Apr 18	Martinsville -- Goody's Body Pain 500	15	29	500	497	0	Running	32,100	76	0	35	-653	J. Burton
636	9	Apr 25	Talladega -- Diehard 500	7	19	188	188	0	Running	44,045	106	0	33	-677	J. Burton
637	10	May 2	California -- California 500	36	41	250	129	0	DNF - Engine	43,975	40	0	37	-812	J. Burton
638	11	May 15	Richmond -- Pontiac Excitement 400	9	36	400	345	0	Running	28,825	55	0	39	-882	Jarrett
639	12	May 30	Charlotte -- Coca-Cola 600	23	28	400	395	0	Running	40,640	79	0	39	-958	Jarrett
640	13	Jun 6	Dover -- MBNA Platinum 400	23	14	400	397	0	Running	45,210	121	0	37	-997	Jarrett
641	14	Jun 13	Michigan -- Kmart 400	35	38	200	196	0	Running	28,780	49	0	38	-1133	Jarrett
642	15	Jun 20	Pocono -- Pocono 500	16	15	200	200	0	Running	46,355	118	0	35	-1190	Jarrett
643	16	Jun 27	Sears Point -- Save Mart/Kragen 350K	15	38	112	106	0	DNF - Crash	32,320	49	0	38	-1291	Jarrett
644	17	Jul 3	Daytona -- Pepsi 400	2	13	160	160	11	Running	55,785	129	5	37	-1342	Jarrett
645	18	Jul 11	New Hampshire -- Jiffy Lube 300	26	27	300	298	0	Running	48,000	82	0	35	-1425	Jarrett
646	19	Jul 25	Pocono -- Pennsylvania 500	35	27	200	199	0	Running	36,565	82	0	35	-1518	Jarrett
647	20	Aug 7	Indianapolis -- Brickyard 400	14	9	160	160	0	Running	137,535	138	0	33	-1565	Jarrett
648	21	Aug 15	Watkins Glen -- Frontier at the Glen	24	32	90	89	0	Running	29,285	67	0	34	-1658	Jarrett
649	22	Aug 22	Michigan -- Pepsi 400	6	38	200	186	0	Running	27,640	49	0	35	-1774	Jarrett
650	23	Aug 28	Bristol -- Goody's Headache Powder 500	35	3	500	500	0	Running	64,190	165	0	33	-1658	Jarrett
651	24	Sep 5	Darlington -- Pepsi Southern 500	26	34	270	237	0	Running	32,840	61	0	32	-1717	Jarrett
652	25	Sep 11	Richmond -- Exide Batteries 400[1]	31	27	400	396	0	Running	33,255	82	0	34	-1800	Jarrett
653	26	Sep 19	New Hampshire -- Dura-Lube/Kmart 300	33	42	300	125	0	DNF - Crash	39,775	37	0	34	-1877	Jarrett
654	27	Sep 26	Dover -- MBNA Gold 400	14	37	400	352	0	DNF - Oil Pump	33,400	52	0	34	-1995	Jarrett
655	28	Oct 3	Martinsville -- NAPA AutoCare 500	8	18	500	497	0	Running	34,155	109	0	34	-2020	Jarrett
656	29	Oct 10	Charlotte -- UAW-GM Quality 500	21	38	334	278	0	Running	26,695	49	0	34	-2122	Jarrett
657	30	Oct 17	Talladega -- Winston 500	2	3	188	188	7	Running	82,235	170	5	33	-2127	Jarrett
658	31	Oct 24	Rockingham -- Pop Secret Popcorn 400	15	19	393	391	0	Running	36,150	106	0	32	-2191	Jarrett
659	32	Nov 7	Phoenix -- Checker Auto Parts/Dura-Lube 500K	7	5	312	312	0	Running	86,240	155	0	31	-2191	Jarrett
660	33	Nov 14	Homestead -- Pennzoil 400	13	41	267	184	0	DNF - Engine	42,500	40	0	32	-2311	Jarrett
661	34	Nov 21	Atlanta -- NAPA 500	15	7	325	325	0	Running	61,955	146	0	31	-2340	Jarrett

[1] -- Relieved by Dick Trickle

Rudd got a taste of what his new venture with Robert Yates Racing would be like at Talladega in 1999. Yates donated an engine to Rudd's team, along with chassis and aerodynamic expertise. With the help, Rudd won the outside pole for the Winston 500.

Rudd chases his new teammate—Dale Jarrett—at Phoenix in 1999. Two months earlier, Rudd had signed to drive for Robert Yates in 2000. Jarrett drove Yates' other car, the No. 88 Quality Care Ford.

2000: Getting Back to Racin'

Years earlier, Robert Yates had an option to put Rudd behind the wheel. He finally exercised that option in 2000. At least, figuratively. In 1981, led by Yates, DiGard Racing signed Ricky Rudd to a five-year deal that guaranteed one year in the powerful No. 88 Gatorade Chevy and included four option years thereafter. Rudd responded with a strong season in 1981—6th in the points, 14 Top 5s, 17 Top 10s—but DiGard never picked up the options. Instead, Bobby Allison was signed to drive the No. 88 in 1982 and Rudd was left to search for another ride. (He ended up with Richard Childress.)

In 2000, Yates pursued and landed Rudd for a second time, and once again put him in one of the series' most powerful cars. Rudd responded just as he had nearly 20 years earlier, posting one of his best years. He introduced his new No. 28 team by winning the outside pole for the Daytona 500 (lining up next to pole winner and teammate Dale Jarrett). Five days later, he led all 50 laps and won his Twin 125 qualifier. At season's end, he was fifth in the final point standings, just the fourth Top 5 points finish of his career.

Given Yates' power and Rudd's experience, most fans expected multiple visits to Victory Lane. It didn't happen. For the second straight year, Rudd went winless, though not for a lack of trying. On five occasions, he appeared headed for victory, only to be sidetracked by a caution or another car:

• At Michigan, he led comfortably with 22 to go when a caution bunched the field. Rusty Wallace got past Rudd and won. Rudd finished second.

• He had the strongest car at Martinsville near the end of the race, but a slow pit stop under caution pushed him back in the field. He finished fourth.

• Another slow pit stop with 27 to go at Charlotte in the fall took him out of the lead and back to sixth. He finished third.

• At Phoenix, he led by three seconds with 16 laps to go when Mike Bliss and Rick Mast crashed each other in front of the No. 28 car. Rudd plowed into Bliss, lost his lead and crawled to a 37th-place finish.

• At Homestead-Miami, Rudd led on lap 211 of 267 when Dale Earnhardt, who was two laps down, rode him into the third groove between turns 1 and 2. The contact knocked Rudd's fender in and ruined his car's aerodynamics. He finished sixth.

While wins were elusive, strong finishes were not. His 12 Top 5s were his best showing since 1985, when he had 13. His 19 Top 10s tied his career high. Qualifying also improved markedly for Rudd, who won poles at Las Vegas and Indianapolis. The Vegas pole was the 25th of his career. He also started on the outside pole five times at Daytona (twice), Michigan, Rockingham, and Homestead.

Rudd's new team didn't escape adversity, however. Though his Speedweeks at Daytona started strong, he finished the Daytona 500 in 15th. He followed with seven finishes outside of the Top 10 in the next eight races. After his 27th at Talladega, he dropped out of the Top 10 in the standings for the first and only time all season. Following Talladega, he had six Top 5s in eight races. He added an eight-race Top 10 streak later in the year to solidify his invitation to NASCAR's banquet at the Waldorf-Astoria Hotel in New York. The annual celebration of the series' Top 10 drivers had gone without a Ricky Rudd appearance for three years starting in 1997. In 2000, he returned in a big way.

2000 Stats Chart

Category	Rudd's Total	Rudd's Rank	2000 Leader
Money	$2,974,970	9th	Bobby Labonte -- 7,361,386
Total Points	4,575	5th	Bobby Labonte -- 5,130
Avg. Start	12.7	5th	Rusty Wallace -- 10.0
Avg. Finish	11.5	5th	Bobby Labonte -- 7.4
Wins	0	--	Tony Stewart -- 6
Top 5s	12	6th	Bobby Labonte -- 19
Top 10s	19	9th	D. Jarrett, D. Earnhardt, B. Labonte -- 24
DNFs	1	50th	J. Mayfield, S. Pruett -- 11
Poles	2	6th	Rusty Wallace -- 9
Front Row Starts	7	2nd	Rusty Wallace -- 11
Laps Led	362	11th	Rusty Wallace -- 1,730
Races Led	14	10th	J. Burton, B. Labonte -- 23
Times Led	32	9th	Rusty Wallace -- 62
Miles Led	547	10th	Rusty Wallace -- 1,869
Times Led Most Laps	1	8th	Rusty Wallace -- 6
Bonus Points	75	10th	Jeff Burton -- 140
Laps Completed	10,048	2nd	Bobby Labonte -- 10,158
Miles Completed	13,011	3rd	Bobby Labonte -- 13,268
Points per Race	134.6	5th	Bobby Labonte -- 150.9
Lead-Lap Finishes	24	5th	D. Earnhardt, B. Labonte -- 28

Rudd made a splash in his Robert Yates Racing debut at Daytona in February of 2000. He won the outside pole for the Daytona 500 and won his Twin 125 qualifying race.

2000 Performance Chart

No 28 Robert Yates Racing Ford

Career Race	Season Race	Date	Race	St.	Fin.	Total Laps	Laps Completed	Laps Led	Condition	Money	Pts.	Bonus Pts.	Point Standing	Behind Leader	Current Leader
662	1	Feb 20	Daytona -- Daytona 500	2	15	200	200	1	Running	$119,475	123	5	14	-62	Jarrett
663	2	Feb 27	Rockingham -- Dura-Lube/Kmart 400	2	6	393	392	0	Running	47,010	150	0	8	-67	Jarrett
664	3	Mar 5	Las Vegas -- Carsdirect.com 400	1	12	148	148	1	Running	83,975	132	5	10	-85	B.Labonte
665	4	Mar 12	Atlanta -- Cracker Barrel Old Country Store 500	34	11	325	324	0	Running	47,940	130	0	7	-130	B.Labonte
666	5	Mar 19	Darlington -- Mall.com 400	22	17	293	292	0	Running	39,440	112	0	8	-147	B.Labonte
667	6	Mar 26	Bristol -- Food City 500	27	14	500	500	0	Running	40,315	121	0	7	-176	B.Labonte
668	7	Apr 2	Texas -- DirecTV 500	20	10	334	334	9	Running	105,125	139	5	7	-207	B.Labonte
669	8	Apr 9	Martinsville -- Goody's Body Pain 500	7	22	500	497	0	Running	36,325	97	0	8	-242	B.Labonte
670	9	Apr 16	Talladega -- DieHard 500	10	27	188	182	0	Running	46,570	82	0	11	-284	Martin
671	10	Apr 30	California -- NAPA Auto Parts 500	3	4	250	250	10	Running	86,525	165	5	10	-265	B.Labonte
672	11	May 6	Richmond -- Pontiac Excitement 400	6	4	400	400	0	Running	63,025	160	0	8	-190	B.Labonte
673	12	May 28	Charlotte -- Coca-Cola 600	20	17	400	399	0	Running	50,395	112	0	9	-253	B.Labonte
674	13	Jun 4	Dover -- MBNA Platinum 400	7	5	400	400	0	Running	78,280	155	0	8	-268	B.Labonte
675	14	Jun 11	Michigan -- Kmart 400	2	12	194	194	40	Running	41,050	132	5	8	-306	B.Labonte
676	15	Jun 18	Pocono -- Pocono 500	3	3	200	200	0	Running	95,870	165	0	8	-265	B.Labonte
677	16	Jun 25	Sears Point -- Save Mart/Kragen 300	10	5	112	112	0	Running	67,915	155	0	6	-270	B.Labonte
678	17	Jul 1	Daytona -- Pepsi 400	2	5	160	160	0	Running	79,900	155	0	6	-242	B.Labonte
679	18	Jul 9	New Hampshire -- Jiffy Lube 300	14	10	273	273	0	Running	68,925	134	0	8	-251	B.Labonte
680	19	Jul 23	Pocono -- Pennsylvania 500	14	38	200	111	0	DNF - Crash	35,150	49	0	10	-357	B.Labonte
681	20	Aug 5	Indianapolis -- Brickyard 400	1	21	160	159	17	Running	120,610	105	5	9	-432	B.Labonte
682	21	Aug 13	Watkins Glen -- Global Crossing at The Glen	9	11	90	90	3	Running	40,580	135	5	8	-457	B.Labonte
683	22	Aug 20	Michigan -- Pepsi 400	4	2	200	200	42	Running	94,530	175	5	7	-452	B.Labonte
684	23	Aug 26	Bristol -- Goracing.com 500	37	10	500	500	0	Running	55,765	134	0	7	-441	B.Labonte
685	24	Sep 3	Darlington -- Southern 500	17	8	328	328	0	Running	52,475	142	0	7	-479	B.Labonte
686	25	Sep 9	Richmond -- Chevrolet Monte Carlo 400	26	9	400	400	0	Running	42,580	138	0	7	-464	B.Labonte
687	26	Sep 17	New Hampshire -- New Hampsire 300	19	3	300	300	0	Running	94,950	165	0	5	-469	B.Labonte
688	27	Sep 24	Dover -- MBNA.com 400	14	3	400	400	1	Running	93,160	170	5	5	-459	B.Labonte
689	28	Oct 1	Martinsville -- NAPA AutoCare 500	11	4	500	500	37	Running	59,275	165	5	6	-428	B.Labonte
690	29	Oct 8	Charlotte -- UAW-GM Quality 500	6	3	334	334	98	Running	104,950	175	10	6	-433	B.Labonte
691	30	Oct 15	Talladega -- Winston 500	11	11	188	188	0	Running	52,930	130	0	5	-435	B.Labonte
692	31	Oct 22	Rockingham -- Pop Secret 400	13	3	393	393	13	Running	65,300	170	5	5	-373	B.Labonte
693	32	Nov 5	Phoenix -- Checker Auto Parts/Dura-Lube 500K	17	37	312	300	41	Running	46,375	57	5	6	-476	B.Labonte
694	33	Nov 12	Homestead -- Pennzoil 400	2	6	267	267	49	Running	86,375	155	5	6	-486	B.Labonte
695	34	Nov 19	Atlanta -- NAPA 500	38	24	325	321	0	Running	48,050	91	0	5	-555	B.Labonte

Rudd hired Michael McSwain (left) in 1999 while still driving the No. 10 Tide Ford. When he signed to drive for Robert Yates, Rudd brought McSwain along.

89

2001: Chasing Gordon for the Championship

In his second season with Robert Yates Racing, Ricky Rudd gave the best indication of just how good the No. 28 team could be. Rudd became Rudd again. He returned to Victory Lane (at Pocono and Richmond), regained his consistency, and like the Rudd of old, started picking fights on the track. More impressively, he gave serious chase for the Winston Cup championship for the first time since 1991.

Similar to 2000, near-victories colored Rudd's performance in the first third of the season. At Martinsville in April, he gave up the lead to teammate Dale Jarrett with just six laps to go. At Michigan, in one of the season's best races, he took the lead from Jeff Gordon with one to go, only to lose it right back to Gordon on the final lap. In both races, Rudd settled for second place.

At Pocono the week after Michigan, however, Rudd finally broke through. Pulling an aggressive three-wide pass on Jarrett and Dale Earnhardt Jr. (who was a lap down) going into Turn 2, he pulled away to a 1.1-second win over Gordon. The victory was a milestone for a variety of reasons. Rudd's win was:

- His first in 44 Pocono starts;
- His first from the pole in his 25-year career;
- The end of a three-year, 89-race winless streak;
- His first for Robert Yates;
- The first for the No. 28 car since Michigan in June of 1997.

Six weeks after his Pocono victory, Rudd pulled into second place in the point standings, behind Gordon. He trailed by just 45 points, his closest look at the points lead since he trailed Dale Earnhardt by four points in 1991. Unfortunately for Rudd, a series of poor finishes doomed his title hopes. He finished 39th in the Brickyard 400 and 42nd at Michigan due to engine problems. In October, consecutive finishes of 21st, 39th, and 26th at Charlotte, Martinsville, and Talladega made his elimination from contention all but certain. Poor finishes at Atlanta and New Hampshire in the final two races allowed Tony Stewart and Sterling Marlin to pass him in the final standings. Stewart finished second to Gordon, while Marlin ended in third. Rudd settled for fourth.

Despite the late breakdown, the 2001 season was one of the best in Rudd's career. His two wins and 14 Top 5 matched career highs. His 22 Top 10s set a new personal best. For the first time in 13 years, he led more than 500 laps. From a NASCAR-history perspective, he became just the sixth driver to start 700 races. He joined the 700 Club at Darlington in March, where he started 10th and finished 8th.

And, like the old days, Rudd wasn't afraid to flex his Yates-aided muscle. At Richmond, he got into a shoving match with Kevin Harvick that ended with Rudd taking the checkered flag for the second time in 2001. Rudd led the race with 18 laps left when Harvick gave him a tap coming off of Turn 2. Rudd fought to keep his car straight down the backstretch. When he recovered, he knocked Harvick out of the way 12 laps later and ran unchallenged to the finish line.

Rudd's fortunes were reversed at Dover, where he enjoyed a comfortable lead with just 55 laps remaining. Rusty Wallace, still angry over a bump he got from Rudd at Bristol a month earlier, nailed the No. 28 in between turns 3 and 4. Rudd slid through Turn 4 and kept his car off the wall, but dropped back to fifth in the running order and never contended for the win again. Not surprisingly, being taken out by a lapped car while leading didn't sit well with Rudd. He called Wallace "Rubberhead" following the race and had to be restrained during their heated conversation.

The incidents recalled Rudd's hot-headed days in the 1980s and early 1990s when he got into major scraps with Earnhardt and Marlin. With his fiery attitude regained and his performance back on track, the question on fans' minds as he headed into his third season with Robert Yates Racing was: Can Rudd do something he's never done before? Can he win a Winston Cup championship?

2001 Stats Chart

Category	Rudd's Total	Rudd's Rank	2001 Leader
Money	$4,878,027	5th	Jeff Gordon -- 10,436,757
Total Points	4,706	4th	Jeff Gordon -- 5,112
Avg. Start	13.1	2nd	Jeff Gordon -- 9.5
Avg. Finish	13.2	4th	Jeff Gordon -- 11.0
Wins	2	5th	Jeff Gordon -- 6
Top 5s	14	3rd	Jeff Gordon -- 18
Top 10s	22	2nd	Jeff Gordon -- 24
DNFs	4	23rd	Todd Bodine -- 12
Poles	1	9th	Jeff Gordon -- 8
Front Row Starts	5	3rd	Jeff Gordon -- 13
Laps Led	569	4th	Jeff Gordon -- 2,320
Races Led	16	6th	Jeff Gordon -- 25
Times Led	30	5th	Jeff Gordon -- 88
Miles Led	697	6th	Jeff Gordon -- 3,030
Times Led Most Laps	0	--	Jeff Gordon -- 11
Bonus Points	80	7th	Jeff Gordon -- 180
Laps Completed	10,536	6th	Bobby Hamilton -- 10,750
Miles Completed	13,846	9th	Sterling Marlin -- 14,104
Points per Race	130.7	4th	Jeff Gordon -- 142.0
Lead-Lap Finishes	26	7th	Sterling Marlin -- 30

2001 Performance Chart
No. 28 Robert yates Racing Ford

Career Race	Season Race	Date	Race	St.	Fin.	Total Laps	Laps Completed	Laps Led	Condition	Money	Pts.	Bonus Pts.	Point Standing	Behind Leader	Current Leader
696	1	Feb 18	Daytona -- Daytona 500	30	4	200	200	0	Running	517,831	160	0	4	-20	M. Waltrip
697	2	Feb 25	Rockingham -- Dura-Lube 400	4	39	393	355	3	Running	63,462	51	5	18	-100	R. Wallace
698	3	Mar 4	Las Vegas -- UAW-DaimlerChrysler 400	25	19	267	266	0	Running	93,372	106	0	15	-151	Marlin
699	4	Mar 11	Atlanta -- Cracker Barrel Old Country Store 500	23	6	325	325	0	Running	77,367	150	0	9	-146	Gordon
700	5	Mar 18	Darlington -- Carolina Dodge Dealers 400	10	8	293	293	0	Running	71,187	142	0	6	-147	D. Jarrett
701	6	Mar 25	Bristol -- Food City 500	14	10	500	500	0	Running	88,237	134	0	7	-128	D. Jarrett
702	7	Apr 1	Texas -- Harrah's 500	6	37	334	264	0	DNF - Engine	73,097	52	0	11	-261	D. Jarrett
703	8	Apr 8	Martinsville -- Virginia 500	4	2	500	500	50	Running	106,047	175	5	8	-266	D. Jarrett
704	9	Apr 22	Talladega -- Talladega 500	32	14	188	188	2	Running	83,407	126	5	8	-249	D. Jarrett
705	10	Apr 29	California -- NAPA Auto Parts 500	6	6	250	250	2	Running	106,697	155	5	6	-190	D. Jarrett
706	11	May 5	Richmond -- Pontiac Excitement 400	3	5	400	400	27	Running	93,297	160	5	6	-148	D. Jarrett
707	12	May 27	Charlotte -- Coca-Cola 600	21	7	400	400	0	Running	102,572	146	0	5	-144	D. Jarrett
708	13	Jun 3	Dover -- MBNA Platinum 400	5	10	400	400	0	Running	91,007	134	0	6	-170	D. Jarrett
709	14	Jun 10	Michigan -- Kmart 400	2	2	200	200	3	Running	123,257	175	5	4	-130	Gordon
710	15	Jun 17	Pocono -- Pocono 500	1	1	200	200	39	Running	158,427	180	5	3	-130	Gordon
711	16	Jun 24	Sears Point -- Dodge/Save Mart 350	22	4	112	112	0	Running	98,847	160	0	3	-145	Gordon
712	17	Jul 7	Daytona -- Pepsi 400	21	14	160	160	0	Running	85,097	121	0	3	-76	Gordon
713	18	Jul 15	Chicago -- Tropicana 400	3	3	267	267	25	Running	112,600	170	5	3	-18	Gordon
714	19	Jul 22	New Hampshire -- New England 300	14	3	300	300	62	Running	105,097	170	5	3	-28	D. Jarrett
715	20	Jul 29	Pocono -- Pennsylvania 500	2	11	200	200	23	Running	73,612	135	5	2	-45	Gordon
716	21	Aug 4	Indianapolis -- Brickyard 400	4	39	160	107	0	Running	114,982	46	0	3	-179	Gordon
717	22	Aug 12	Watkins Glen -- Global Crossing at The Glen	2	4	90	90	2	Running	96,322	165	5	2	-194	Gordon
718	23	Aug 19	Michigan -- Pepsi 400	3	42	162	120	51	DNF - Engine	64,957	42	5	2	-298	Gordon
719	24	Aug 25	Bristol -- Bristol 500	5	4	500	500	3	Running	124,527	165	5	2	-308	Gordon
720	25	Sep 2	Darlington -- Southern 500	26	7	367	367	0	Running	85,657	146	0	2	-342	Gordon
721	26	Sep 8	Richmond -- Chevrolet Monte Carlo 400	9	1	400	400	88	Running	158,427	180	5	2	-222	Gordon
722	27	Sep 23	Dover -- MBNA.com 400	4	3	400	400	169	Running	117,507	170	5	2	-212	Gordon
723	28	Sep 30	Kansas -- Protection One 400	8	3	267	267	20	Running	138,947	170	5	2	-222	Gordon
724	29	Oct 7	Charlotte -- UAW-GM Quality 500	19	21	334	331	0	Running	69,772	100	0	2	-237	Gordon
725	30	Oct 14	Martinsville -- Old Dominion 500	19	39	500	397	0	DNF - Engine	59,647	46	0	2	-334	Gordon
726	31	Oct 21	Talladega -- Alabama 500	23	26	188	187	0	DNF - Accident	73,742	85	0	2	-395	Gordon
727	32	Oct 28	Phoenix -- Checker Auto Parts/Dura-Lube 500	21	3	312	312	0	Running	139,797	165	0	2	-380	Gordon
728	33	Nov 4	Rockingham -- Pop Secret 400	37	8	393	393	0	Running	75,572	142	0	2	-326	Gordon
729	34	Nov 11	Homestead -- Pennzoil 400	4	21	267	267	0	Running	72,447	100	0	2	-305	Gordon
730	35	Nov 18	Atlanta -- NAPA 500	37	35	325	319	0	Running	78,397	58	0	3	-402	Gordon
731	36	Nov 23	New Hampshire -- New England 300	2	13	300	299	0	Running	76,622	124	0	4	-406	Gordon

When Rudd won the 2001 Pocono 500, it marked the first time in his 710-race career that he won a race from the pole.

Rudd celebrates his Pocono victory. It was his first win for Robert Yates.

Robert Yates (center) joins Rudd and Michael McSwain (right) after Rudd's victory in the Chevrolet Monte Carlo 400 at Richmond.

The Tracks

## Chapter 4

Ricky Rudd's Performance on Current and Former Winston Cup Tracks

The Winston Cup schedule includes a variety of tracks, from short tracks (less than 1 mile, such as Bristol) to 1-mile ovals (Dover) to speedways (less than 2 miles, such as Charlotte) to superspeedways (2 miles or greater, such as Talladega) to road courses (Watkins Glen). Each track demands a different touch, a different set of skills. Over the course of a driver's career, patterns emerge that provide a glimpse into the style and skill of a driver. This section lays out in detail Rudd's career on each Winston Cup track.

For each track on which Rudd competed at least three times there is a statistical comparison to determine his place in the track's history. This comparison extends to 22 different statistical categories. Rudd's total for each category is listed, along with his rank and that category's leader. If Rudd is the leader in a category, the second-place driver is listed in parentheses with his total. For the older tracks—that is, tracks that have been part of the Winston Cup circuit for more than 35 years—the comparison is limited to the Modern Era (1972 to the present).

Accompanying the statistical comparison is a track summary that puts Rudd's career at the track in context or details memorable moments. Perhaps most useful to understanding Rudd's development at each track is the inclusion of a "performance chart" that lists in detail every race he started at the track. Listed for each race are the year, date, and race name, along with Rudd's start, finish, total laps, laps completed, laps led, race-ending condition, money, points earned, and bonus points.

Few drivers have witnessed the growth of NASCAR first-hand quite like Ricky Rudd. In 1975 at North Wilkesboro, he won $345 after finishing 28th in the Gwyn Staley Memorial. In 1998, he won $571,000 after winning the Brickyard 400.

During the 1980s and early 1990s, Rudd and Rusty Wallace were the best Winston Cup road course racers. Their late-race battles at Sears Point and Watkins Glen were legendary.

Rudd's 1995 victory at Phoenix was the 16th of his career.

Atlanta Motor Speedway

Atlanta Motor Speedway has rarely been a memorable track for Ricky Rudd during his career. Unfortunately, it may ultimately be the most unforgettable.

In November of 1990, during the season-ending Atlanta Journal 500, Rudd lost control of his car on pit road while approaching his team's stall. His car spun out and slammed into the jacked car of race leader Bill Elliott. The collision struck and critically injured Elliott's right-rear tire changer Mike Rich. After being rushed from the scene to an area hospital, Rich died of a heart attack two hours later. Also injured in the accident were Tommy Cole, Elliott's jackman, and Dan Elliott, Bill's brother and front tire changer. Elliott and Cole were not seriously injured.

The result of Rich's death was a series of enacted measures that attempted to eliminate similar pit road incidents. After a period of experimentation with pit-road rules, the legacy of the Rudd-Elliott tragedy was the introduction of a pit-road speed limit and managed yellow-flag pit stops.

Before and after the 1990 incident, Rudd's performance at Atlanta never approached his consistency on the short tracks and road courses. He pulled off a win in 1987, but otherwise had just six Top 5s in his first 48 career Atlanta starts. His inability to get to the front of the field created mind-boggling statistics: Through 2001, he completed 14,016 laps but led just 94 of them. In the decade leading up to the 2002 season, he led just 17 of 6,429 laps run at the 1.5-mile oval. Not since 1996 has he scored back-to-back Top 10s. The last time he had back-to-back Top 5s was 1993.

Atlanta Stats Chart

Atlanta Record Book - Modern Era (min. 5 starts)

Category	Rudd's Total	Rudd's Rank	Modern Era Atlanta Leader
Money	$1,062,909	9th	Dale Earnhardt -- 1,796,225
Starts	48	4th	Darrell Waltrip -- 56
Total Points[1]	5,695	5th	Dale Earnhardt -- 6,715
Avg. Start	17.3	32nd	David Pearson -- 4.7
Avg. Finish	16.0	14th	Dale Earnhardt -- 9.6
Wins	1	15th	Dale Earnhardt -- 9
Winning Pct.	2.1	22nd	Bobby Labonte -- 27.8
Top 5s	7	18th	Dale Earnhardt -- 26
Top 10s	22	4th	Dale Earnhardt -- 30
DNFs	10	16th	Dave Marcis -- 19
Poles	0	--	Buddy Baker -- 5
Front Row Starts	3	12th	Dale Earnhardt -- 10
Laps Led	94	33rd	Dale Earnhardt -- 2,647
Pct. Laps Led	0.6	53rd	Cale Yarborough -- 21.2
Races Led	11	17th	Dale Earnhardt -- 32
Times Led	14	24th	Dale Earnhardt -- 125
Times Led Most Laps	0	--	Dale Earnhardt -- 9
Bonus Points[1]	55	18th	Dale Earnhardt -- 205
Laps Completed	14,016	3rd	Darrell Waltrip -- 14,818
Pct. Laps Completed	90.4	18th	Kenny Irwin -- 99.1
Points per Race[1]	118.6	16th	Dale Earnhardt -- 146.0
Lead-Lap Finishes	11	7th	Dale Earnhardt—26

[1]—Since implementation of current point system in 1975

Stealing a Victory

Only Donnie Allison in 1978 earned an Atlanta victory with fewer laps led than Ricky Rudd in 1987. A look at the most "efficient" wins in Atlanta's Modern Era.

Driver	Laps Led	Race
Donnie Allison	3	1978 Dixie 500
Ricky Rudd	7	1987 Motorcraft Quality Parts 500
Bobby Labonte	13	2001 NAPA 500
Darrell Waltrip	15	1977 Dixie 500
Kevin Harvick	18	2001 Cracker Barrel 500

Atlanta Longevity Record Watch (Modern Era)

Atlanta Starts		Atlanta Laps Completed	
Driver	No. of Starts	Driver	Laps Completed
Darrell Waltrip	56	Darrell Waltrip	14,818
Dave Marcis	52	Bill Elliott	14,103
Bill Elliott	50	Ricky Rudd	14,016
Ricky Rudd	48	Dale Earnhardt	13,834
Terry Labonte	47	Terry Labonte	13,611

Memorable Atlanta Moments

1997 Motorcraft Quality Parts 500-Late-race difficulties ruined a dominating day for race leader Dale Earnhardt and opened the door for an improbable Rudd victory. Earnhardt led 196 of 328 laps and appeared invincible until he experienced mechanical problems with just 45 laps to go. His trouble allowed the rest of the field to get back into contention. After a late restart, Rudd passed leader Benny Parsons with just 7 laps to go and won by four car lengths. Rudd led just 7 laps, the second fewest by an Atlanta winner in the Modern Era. He surpassed this unusual statistic with his 1988 win at Watkins Glen, during which he led only 4 laps.

Atlanta Performance Chart

Atlanta Motor Speedway
Hampton, Ga. — 1.5 miles — 24° banking

Year	Date	Race	St.	Fin.	Total Laps	Laps Completed	Laps Led	Condition	Money	Pts	Bonus Pts.
1975	Mar 23	Atlanta 500	33	25	328	130	0	DNF - Engine	$1,200	88	0
1977	Nov 6	Dixie 500	11	8	268	266	0	Running	6,150	142	0
1978	Nov 5	Dixie 500	15	8	328	322	11	Running	5,900	147	5
1979	Mar 18	Atlanta 500	8	9	328	325	0	Running	5,720	138	0
	Nov 4	Dixie 500	6	8	328	324	0	Running	6,285	142	0
1980	Mar 16	Atlanta 500	5	31	328	147	6	DNF - Crash	1,420	75	5
1981	Mar 15	Coca-Cola 500	16	22	328	280	0	Running	7,760	97	0
	Nov 8	Atlanta Journal 500	14	39	328	36	0	DNF - Engine	6,070	46	0
1982	Mar 21	Coca-Cola 500	2	25	287	221	0	DNF - Engine	4,160	88	0
	Nov 7	Atlanta Journal 500	20	7	328	326	2	Running	7,255	151	5
1983	Mar 27	Coca-Cola 500	20	10	328	326	0	Running	6,805	134	0
	Nov 6	Atlanta Journal 500	18	26	328	148	0	DNF - Engine	3,000	85	0
1984	Mar 18	Coca-Cola 500	2	8	328	326	0	Running	12,825	142	0
	Nov 11	Atlanta Journal 500	13	3	328	328	0	Running	19,350	165	0
1985	Mar 17	Coca-Cola 500	5	4	328	327	30	Running	15,825	165	5
	Nov 3	Atlanta Journal 500	7	31	328	208	0	DNF - Piston	7,650	70	0
1986	Mar 16	Motorcraft 500	23	26	328	301	0	Running	9,695	85	0
	Nov 2	Atlanta Journal 500	25	25	328	301	0	Running	9,435	88	0
1987	Mar 15	Motorcraft Quality Parts 500	6	1	328	328	7	Running	62,400	180	5
	Nov 22	Atlanta Journal 500	14	3	328	328	19	Running	22,585	170	5
1988	Mar 20	Motorcraft Quality Parts 500	28	24	328	253	0	DNF - Engine	5,430	91	0
	Nov 20	Atlanta Journal 500	5	4	328	328	1	Running	14,725	165	5
1989	Mar 19	Motorcraft Quality Parts 500	15	24	328	270	0	DNF - Engine	5,730	91	0
	Nov 19	Atlanta Journal 500	33	14	328	325	1	Running	10,350	126	5
1990	Mar 18	Motorcraft Quality Parts 500	4	27	328	307	0	Running	6,545	82	0
	Nov 18	Atlanta Journal 500	10	16	328	325	0	Running	7,550	115	0
1991	Mar 18	Motorcraft Quality Parts 500	11	6	328	328	0	Running	17,750	150	0
	Nov 17	Hardee's 500	29	11	328	326	0	Running	12,800	130	0
1992	Mar 15	Motorcraft Quality Parts 500	24	12	328	328	0	Running	15,425	127	0
	Nov 15	Hooters 500	16	25	328	300	0	DNF - Engine	12,735	88	0
1993	Mar 20	Motorcraft Quality Parts 500	14	5	328	327	0	Running	26,550	155	0
	Nov 14	Hooters 500	13	2	328	328	5	Running	57,225	175	5
1994	Mar 13	Purolator 500	22	9	328	326	0	Running	12,350	138	0
	Nov 13	Hooters 500	8	14	328	324	0	Running	17,200	121	0
1995	Mar 12	Purolator 500	6	8	328	327	0	Running	26,200	142	0
	Nov 12	NAPA 500	2	10	328	327	11	Running	29,775	139	5
1996	Mar 10	Purolator 500	20	8	328	327	1	Running	29,650	147	5
	Nov 10	NAPA 500	28	8	328	328	0	Running	34,100	142	0
1997	Mar 9	Primestar 500	25	30	328	293	0	Running	32,975	73	0
	Nov 16	NAPA 500	11	37	325	242	0	DNF - Handling	36,030	52	0
1998	Mar 8	Primestar 500	23	23	325	322	0	Running	38,555	94	0
	Nov 8	NAPA 500	34	24	221	221	0	Running	44,225	91	0
1999	Mar 14	Cracker Barrel 500	41	25	325	322	0	Running	33,985	88	0
	Nov 21	NAPA 500	15	7	325	325	0	Running	61,955	146	0
2000	Mar 12	Cracker Barrel 500	34	11	325	324	0	Running	47,940	130	0
	Nov 19	NAPA 500	38	24	325	321	0	Running	48,050	91	0
2001	Mar 11	Cracker Barrel 500	23	6	325	325	0	Running	77,367	150	0
	Nov 18	NAPA 500	37	35	325	319	0	Running	78,397	58	0

Despite joining the well-financed, high-powered Robert Yates Racing in 2000, Rudd's luck at Atlanta hasn't improved. In his first four Atlanta races with Yates, his average finish was 19th, while his career average finish is 17th.

Bristol Motor Speedway

It takes a tough SOB to handle the half-mile track at Bristol Motor Speedway. Ricky Rudd proved immediately that he was tough enough to go door-to-door with NASCAR's best. In just the second Grand National start of his life—in March of 1975—the 18-year-old Rudd climbed from his 23rd starting position to finish 10th.

That 1975 Bristol event was Rudd's second race ever in a stock car. He has displayed his short-track talents ever since. He finished 7 of his first 10 Bristol races in the Top 10. In 1981, he ran as the runner-up in both of the Tennessee track's events—losing to the track's acknowledged master, Darrell Waltrip, both times. In 1984, he won his only Bristol pole.

The only hole in Rudd's impressive BMS resume—and it's a glaring one—is his failure to win a race. He has certainly been strong on the high banks throughout his career. He has finished second or third at Bristol nine times. Only Waltrip had more close calls. During one 11-race stretch between 1985 and 1990, Rudd managed six second- or third-place finishes. In the track's Modern Era history, only Waltrip, Dale Earnhardt, and Terry Labonte have more Top 10s.

Besides revealing his talent and toughness, Rudd has also shown his SOB side regularly at Bristol. Among other incidents, he has gotten into angry scuffles with Earnhardt, Sterling Marlin, Brett Bodine, and Rusty Wallace over the years. As part of their continuing late 1980s acrimony, Rudd rubbed with Earnhardt in the final laps of the 1990 spring race, cutting down a tire on Earnhardt's car. Earnhardt, who led 350 of the race's first 410 laps, was in the lead at the time, while Rudd was riding around in a lapped car. The contact knocked Earnhardt from a sure victory to a ninth-place finish.

Rudd was on the reverse end of the same situation in 1993. Fighting among the leaders, Brett Bodine took Rudd's car out of contention with a well-placed bump. Bodine was simply getting Rudd back for a similar incident a few weeks earlier at North Wilkesboro. More recently, Wallace and Rudd traded hatred in the closing laps of the 2001 night race. Rudd plowed into Wallace to take over the fourth position with less than five laps remaining. After the checkers fell, Wallace returned the favor and spun out Rudd on the cool-down lap. If it takes a tough SOB to race at Bristol, Rudd has shown over 26 years that he is up to the task.

Bristol Stats Chart

Bristol Record Book - Modern Era (min. 5 starts)

Category	Rudd's Total	Rudd's Rank	Modern Era Bristol Leader
Money	$1,016,990	6th	Rusty Wallace -- 1,428,210
Starts	48	2nd	Darrell Waltrip -- 52
Total Points[1]	6,158	4th	Darrell Waltrip -- 7,205
Avg. Start	12.5	20th	Cale Yarborough -- 2.5
Avg. Finish	13.1	18th	Cale Yarborough -- 6.6
Wins	0	--	Darrell Waltrip -- 12
Winning Pct.	0.0	--	Cale Yarborough -- 56.3
Top 5s	13	9th	Darrell Waltrip -- 26
Top 10s	28	4th	Terry Labonte -- 33
DNFs	11	4th	J.D. McDuffie -- 15
Poles	1	14th	M. Martin, R. Wallace, C. Yarborough -- 7
Front Row Starts	2	16th	Rusty Wallace -- 12
Laps Led	604	12th	Cale Yarborough -- 3,872
Pct. Laps Led	2.6	25th	Cale Yarborough -- 50.3
Races Led	9	14th	D. Earnhardt, D. Waltrip -- 30
Times Led	24	12th	Darrell Waltrip -- 94
Times Led Most Laps	1	10th	Darrell Waltrip -- 10
Bonus Points[1]	50	14th	Darrell Waltrip -- 200
Laps Completed	21,083	2nd	Darrell Waltrip -- 22,964
Pct. Laps Completed	89.1	31st	Kevin Lepage -- 99.2
Points per Race[1]	128.3	17th	Cale Yarborough -- 158.1
Lead-Lap Finishes	17	4th	Darrell Waltrip -- 24

[1] -- Since implementation of current point system in 1975

Longevity Record Watch

Bristol Starts Driver	No. of Starts	Bristol Laps Completed Driver	Laps Completed	Bristol Top 10s Driver	Top 10s
Darrell Waltrip	52	Darrell Waltrip	22,964	Terry Labonte	33
Dave Marcis	48	Ricky Rudd	21,083	Darrell Waltrip	32
Ricky Rudd	48	Terry Labonte	20,463	Dale Earnhardt	30
Terry Labonte	46	Dale Earnhardt	20,038	Ricky Rudd	28
Dale Earnhardt	43	Dave Marcis	18,561	Rusty Wallace	25

Memorable Bristol Moments

1999 Goody's 500—A wild Bristol night race ended with Terry Labonte getting spun out twice within 10 laps while in the lead. After getting tapped by Darrell Waltrip with 10 to go, Labonte used a banzai run in the closing laps to retake the lead from Dale Earnhardt. On the final lap of the race, Earnhardt tagged Labonte's rear bumper between Turns 1 and 2 and sent the two-time champion into another spin. The incident cleared the way for an Earnhardt win. An innocent bystander throughout, Rudd became involved when he collided with the sliding Labonte in Turn 2. Despite a flattened front end, Rudd recovered to finish in third place, his 12th Bristol Top 5.

Bristol Performance Chart

Bristol Motor Speedway
Bristol, Tenn. — .533 miles — 36° banking

Year	Date	Race	St.	Fin.	Total Laps	Laps Completed	Laps Led	Condition	Money	Pts	Bonus Pts.
1975	Mar 16	Southeastern 500	23	10	500	456	0	Running	$800	134	0
1977	Apr 17	Southeastern 500	14	10	500	465	0	Running	1,900	134	0
	Aug 28	Volunteer 500	11	16	400	220	0	Running	590	115	0
1979	Apr 1	Southeastern 500	15	10	500	485	0	Running	3,120	134	0
	Aug 25	Volunteer 500	11	9	500	493	0	Running	3,030	138	0
1980	Aug 23	Busch Volunteer 500	9	28	500	135	0	DNF - Mechanical	720	79	0
1981	Mar 29	Valleydale 500	5	2	500	500	0	Running	14,375	170	0
	Aug 22	Busch 500	3	2	500	499	92	Running	12,375	175	5
1982	Mar 14	Valleydale 500	7	27	500	217	0	DNF - Valve	1,110	82	0
	Aug 28	Busch 500	6	7	500	498	0	Running	4,140	146	0
1983	May 21	Valleydale 500	3	26	500	393	0	DNF - Engine	1,120	85	0
	Aug 27	Busch 500	4	14	419	396	0	Running	3,110	121	0
1984	Apr 1	Valleydale 500	1	6	500	498	0	Running	10,630	150	0
	Aug 25	Busch 500	7	16	500	442	0	DNF - Rear End	7,850	115	0
1985	Apr 6	Valleydale 500	6	2	500	500	163	Running	18,050	175	5
	Aug 24	Busch 500	6	9	500	495	0	Running	7,450	138	0
1986	Apr 6	Valleydale 500	8	2	500	500	0	Running	20,125	170	0
	Aug 23	Busch 500	4	23	500	250	0	DNF - Crash	7,910	94	0
1987	Apr 12	Valleydale Meats 500	15	3	500	500	0	Running	17,175	165	0
	Aug 22	Busch 500	7	3	500	500	0	Running	20,275	165	0
1988	Apr 10	Valleydale Meats 500	10	20	500	378	1	DNF - Crash	4,800	108	5
	Aug 27	Busch 500	19	16	500	451	10	DNF - Engine	4,850	120	5
1989	Apr 9	Valleydale Meats 500	18	8	500	500	0	Running	7,325	142	0
	Aug 26	Busch 500	6	3	500	500	0	Running	19,200	165	0
1990	Apr 8	Valleydale Meats 500	13	3	500	500	0	Running	19,775	165	0
	Aug 25	Busch 500	7	10	500	499	0	Running	10,100	134	0
1991	Apr 17	Valleydale Meats 500	4	5	500	500	145	Running	37,950	165	10
	Aug 24	Bud 500	17	5	500	499	0	Running	16,450	155	0
1992	Apr 5	Food City 500	17	6	500	497	0	Running	16,485	150	0
	Aug 29	Bud 500	2	8	500	499	139	Running	16,875	147	5
1993	Apr 4	Food City 500	9	26	500	369	0	DNF - Crash	12,500	85	0
	Aug 28	Bud 500	3	22	500	414	0	Running	13,900	97	0
1994	Apr 10	Food City 500	11	32	500	187	0	DNF - Crash	6,625	67	0
	Aug 27	Goody's 500	33	12	500	499	0	Running	16,540	127	0
1995	Apr 2	Food City 500	13	5	500	500	0	Running	32,260	155	0
	Aug 26	Goody's 500	8	36	500	138	0	DNF - Crash	23,510	55	0
1996	Mar 31	Food City 500	9	14	342	340	8	Running	26,115	126	5
	Aug 24	Goody's 500	13	9	500	500	0	Running	32,115	138	0
1997	Apr 13	Food City 500	22	27	500	483	0	Running	27,991	82	0
	Aug 23	Goody's 500	39	19	500	496	0	Running	30,750	106	0
1998	Mar 29	Food City 500	35	30	500	482	0	Running	34,485	73	0
	Aug 22	Goody's 500	3	9	500	500	43	Running	45,540	143	5
1999	Apr 11	Food City 500	5	38	500	410	0	DNF - Handling	32,250	49	0
	Aug 28	Goody's 500	35	3	500	500	0	Running	64,190	165	0
2000	Mar 26	Food City 500	27	14	500	500	0	Running	40,315	121	0
	Aug 26	Goracing.com 500	37	10	500	500	0	Running	55,765	134	0
2001	Mar 25	Food City 500	14	10	500	500	0	Running	88,237	134	0
	Aug 25	Bristol 500	5	4	500	500	3	Running	124,527	165	5

Bristol has been one of Rudd's best tracks. He has more Top 10 finishes (28) at the half-mile oval than at any other Winston Cup track.

After becoming a car owner, Rudd's performance at Bristol slipped. He finished in the Top 5 just two times in 12 starts.

California Speedway

NASCAR's new tracks generally have been kind to "Old Man" Rudd. California Speedway has been one of the kindest. In the 2-mile track's first five races, he was strong in four. The lone off-race—the 1999 California 500—was the result of late engine trouble; his engine gave out and began leaving a trail of flaming oil. Rudd finished the race in 41st.

But even that 1999 trip to Fontana, California, inspires warm feelings. Shortly after that race, Rudd hired Michael McSwain as his crew chief. Rudd took two months to interview a variety of candidates before selecting McSwain to guide his team. The two developed such a trusted relationship, Rudd insisted on bringing his crew chief with him when he signed to drive for Robert Yates Racing later that year. In their first two visits to California as a team, Rudd and McSwain posted solid finishes. Rudd led 10 laps and finished fourth in 2000, then followed up with a sixth-place finish in 2001.

While his California starts with Robert Yates Racing have been strong, his first two races with his former Tide team were much more eventful. In the inaugural race in 1997, he qualified horribly and needed a provisional to make the event. Starting 39th, he stretched his fuel mileage to its limits and climbed all the way to third place at the finish. Rudd was so close on fuel that when his team took the No. 10 Tide Ford to the gas pumps after the race, 21.9 gallons of fuel were poured into the car's 22-gallon fuel cell.

The following year, Rudd enjoyed another strong car. However, on the team's first pit stop, Rudd's clutch broke and was inoperable the rest of the race. He was forced to go to the end of the longest line on restarts to avoid becoming a bottleneck as he slowly got back up to speed. Despite the mechanical problems and the regular loss of track position, he was strong enough to finish 11th.

California Stats Chart

California Record Book - All-Time (min. 2 starts)

Category	Rudd's Total	Rudd's Rank	All-Time California Leader*
Money	$373,747	8th	Jeff Gordon -- 627,667
Starts	5	T-1st	21 Others with 5 Starts
Total Points	655	3rd	Jeff Gordon -- 840
Avg. Start	21.4	24th	Mark Martin -- 6.6
Avg. Finish	13.0	6th	Jeff Gordon -- 3.8
Wins	0	--	Jeff Gordon -- 2
Winning Pct.	0.0	--	Jeff Gordon -- 40.0
Top 5s	2	3	Jeff Gordon -- 4
Top 10s	3	3	J. Gordon, J. Mayfield -- 4
DNFs	1	7	Mark Martin -- 3
Poles	0	--	5 Tied with 1 Pole
Front Row Starts	0	--	9 Drivers with 1 FRS
Laps Led	12	14	Jeff Gordon -- 329
Pct. Laps Led	1.0	16	Jeff Gordon -- 26.3
Races Led	2	8	Mark Martin -- 5
Times Led	2	14	Jeff Gordon -- 24
Times Led Most Laps	0	--	Jeff Gordon -- 2
Bonus Points	10	10	J. Gordon, M. Martin -- 30
Laps Completed	1,129	18	Jeff Gordon -- 1,250
Pct. Laps Completed	90.3	39	5 Tied at 100 percent
Points per Race	131.0	6	Jeff Gordon -- 168.0
Lead-Lap Finishes	4	2	Jeff Gordon --5

* -- Second-place driver listed in parentheses if Rudd is category leader

California Performance Chart

California Speedway
Fontana, Calif. — 2.0 miles — 14° banking

Year	Date	Race	St.	Fin.	Total Laps	Laps Completed	Laps Led	Condition	Money	Pts	Bonus Pts.
1997	Jun 22	California 500	39	3	250	250	0	Running	$78,525	165	0
1998	May 3	California 500	23	11	250	250	0	Running	58,025	130	0
1999	May 2	California 500	36	41	250	129	0	DNF - Engine	43,975	40	0
2000	Apr 30	NAPA Auto Parts 500	3	4	250	250	10	Running	86,525	165	5
2001	Apr 29	NAPA Auto Parts 500	6	6	250	250	2	Running	106,697	155	5

Rudd's best California race came in the 2-mile track's 1997 inaugural event. He needed a provisional to make the field and started 39th. However, excellent fuel management allowed him to climb to a third-place finish.

Darlington Raceway

Egg-shaped and one-grooved, Darlington Raceway has been a tricky track for Ricky Rudd throughout his career. Six of his first 50 starts on the 1.366-mile track ended early due to crashes—the greatest number of crash-related DNFs of any Winston Cup track in his career. During one stretch beginning in 1985, he wrecked out of three consecutive spring races. Even when he doesn't wreck, Rudd often feels a little battered. In the 2001 Southern 500, he went through the final two turns of the race sideways in a near-wreck as the bunched up field scrambled for top finishes. He finished the race seventh.

Since 1990, Rudd has just one DNF and his finishes have shown accompanying improvement. Before 1990, his average finish at Darlington was 17th; since then it has improved to 14th. In 26 races through 2001, he managed 14 Top 10 finishes. With Robert Yates Racing, his performance received a noticeable jolt. With an 8th-place and a 7th-place finish in 2001, his average Darlington finish for the season (7.5) was his best since 1994.

Darlington Stats Chart

Darlington Record Book - Modern Era (min. 5 starts)

Category	Rudd's Total	Rudd's Rank	Modern Era Darlington Leader
Money	$986,753	8th	Dale Earnhardt --1,403,125
Starts	50	3rd	Darrell Waltrip -- 55
Total Points[1]	5,971	4th	Bill Elliott -- 6,781
Avg. Start	14.5	20th	David Pearson -- 4.8
Avg. Finish	15.8	18th	Tony Stewart -- 8.5
Wins	1	12th	Dale Earnhardt -- 9
Winning Pct.	2.0	20th	David Pearson -- 29.6
Top 5s	7	18th	Bill Elliott -- 20
Top 10s	25	2nd	Bill Elliott -- 31
DNFs	12	13th	B. Baker, R. Petty -- 19
Poles	0	--	David Pearson -- 10
Front Row Starts	1	22nd	David Pearson -- 14
Laps Led	239	22nd	Dale Earnhardt -- 2,648
Pct. Laps Led	1.4	35th	Dale Earnhardt -- 17.7
Races Led	15	12th	Darrell Waltrip -- 32
Times Led	24	19th	Dale Earnhardt -- 116
Times Led Most Laps	0	--	Dale Earnhardt -- 10
Bonus Points[1]	75	16th	Darrell Waltrip -- 190
Laps Completed	14,890	3rd	Darrell Waltrip -- 16,395
Pct. Laps Completed	87.3	26th	Tony Stewart -- 100.
Points per Race[1]	119.4	20th	Jeff Burton -- 145.3
Lead-Lap Finishes	11	9th	Bill Elliott -- 20

[1] -- Since implementation of current point system in 1975

Darlington Longevity Record Watch (Modern Era)

Darlington Starts		Darlington Laps Completed		Darlington Top 10s	
Driver	No. of Starts	Driver	Laps Completed	Driver	Top 10s
Darrell Waltrip	55	Darrell Waltrip	16,395	Bill Elliott	31
Dave Marcis	52	Bill Elliott	15,794	Ricky Rudd	25
Ricky Rudd	50	Ricky Rudd	14,890	Dale Earnhardt	24
Terry Labonte	47	Dave Marcis	14,372	Darrell Waltrip	23
Bill Elliott	47	Dale Earnhardt	14,011	Mark Martin	20

Memorable Darlington Moments

1991 TranSouth 500—Rudd won an oval race for the first time since 1987 by using a calculating, deliberate race strategy. More importantly, his win lifted him into the Winston Cup points lead for the first and only time in his career. With 37 laps to go, Davey Allison enjoyed a 15-second lead over Rudd. But Rudd knew Allison's lead was artificial—the result of being out of sync with the rest of the field on pit stops. When Allison dipped into the pits, he handed the lead to Rudd, who won by nearly half a lap. With the win, Rudd took an 80-point lead over Dale Earnhardt in the standings. Rudd gave the points lead back a month later and finished the 1991 season as the championship runner-up, 195 points behind Earnhardt.

Rudd finished eighth or better in three of his first four Darlington starts for Robert Yates Racing.

Darlington Performance Chart

Darlington Raceway
Darlington, S.C. — 1.366 miles — 23-25° banking

Year	Date	Race	St.	Fin.	Total Laps	Laps Completed	Laps Led	Condition	Money	Pts	Bonus Pts.
1977	Apr 3	Rebel 500	27	22	367	259	0	DNF - Engine	$1,300	97	0
	Sep 5	Southern 500	18	7	367	360	0	Running	7,400	146	0
1978	Apr 9	Rebel 500	18	10	367	349	2	Running	5,290	139	5
	Sep 4	Southern 500	13	36	367	122	1	DNF - Crash	3,025	60	5
1979	Apr 8	CRC Chemicals Rebel 500	4	8	367	360	19	Running	5,950	147	5
	Sep 3	Southern 500	14	8	367	361	0	Running	7,105	142	0
1980	Apr 13	CRC Chemicals Rebel 500	4	19	189	172	0	Running	2,965	106	0
	Sep 1	Southern 500	16	34	367	201	0	DNF - Steering	2,025	61	0
1981	Apr 12	CRC Chemicals Rebel 500	10	11	367	359	0	Running	8,225	130	0
	Sep 7	Southern 500	7	23	367	343	0	DNF - Crash	7,850	94	0
1982	Apr 4	CRC Chemicals Rebel 500	7	29	367	133	0	DNF - Transmission	3,050	76	0
	Sep 6	Southern 500	6	31	367	168	1	DNF - Engine	4,175	75	5
1983	Apr 10	TranSouth 500	8	4	367	366	0	Running	9,905	160	0
	Sep 5	Southern 500	8	25	367	272	76	DNF - Engine	7,415	93	5
1984	Apr 15	TranSouth 500	3	9	367	358	1	Running	11,400	143	5
	Sep 2	Southern 500	11	5	367	364	0	Running	17,050	155	0
1985	Apr 14	TranSouth 500	9	25	367	249	0	DNF - Crash	8,200	88	0
	Sep 1	Southern 500	11	6	367	366	0	Running	13,450	150	0
1986	Apr 13	TranSouth 500	8	26	367	207	1	DNF - Crash	9,605	90	5
	Aug 31	Southern 500	15	6	367	367	0	Running	15,735	150	0
1987	Mar 29	TranSouth 500	10	30	367	144	12	DNF - Crash	9,885	78	5
	Sep 6	Southern 500	12	7	202	202	0	Running	15,055	146	0
1988	May 27	TranSouth 500	10	30	367	208	0	DNF - Engine	4,635	73	0
	Sep 4	Southern 500	29	10	367	366	6	Running	13,130	139	5
1989	Apr 2	TranSouth 500	25	12	367	365	0	Running	7,425	127	0
	Sep 3	Heinz Southern 500	8	3	367	367	0	Running	26,865	165	0
1990	Apr 1	TranSouth 500	10	24	367	294	0	Running	6,480	91	0
	Sep 2	Heinz Southern 500	5	7	367	367	6	Running	12,755	151	5
1991	Apr 7	TranSouth 500	13	1	367	367	69	Running	62,185	180	5
	Sep 1	Heinz Southern 500	18	15	367	363	0	Running	14,100	118	0
1992	Mar 29	TranSouth 500	18	5	367	366	0	Running	21,020	155	0
	Sep 6	Mountain Dew Southern 500	18	10	298	297	3	Running	18,470	139	5
1993	Mar 28	TranSouth 500	13	19	367	353	0	Running	12,100	106	0
	Sep 5	Mountain Dew Southern 500	16	6	351	350	0	Running	16,940	150	0
1994	Mar 27	TranSouth 500	25	9	293	292	0	Running	9,260	138	0
	Sep 4	Southern 500	18	4	367	367	3	Running	24,715	165	5
1995	Mar 26	TranSouth 500	4	41	293	74	0	DNF - Crash	21,409	40	0
	Sep 3	Southern 500	2	6	367	367	37	Running	34,865	155	5
1996	Mar 24	TranSouth 500	24	9	293	292	0	Running	27,560	138	0
	Sep 1	Southern 500	18	16	367	365	2	Running	27,805	120	5
1997	Mar 23	TranSouth Financial 400	16	23	293	291	0	Running	26,055	94	0
	Aug 31	Mountain Dew Southern 500	21	5	367	367	0	Running	39,345	155	0
1998	Mar 22	TranSouth Financial 400	18	33	293	288	0	Running	32,745	64	0
	Sep 6	Southern 500	14	22	367	362	0	Running	38,095	97	0
1999	Mar 21	TranSouth Financial 400	41	27	164	163	0	Running	31,400	82	0
	Sep 5	Pepsi Southern 500	26	34	270	237	0	Running	32,840	61	0
2000	Mar 19	Mall.com 400	22	17	293	292	0	Running	39,440	112	0
	Sep 3	Southern 500	17	8	328	328	0	Running	52,475	142	0
2001	Mar 18	Carolina Dodge Dealers 400	10	8	293	293	0	Running	71,187	142	0
	Sep 2	Southern 500	26	7	367	367	0	Running	85,657	146	0

Demolition Derby

Tracks on which Ricky Rudd has suffered the most race-ending crashes

Track	No. of Crash-related DNFs
Darlington	6
Charlotte	5
Bristol	5
Dover	4
Rockingham	4
Talladega	4

Daytona International Speedway

Back when Ricky Rudd's dad was buying opportunities for his teenage son to race a stock car—in 1975 and 1976—one of the tracks he chose was Daytona. It was a gutsy place to race, given Ricky's inexperience in heavy Grand National cars or with the high speeds of a superspeedway. But if the young Rudd revealed anything during his early career, it was an almost virtuoso ability to learn different forms of racing quickly. Whether he raced go-karts, motorcycles, or stock cars, he figured out a way to go fast and work his way to the front.

Rudd's learn-quick experience held true at Daytona. Starting the Firecracker 400 on July 4, 1976—just his seventh Grand National start—he qualified 22nd and scaled the field to a 10th-place finish. When he got his first competitive ride with DiGard Racing in 1981, he finished third in his first crack at the Daytona 500. In 1983, he won the pole for the Daytona 500 (with an assist from Cale Yarborough, who crashed in qualifying after posting the fastest time). In 1984, in his first race with Bud Moore, he survived a horrific crash in the Busch Clash that left his face so swollen and bruised his could barely keep his eyes open. Three days later, he recorded a lap of 194 miles per hour in practice. In 1985, he started and finished both Daytona races in the Top 10 for the first time in his career. In 1993, he was part of Rick Hendrick's near sweep of the top spots in the Pepsi 400, finishing fourth. In 1999, he started a string of three straight outside poles.

In other words, Rudd possesses a long and storied record of accomplishments at NASCAR's flagship track. A victory, however, is not among his Daytona achievements. Despite his early success and later experience, the 2.5-mile oval has resisted his every effort. Dale Earnhardt's failure to win the Daytona 500, despite his otherwise amazing performance there, became an annual rite of spring until 1998. Rudd couldn't win the Great American race in his first 24 starts. When he finally pulls into the most famous Victory Lane in stock car racing, expect a celebration that is every bit as giddy as Earnhardt's in 1998.

Daytona Stats Chart

Daytona Record Book - Modern Era (min. 5 starts)

Category	Rudd's Total	Rudd's Rank	Modern Era Daytona Leader
Money	$2,125,288	10th	Dale Earnhardt -- 4,441,856
Starts	50	3rd	Dave Marcis -- 56
Total Points[1]	5,749	3rd	Dale Earnhardt -- 6,507
Avg. Start	17.9	32nd	Bobby Isaac -- 4.2
Avg. Finish	17.0	17th	Dale Earnhardt -- 10.7
Wins	0	--	Richard Petty -- 7
Winning Pct.	0.0	--	Jeff Gordon -- 22.2
Top 5s	6	15th	Dale Earnhardt -- 22
Top 10s	20	5th	Dale Earnhardt -- 34
DNFs	11	16th	A.J. Foyt -- 23
Poles	1	16th	Cale Yarborough -- 8
Front Row Starts	5	5th	Cale Yarborough -- 13
Laps Led	46	34th	Dale Earnhardt -- 1,286
Pct. Laps Led	0.5	51st	Dale Earnhardt Jr. -- 17.9
Races Led	12	17th	Dale Earnhardt -- 36
Times Led	14	26th	Dale Earnhardt -- 173
Times Led Most Laps	0	--	Dale Earnhardt -- 7
Bonus Points[1]	60	18th	Dale Earnhardt -- 215
Laps Completed	7,797	4th	Darrell Waltrip -- 8,482
Pct. Laps Completed	87.4	32nd	Rick Mast -- 99.3
Points per Race[1]	115.0	19th	Dale Earnhardt -- 141.5
Lead-Lap Finishes	22	4th	Dale Earnhardt -- 28

[1] -- Since implementation of current point system in 1975

Memorable Daytona Moments

1993 Pepsi 400—In one of the most successful days in Hendrick Motorsports history, Rudd and teammates Ken Schrader and Jeff Gordon finished 3-4-5 in Daytona's annual Fourth of July celebration. Rudd came home in fourth, sandwiched between Schrader (third) and Gordon (fifth). Rudd started the race in 10th, led a single lap, and matched his second-best finish at Daytona.

Daytona Longevity Record Watch (Modern Era)

Daytona Starts		Daytona Laps Completed	
Driver	No. of Starts	Driver	Laps Completed
Dave Marcis	56	Darrell Waltrip	8,482
Darrell Waltrip	55	Dave Marcis	8,270
Ricky Rudd	50	Bill Elliott	8,071
Bill Elliott	49	Ricky Rudd	7,797
Terry Labonte	46	Terry Labonte	7,504

Daytona Performance Chart

Daytona International Speedway
Daytona Beach, Fla. — 2.5 miles — 31° banking

Year	Date	Race	St.	Fin.	Total Laps	Laps Completed	Laps Led	Condition	Money	Pts	Bonus Pts.
1976	Jul 4	Firecracker 400	22	10	160	152	0	Running	$2,590	134	0
1977	Feb 20	Daytona 500	21	22	200	135	0	DNF - Rear End	2,935	97	0
	Jul 4	Firecracker 400	17	36	160	45	0	DNF - Transmission	910	55	0
1978	Feb 19	Daytona 500	36	37	200	21	0	DNF - Handling	4,375	52	0
	Jul 4	Firecracker 400	25	21	160	143	0	DNF - Engine	2,970	100	0
1979	Feb 18	Daytona 500	11	31	200	79	0	DNF - Engine	4,110	70	0
	Jul 4	Firecracker 400	19	13	160	155	0	Running	5,075	124	0
1980	Jul 4	Firecracker 400	28	13	160	155	0	Running	5,065	124	0
1981	Feb 15	Daytona 500	5	3	200	200	9	Running	53,115	170	5
	Jul 4	Firecracker 400	12	40	160	16	0	DNF - Crash	6,625	43	0
1982	Feb 14	Daytona 500	16	35	200	51	0	DNF - Engine	6,050	58	0
	Jul 4	Firecracker 400	2	7	160	160	0	Running	10,420	146	0
1983	Feb 20	Daytona 500	1	24	200	182	1	DNF - Mechanical	16,515	96	5
	Jul 4	Firecracker 400	6	21	160	149	0	Running	4,315	100	0
1984	Feb 19	Daytona 500	14	7	200	199	0	Running	38,700	146	0
	Jul 4	Pepsi Firecracker 400	22	15	160	156	0	Running	11,950	118	0
1985	Feb 17	Daytona 500	9	5	200	199	0	Running	52,900	155	0
	Jul 4	Pepsi Firecracker 400	3	7	160	160	0	Running	14,500	146	0
1986	Feb 16	Daytona 500	22	11	200	198	0	Running	32,690	130	0
	Jul 4	Firecracker 400	33	6	160	160	0	Running	17,200	150	0
1987	Feb 15	Daytona 500	31	9	200	200	0	Running	38,425	138	0
	Jul 4	Pepsi Firecracker 400	17	14	160	159	0	Running	12,855	121	0
1988	Feb 14	Daytona 500	27	17	200	200	0	Running	20,125	112	0
	Jul 2	Pepsi Firecracker 400	12	22	160	158	2	Running	6,230	102	5
1989	Feb 19	Daytona 500	36	19	200	197	2	Running	19,120	111	5
	Jul 1	Pepsi 400	38	9	160	160	0	Running	16,842	138	0
1990	Feb 18	Daytona 500	19	4	200	200	1	Running	77,050	165	5
	Jul 7	Pepsi 400	9	13	160	158	0	Running	10,135	124	0
1991	Feb 17	Daytona 500 by STP	9	9	200	199	0	Running	52,600	138	0
	Jul 6	Pepsi 400	13	9	160	160	8	Running	16,500	143	5
1992	Feb 16	Daytona 500 by STP	8	40	200	79	0	DNF - Engine	34,350	43	0
	Jul 4	Pepsi 400	5	7	160	160	2	Running	20,875	151	5
1993	Feb 14	Daytona 500 by STP	12	30	200	177	0	Running	31,285	73	0
	Jul 3	Pepsi 400	10	4	160	160	1	Running	28,250	165	5
1994	Feb 20	Daytona 500	20	8	200	200	0	Running	56,465	142	0
	Jul 2	Pepsi 400	31	17	160	160	3	Running	13,985	117	5
1995	Feb 19	Daytona 500	18	13	200	200	0	Running	60,620	124	0
	Jul 1	Pepsi 400	14	8	160	160	5	Running	31,775	147	5
1996	Feb 18	Daytona 500	10	9	200	200	0	Running	79,987	138	0
	Jul 6	Pepsi 400	39	33	117	116	0	Running	28,255	64	0
1997	Feb 16	Daytona 500	13	9	200	200	0	Running	88,590	138	0
	Jul 5	Pepsi 400	13	34	160	155	0	DNF - Crash	29,985	61	0
1998	Feb 15	Daytona 500	40	42	200	117	0	DNF - Valve Spring	86,480	37	0
	Oct 17	Pepsi 400	41	27	160	159	0	Running	42,715	82	0
1999	Feb 14	Daytona 500	29	30	200	168	0	Running	102,226	73	0
	Jul 3	Pepsi 400	2	13	160	160	11	Running	55,785	129	5
2000	Feb 20	Daytona 500	2	15	200	200	1	Running	119,475	123	5
	Jul 1	Pepsi 400	2	5	160	160	0	Running	79,900	155	0
2001	Feb 18	Daytona 500	30	4	200	200	0	Running	517,831	160	0
	Jul 7	Pepsi 400	21	14	160	160	0	Running	85,097	121	0

No matter what color his car or how powerful the team, Ricky Rudd has yet to win a race at Daytona. Through 2001, he was 0-for-50 at the 2.5-mile track.

Winless at Daytona

Ricky Rudd is fast approaching the Modern Era Daytona record for most starts without a victory

Driver	No. of Starts
Dave Marcis	56
Ricky Rudd	50
Terry Labonte	46
Kyle Petty	40
Rusty Wallace	37

Dover Downs International Speedway

Ricky Rudd's education at Dover Downs International Speedway followed a logical sequence: first learn to start, then learn to finish. After a shaky beginning, he grew to do both very well. In fact, statistically speaking, Rudd is one of the best drivers in Dover history. No driver has more Top 10s on the banked track (he is tied with Richard Petty at 26). Rudd is also at the top of the heap with 6,105 total points earned at Dover; he passed Darrell Waltrip in 2001 after amassing his 6,105th point.

Rudd's approach to Dover was methodical. In his first four races on the banked 1-mile oval, Rudd neither started nor finished better than 12th. Each effort was cut short by some sort of problem, whether of mechanical or human origin. Beginning in 1981, however, his fortunes at Dover changed. In his next 11 visits, he won four poles and never started worse than seventh. After getting the hang of qualifying, he developed the ability to finish just as well. He produced victories in 1986 and 1987, then wins in 1992 and 1997. If not for a blatantly intentional take-out by Rusty Wallace, he would have claimed his fifth Dover victory in 2001.

Rudd's four wins make Dover his winningest track (Martinsville, with three wins, is next). Indicating the portability of his talent, those four victories came with three different teams. His first two wins were powered by Bud Moore-owned Fords. He earned his 1992 triumph in Rick Hendrick's No. 5 Tide Chevy, and he owned his own car when he won in 1997. His close call in 2001 was in Robert Yates' No. 28 Ford.

Dover Stats Chart

Dover Record Book - All-Time (min. 5 starts)

Category	Rudd's Total	Rudd's Rank	All-Time Dover Leader*
Money	$1,287,644	3rd	Mark Martin -- 1,377,427
Starts	47	3rd	Dave Marcis -- 54
Total Points[1]	6,105	1st	(Darrell Waltrip -- 6,075)
Avg. Start	11.8	21st	Bobby Isaac -- 2.2
Avg. Finish	13.0	15th	Tony Stewart -- 3.3
Wins	4	4th	B. Allison, R. Petty -- 7
Winning Pct.	8.5	11th	Tony Stewart -- 33.3
Top 5s	14	4th	Dale Earnhardt -- 19
Top 10s	26	1st	(Richard Petty -- 26)
DNFs	11	12th	J.D. McDuffie -- 27
Poles	4	2nd	David Pearson -- 6
Front Row Starts	6	4th	David Pearson -- 9
Laps Led	935	12th	Bobby Allison -- 2,801
Pct. Laps Led	4.1	22nd	David Pearson -- 26.9
Races Led	16	6th	Dale Earnhardt -- 26
Times Led	32	14th	Bobby Allison -- 84
Times Led Most Laps	2	12th	Bobby Allison -- 7
Bonus Points[1]	90	9th	Dale Earnhardt -- 150
Laps Completed	20,246	3rd	Darrell Waltrip -- 22,539
Pct. Laps Completed	89.6	18th	Tony Stewartv99.9
Points per Race[1]	129.9	14th	Tony Stewart -- 171.0
Lead-Lap Finishes	9	8th	Mark Martin -- 14

[1] -- Since implementation of current point system in 1975

* -- Second-place driver listed in parentheses if Rudd is category leader

Memorable Dover Moments

1986 Delaware 500—Despite falling a lap behind early, Rudd battled back to lead 141 of 500 laps en route to his first victory on a 1-mile oval. His five previous wins had come on road courses and short tracks.

1987 Delaware 500—A day after notifying Bud Moore that he would not be returning to drive the No. 15 Ford in 1988, Rudd turned in one of the most dominating performances of his career. Starting 13th, he took the lead by lap 49 and led a total of 373 laps. He took the lead for the final time with 29 laps to go and won by 20 car lengths over Davey Allison. Though an impressive showing, Rudd's 373 laps led rank only 12th in track history for most laps led in a single race (Richard Petty holds the record for leading 491 of 500 laps in 1974).

Longevity Record Watch

Dover Starts		Dover Laps Completed	
Driver	No. of Starts	Driver	Laps Completed
Dave Marcis	54	Darrell Waltrip	22,539
Darrell Waltrip	53	Dave Marcis	21,347
Ricky Rudd	47	Ricky Rudd	20,246
Richard Petty	46	Terry Labonte	19,615
Terry Labonte	46	Dale Earnhardt	19,211

Dover Performance Chart

Dover Downs International Speedway
Dover, Del. — 1.0 miles — 24° banking

Year	Date	Race	St.	Fin.	Total Laps	Laps Completed	Laps Led	Condition	Money	Pts	Bonus Pts.
1976	May 16	Mason-Dixon 500	17	33	500	247	0	DNF - Accident	$555	64	0
1977	May 15	Mason-Dixon 500	20	27	500	190	0	DNF - Mechanical	1,125	82	0
	Sep 18	Delaware 500	12	32	500	178	0	DNF - Engine	530	67	0
1979	May 20	Mason-Dixon 500	16	14	500	480	1	DNF - Crash	2,830	126	5
	Sep 16	CRC Chemicals 500	14	8	500	496	0	Running	4,400	142	0
1981	May 17	Mason-Dixon 500	4	5	500	490	0	Running	9,450	155	0
	Sep 20	CRC Chemicals 500	1	5	500	495	55	Running	11,375	160	5
1982	May 16	Mason-Dixon 500	4	22	500	271	0	DNF - Engine	2,620	97	0
	Sep 19	CRC Chemicals 500	1	11	500	478	2	DNF - Crash	6,875	135	5
1983	May 15	Mason-Dixon 500	2	24	500	277	0	DNF - Engine	3,140	91	0
	Sep 18	Budweiser 500	2	13	500	467	0	Running	4,855	124	0
1984	May 20	Budweiser 500	1	8	500	497	13	Running	14,200	147	5
	Sep 16	Delaware 500	7	3	500	498	1	Running	17,200	170	5
1985	May 19	Budweiser 500	5	4	500	498	0	Running	15,375	160	0
	Sep 15	Delaware 500	7	3	500	499	55	Running	31,450	170	5
1986	May 18	Budweiser 500	1	4	500	498	0	Running	18,875	160	0
	Sep 14	Delaware 500	11	1	500	500	141	Running	51,500	185	10
1987	May 31	Budweiser 500	11	12	500	490	1	Running	11,300	132	5
	Sep 20	Delaware 500	13	1	500	500	373	Running	54,550	185	10
1988	Jun 5	Budweiser 500	20	19	500	493	0	Running	5,200	106	0
	Sep 18	Delaware 500	19	10	500	497	0	Running	10,650	134	0
1989	Jun 4	Budweiser 500	7	6	500	500	0	Running	11,675	150	0
	Sep 17	Peak Performance 500	14	5	500	498	0	Running	18,375	155	0
1990	Jun 3	Budweiser 500	20	11	500	499	0	Running	9,025	130	0
	Sep 16	Peak Antifreeze 500	20	32	500	246	0	DNF - Mechanical	5,600	67	0
1991	Jun 2	Budweiser 500	13	10	500	497	0	Running	18,000	134	0
	Sep 15	Peak Antifreeze 500	24	7	500	493	1	Running	15,800	151	5
1992	May 31	Budweiser 500	13	6	500	498	58	Running	21,215	155	5
	Sep 20	Peak Antifreeze 500	6	1	500	500	32	Running	64,965	180	5
1993	Jun 6	Budweiser 500	15	35	500	121	0	DNF - Crash	12,115	58	0
	Sep 19	SplitFire Spark Plug 500	22	21	500	458	0	DNF - Flagged	13,205	100	0
1994	Jun 5	Bud 500	18	19	500	489	0	Running	11,465	106	0
	Sep 18	SplitFire 500	16	18	500	496	0	Running	15,450	109	0
1995	Jun 4	Miller 500	29	31	500	436	0	Running	25,665	70	0
	Sep 17	MBNA 500	6	10	500	498	0	Running	33,665	134	0
1996	Jun 2	Miller 500	16	8	500	499	0	Running	32,765	142	0
	Sep 16	MBNA 500	14	34	500	433	0	Running	28,430	61	0
1997	Jun 1	Miller 500	13	1	500	500	31	Running	95,255	180	5
	Sep 21	MBNA 400	16	6	400	399	0	Running	34,440	150	0
1998	May 31	MBNA Platinum 400	5	6	400	399	1	Running	49,275	155	5
	Sep 20	MBNA Gold 400	11	13	400	399	0	Running	35,140	124	0
1999	Jun 6	MBNA Platinum 400	23	14	400	397	0	Running	45,210	121	0
	Sep 26	MBNA Gold 400	14	37	400	352	0	DNF - Oil Pump	33,400	52	0
2000	Jun 4	MBNA Platinum 400	7	5	400	400	0	Running	78,280	155	0
	Sep 24	MBNA.com 400	14	3	400	400	1	Running	93,160	170	5
2001	Jun 3	MBNA Platinum 400	5	10	400	400	0	Running	91,007	134	0
	Sep 23	MBNA Cal Ripken Jr. 400	4	3	400	400	169	Running	117,507	170	5

Dover is one of Ricky Rudd's best tracks. He has four wins and four poles on the 1-mile oval.

In the first Winston Cup race after the September 11 terrorist attacks, Robert Yates Racing showed its colors with American flag decals.

Most Top 10s

A look at the drivers who have earned the most Top 10s in Dover history

Driver	Top 10s
Ricky Rudd	26
Richard Petty	26
Bobby Allison	25
Dale Earnhardt	25
Darrell Waltrip	21

Most Driver Points

A look at the drivers who have earned the most points at Dover since 1975

Driver	Top 10s
Ricky Rudd	6,105
Darrell Waltrip	6,075
Dale Earnhardt	5,953
Terry Labonte	5,403

Homestead-Miami Speedway

After 26 seasons and 700-plus races, it's hard to imagine that the no-nonsense Ricky Rudd would feel sentimental or nostalgic about very much in racing. But his battle with Dale Earnhardt in the 2000 Pennzoil 400 must have seemed like old times. Rudd was in the lead with 56 laps to go when Earnhardt rubbed his lapped car against Rudd's No. 28 Ford between turns 1 and 2 of the flat 1.5-mile track. The contact pushed Rudd out of Miami-Homestead's single groove and allowed Tony Stewart to sneak inside and assume the lead. Besides costing him the lead, Earnhardt's bump also damaged the left-front fender on Rudd's car, ruining his aerodynamic balance. He dropped back to an eventual sixth-place finish, while Stewart cruised to victory.

Though Miami-Homestead is one of NASCAR's newest tracks, the Earnhardt-Rudd get-together was a reminder of the two veterans' by-gone battles. More than a decade before Homestead-Miami appeared on the Winston Cup schedule, the older tracks—North Wilkesboro, Bristol, Richmond, and Rockingham—were the site of their intense slugfests. Each got the better of the other at various points. When the venom disappeared and hard racing took its place, Earnhardt and Rudd staged fantastic exhibitions of hard, but clean racing—most memorably at another new, flat track (New Hampshire) in 1994 and at Richmond in 1991.

As events turned out, the 2000 Homestead was the last such battle for the two long-time rivals. Four months later, Earnhardt was killed in a last-lap crash in the Daytona 500. Due to his massive presence in NASCAR, every driver in the Winston Cup series had a connection to Earnhardt that was severed on February 18, 2001. For Rudd, that day marked the loss of one of his most intense, but respectful on-track rivalries.

Homestead Stats Chart

Homestead Record Book - All-Time (min. 2 starts)

Category	Rudd's Total	Rudd's Rank	All-Time Homestead Leader
Money	$201,322	13th	Tony Stewart -- 628,940
Starts	3	T-1st	28 Others with 3 Starts
Total Points	295	15th	Bobby Labonte -- 487
Avg. Start	6.3	2nd	Casey Atwood -- 3.5
Avg. Finish	22.7	25th	Bobby Labonte -- 4.7
Wins	0	--	Tony Stewart -- 2
Winning Pct.	0.0	--	Tony Stewart -- 66.7
Top 5s	0	--	Four with 2 Top 5s
Top 10s	1	8th	Bobby Labonte -- 3
DNFs	1	3rd	S. Compton, D. Waltrip -- 2
Poles	0	--	B. Elliott, D. Green, S. Park -- 1
Front Row Starts	1	T-1st	Six with 1 Front Row Start
Laps Led	49	5th	Tony Stewart -- 282
Pct. Laps Led	6.1	6th	Tony Stewart -- 35.2
Races Led	1	5th	Tony Stewart -- 3
Times Led	6	2nd	Tony Stewart -- 14
Times Led Most Laps	0	--	Tony Stewart -- 2
Bonus Points	5	5th	Tony Stewart -- 25
Laps Completed	718	25th	B. Labonte, M. Martin, T. Stewart -- 801
Pct. Laps Completed	89.6	38th	Four with 100 percent Laps Completed
Points per Race	98.3	21st	Bobby Labonte -- 162.3
Lead-Lap Finishes	2	4th	B. Labonte, M. Martin, T. Stewart -- 3

Homestead-Miami Speedway Performance Chart

Homestead Motorsports Complex

Homestead, Fla. — 1.5 miles — 8° banking

Year	Date	Race	St.	Fin.	Total Laps	Laps Completed	Laps Led	Condition	Money	Pts	Bonus Pts.
1999	Nov 14	Jiffy Lube Miami 400	13	41	267	184	0	DNF - Engine	$42,500	40	0
2000	Nov 12	Pennzoil 400	2	6	267	267	49	Running	86,375	155	5
2001	Nov 11	Pennzoil 400	4	21	267	267	0	Running	72,447	100	0

Rudd's crew works to get him back on the track . . . but it wouldn't last. He suffered engine trouble and dropped out of the 1999 Jiffy Lube Miami 400 after 184 laps.

Indianapolis Motor Speedway

Though Ricky Rudd has yet to win any of NASCAR's traditional major events—the Daytona 500, Coca-Cola 600, and Southern 500—he can claim an early victory in the newest major, the Brickyard 400. Since joining the Winston Cup schedule in 1994, the Brickyard assumed immediate importance in the stock car world. The track's hallowed history, its massive crowds (in excess of 300,000), and record-setting purses gave it instant credibility. Even its first two stock car winners—Jeff Gordon and Dale Earnhardt—helped raise the annual August event's standing.

The event's elevated importance made Rudd's 1997 Brickyard victory all the more improbable. In 75 attempts at winning the big ones at Charlotte, Darlington and Daytona, he had never finished better than third. At Indy, the big teams—Hendrick Motorsports, Richard Childress Racing, and Robert Yates Racing—seemed to have the early advantage. They had swept the first three victories and had won two of the first three poles. Rudd Performance Motorsports, meanwhile, was going in the opposite direction. Locked into inadequate sponsorship funding—a short-sighted Rudd signed a five-year deal with Tide without foreseeing NASCAR's escalating costs—RPM was losing ground quickly to the multicar operations.

Earlier in the 1997 season, Rudd stole a win at Dover after the big teams' lead drivers—Gordon, Dale Jarrett, and Ernie Irvan—dropped out due to engine woes and crashes. The victory illustrated how the single-car teams could expect to win: If you can't outrun them, try to outsmart them; if all else fails, pray for luck. At Indianapolis two months after his Dover miracle, Rudd stole another one. Realizing long green-flag runs could play into his hands, he dropped back into a fuel-conserving strategy. With 46 laps remaining in the 160-lap event, he visited pit road for the final time. With 13 to go, the race's top cars turned down pit road during the final caution of the afternoon. Rudd stayed out and took the lead. Then he took advantage. On the restart, he built a comfortable lead while the race's top cars fought frantically to get by slower lapped cars. Cruising in clean air up front, Rudd eased to a two car-length victory over Bobby Labonte.

The win was the 19th of Rudd's career, but is clearly the most significant. A former go-kart champion as a kid, he had traveled to Indianapolis to race as a youngster and had toured the Speedway. He had even contemplated pursuing an open-wheel driving career that ultimately might have led him to the Indianapolis 500. Indicating the magnitude of the win, Rudd's winner's prize of $571,000 exceeded his winnings in nine entire seasons.

Though his name is etched in the track's record book, Rudd cannot call Indianapolis one of his best tracks. Including his win, he has just three Top 10s in his eight Brickyard starts. On the other hand, he has four finishes of 20th or worse. Even since joining Yates' powerhouse, his luck has been minimal. In his first Brickyard 400 in the No. 28 Ford, he won the pole, but dropped to a 21st-place finish. In 2001, engine difficulties ruined his chances early. He finished a career-worst 39th.

Indianapolis Stats Chart

Indianapolis Record Book - All-Time (min. 3 starts)

Category	Rudd's Total	Rudd's Rank	All-Time Indianapolis Leader
Money	$1,278,297	6th	Jeff Gordon -- 2,704,528
Starts	8	T-1st	15 Others with 8 Starts
Total Points	927	8th	Bobby Labonte -- 1,162
Avg. Start	14.8	10th	Mike Skinner -- 9.3
Avg. Finish	17.3	15th	Mike Skinner -- 8.5
Wins	1	3rd	Jeff Gordon -- 3
Winning Pct.	12.5	4th	Jeff Gordon -- 37.5
Top 5s	1	8th	Jeff Gordon -- 5
Top 10s	3	8th	Rusty Wallace -- 7
DNFs	1	14th	C. Little, D. Marcis -- 3
Poles	1	3rd	Jeff Gordon -- 3
Front Row Starts	1	4th	Jeff Gordon -- 3
Laps Led	33	11th	Jeff Gordon -- 306
Pct. Laps Led	2.6	13th	Jeff Gordon -- 23.9
Races Led	3	8th	Jeff Gordon -- 7
Times Led	4	10th	Jeff Gordon -- 23
Times Led Most Laps	0	--	Jeff Gordon -- 2
Bonus Points	15	9th	Jeff Gordon -- 45
Laps Completed	1,220	7th	B. Elliott, B. Labonte -- 1,279
Pct. Laps Completed	95.3	27th	M. Shepherd, M. Skinner, T. Stewart -- 100.0
Points per Race	115.9	14th	Bobby Labonte -- 145.3
Lead-Lap Finishes	4	14th	B. Elliott, B. Labonte, R. Wallace -- 7

Indianapolis Performance Chart

Indianapolis Motor Speedway

Indianapolis, Ind. — 2.5 miles — 9-12° banking

Year	Date	Race	St.	Fin.	Total Laps	Laps Completed	Laps Led	Condition	Money	Pts	Bonus Pts.
1994	Aug 6	Brickyard 400	8	11	160	160	0	Running	$57,100	130	0
1995	Aug 5	Brickyard 400	22	20	160	159	0	Running	73,450	103	0
1996	Aug 3	Brickyard 400	35	6	160	160	1	Running	118,385	155	5
1997	Aug 3	Brickyard 400	7	1	160	160	15	Running	571,000	180	5
1998	Aug 1	Brickyard 400	27	31	160	155	0	DNF - Crash	85,685	70	0
1999	Aug 7	Brickyard 400	14	9	160	160	0	Running	137,535	138	0
2000	Aug 5	Brickyard 400	1	21	160	159	17	Running	120,610	105	5
2001	Aug 7	Brickyard 400	4	39	160	107	0	Running	114,982	46	0

The biggest win of Ricky Rudd's career came at Indianapolis, when he won the 1997 Brickyard 400.

In his first Brickyard 400 with the powerful Robert Yates Racing team, Rudd won the pole for the 2000 race.

Las Vegas Motor Speedway

Ricky Rudd has yet to figure out the new Las Vegas Motor Speedway. In the track's first four races, he failed to crack the Top 10. The highlight of his Vegas experience was his pole-winning qualifying run in 2000. The pole culminated an auspicious beginning to his new partnership with Robert Yates Racing. In his first three RYR races, he qualified second for the season-opening Daytona 500, second at Rockingham and first at Las Vegas. Unfortunately for Rudd, his success didn't extend to the end of the race. He finished 12th at Vegas after his pole start and led just one lap.

Rudd's other Vegas races haven't been nearly as eventful. His 12th-place finish in the track's inaugural race in March of 1998 was nondescript, but stood as his best effort since September of the previous season. In 1999, he dropped out early due to a blown engine and finished 43rd—one of only two 43rd-place finishes in his career. (The other occurred at Rockingham in 1998.) In 2001, he endured another difficult Vegas race, starting 25th and finishing 19th after cutting a tire early.

Las Vegas Stats Chart

Las Vegas Record Book - All-Time (min. 2 starts)

Category	Rudd's Total	Rudd's Rank	All-Time Las Vegas Leader
Money	$306,522	16th	Jeff Burton -- 966,615
Starts	4	T-1st	21 Others with 4 Starts
Total Points	399	18th	Mark Martin -- 654
Avg. Start	19.8	19th	(Bobby Labonte -- 5.8)
Avg. Finish	21.5	27th	Mark Martin -- 5.0
Wins	0	--	Jeff Burton -- 2
Winning Pct.	0.0	--	Jeff Burton -- 50.0
Top 5s	0	--	Jeff Burton -- 3
Top 10s	0	--	Mark Martin -- 4
DNFs	1	4th	R. Craven, H. Stricklin, K. Wallace -- 2
Poles	1	2nd	(B. Labonte, R. Rudd -- 1)
Front Row Starts	1	2nd	(Six with 1 Front Row Start)
Laps Led	1	28th	Jeff Burton -- 204
Pct. Laps Led	0.1	29th	Jeff Burton -- 21.5
Races Led	1	11th	Mark Martin -- 4
Times Led	1	15th	Mark Martin -- 13
Times Led Most Laps	0	--	J. Burton, M. Martin -- 2
Bonus Points	5	11th	Mark Martin -- 30
Laps Completed	795	18th	Mark Martin -- 949
Pct. Laps Completed	83.8	42nd	D. Earnhardt, M. Martin -- 100.0
Points per Race	99.8	27th	Mark Martin -- 163.5
Lead-Lap Finishes	1	15th	Mark Martin -- 4

Las Vegas Performance Chart

Las Vegas Motor Speedway
Las Vegas, Nev. — 1.5 miles — 12° banking

Year	Date	Race	St.	Fin.	Total Laps	Laps Completed	Laps Led	Condition	Money	Pts	Bonus Pts.
1998	Mar 1	Las Vegas 400	19	12	267	266	0	Running	$77,200	127	0
1999	Mar 7	Las Vegas 400	34	43	267	115	0	DNF - Engine	51,975	34	0
2000	Mar 5	Carsdirect.com 400	1	12	148	148	1	Running	83,975	132	5
2001	Mar 4	UAW-Daimler Chrysler 400	25	19	267	266	0	Running	93,372	106	0

Ricky Rudd won the pole for the 2000 Las Vegas race, but quickly dropped to a 12th-place finish.

Lowe's Motor Speedway at Charlotte

Similar to NASCAR's other speedways (tracks greater than 1 mile, but less than 2 miles), Lowe's Motor Speedway near Charlotte, N.C., has been a mixed bag for Ricky Rudd. Only Darrell Waltrip owns more Top 10 finishes on the 1.5-mile track in the Modern Era. And, given a couple of more seasons, Rudd should soon take over most of the longevity records (starts, laps completed, points earned) in the track's history.

Wins, however, have escaped Rudd's grasp. In his first 51 starts, he did not finish a race in first place, an amazing statistic for one of the Winston Cup series' most consistent drivers. No other competitive driver even approaches Rudd's winless record at Charlotte. Dave Marcis, the exemplar of uncompetitive drivers in NASCAR history, is the only driver with more than 40 winless Charlotte starts.

Not winning and not being competitive are different things, of course. Rudd had close calls in the 1994 Coca-Cola 600 and in the 2000 fall race. He led the 600 with 10 laps to go before a final fuel stop handed the race back to Jeff Gordon. In 2000, he led with just 17 to go before a late caution erased his advantage. A slow pit stop dropped him back to sixth and out of contention.

In 1980, Rudd's strong performance at Charlotte caught the notice of a young engine builder named Robert Yates. Then the lead technician for the powerful DiGard Racing team, Yates watched Rudd nearly win the pole for the National 500. He started second and raced among the Top 5 all afternoon, to finish fourth. DiGard at the time was involved in interminable squabbles with its driver, Darrell Waltrip, over contract terms. Waltrip finally won his freedom from DiGard in late 1980 and bolted to Junior Johnson's team. Yates talked DiGard's ownership, left without a driver, into signing Rudd for the 1981 season (plus options on the next four seasons, which were never exercised). Driving the No. 88 DiGard car was, at the time, the biggest break of Rudd's career.

Lowe's Stats Chart

Charlotte Record Book - Modern Era (min. 5 starts)

Category	Rudd's Total	Rudd's Rank	Modern Era Charlotte Leader
Money	$1,256,699	10th	Dale Earnhardt -- 1,934,793
Starts	51	2nd	Darrell Waltrip -- 55
Total Points[1]	6,072	3rd	Darrell Waltrip -- 6,379
Avg. Start	16.8	28th	David Pearson -- 3.8
Avg. Finish	15.8	14th	Tony Stewart -- 7.7
Wins	0	--	Darrell Waltrip -- 6
Winning Pct.	0.0	--	Jeff Gordon -- 22.2
Top 5s	8	15th	Darrell Waltrip -- 19
Top 10s	24	2nd	Darrell Waltrip -- 29
DNFs	8	29th	Dave Marcis -- 30
Poles	1	14th	David Pearson -- 13
Front Row Starts	2	18th	David Pearson -- 16
Laps Led	255	27th	Bobby Allison -- 1,844
Pct. Laps Led	1.4	40th	Bobby Allison -- 16.3
Races Led	8	25th	Dale Earnhardt -- 30
Times Led	18	28th	Dale Earnhardt -- 120
Times Led Most Laps	2	9th	Bobby Allison -- 8
Bonus Points[1]	50	25th	Dale Earnhardt -- 175
Laps Completed	16,967	2nd	Darrell Waltrip -- 18,239
Pct. Laps Completed	91.1	19th	Tony Stewart -- 99.8
Points per Race[1]	119.1	19th	Tony Stewart -- 150.3
Lead-Lap Finishes	11	9th	Dale Earnhardt -- 18

[1] -- Since implementation of current point system in 1975

Memorable Charlotte Memories

1994 Mello Yello 500—Angered by a late-race bump, Rudd tailgated and crashed Jeff Gordon in Turn 1 with just 10 laps to go. Both drivers were sent hurtling into the wall as a result of the contact and totaled their cars. NASCAR reviewed videotape and Rudd's postrace comments, which confirmed that his move was intentional, and levied one of the stiffest penalties in Rudd's career. NASCAR fined him $10,000 and put him on probation for the remainder of the season (three races). The veteran was unrepentant for his actions, claiming to be sorry only for the wrecked cars. Rudd also made the preposterous claim that Gordon's lack of talent contributed to the crash, saying similar racing with a better driver would not have resulted in a wreck.

Winless at Charlotte

Ricky Rudd holds the Modern Era for most starts at Charlotte without a win

Driver	No. of Starts
Ricky Rudd	51
Dave Marcis	46
Morgan Shepherd	36
Michael Waltrip	34

Lowe's Performance Chart

Lowe's Motor Speedway
Charlotte, N.C. — 1.5 miles — 24° banking

Year	Date	Race	St.	Fin.	Total Laps	Laps Completed	Laps Led	Condition	Money	Pts	Bonus Pts.
1976	Oct 10	National 500	33	16	334	318	0	Running	$1,995	115	0
1977	May 29	World 600	18	17	400	384	2	Running	2,960	117	5
	Oct 9	NAPA National 500	21	24	334	232	0	Running	1,750	91	0
1978	May 28	World 600	20	28	400	331	0	Running	3,430	79	0
	Oct 8	NAPA National 500	13	23	334	308	0	Running	3,710	94	0
1979	May 27	World 600	10	6	400	397	0	Running	14,845	150	0
	Oct 7	NAPA National 500	21	11	334	327	0	Running	6,105	130	0
1980	May 25	World 600	13	9	400	394	0	Running	7,425	138	0
	Oct 5	National 500	2	4	334	334	1	Running	15,350	165	5
1981	May 24	World 600	13	4	400	397	0	Running	18,975	160	0
	Oct 11	National 500	8	3	334	334	0	Running	29,925	165	0
1982	May 30	World 600	10	7	400	397	0	Running	11,130	146	0
	Oct 10	National 500	6	31	334	122	0	DNF - Engine	3,445	70	0
1983	May 29	World 600	9	32	400	245	0	Running	3,425	67	0
	Oct 9	Miler High Life 500	13	9	334	334	1	Running	8,265	143	5
1984	May 27	World 600	10	11	400	395	0	Running	14,025	130	0
	Oct 7	Miler High Life 500	7	8	334	332	0	Running	14,225	142	0
1985	May 26	Coca-Cola World 600	17	13	400	391	0	Running	13,255	124	0
	Oct 6	Miler High Life 500	8	15	334	320	0	Running	11,350	118	0
1986	May 25	Coca-Cola 600	13	8	400	399	0	Running	18,200	142	0
	Oct 5	Oakwood Homes 500	16	4	334	333	0	Running	25,700	160	0
1987	May 24	Coca-Cola 600	25	25	400	254	0	DNF - Crash	11,950	88	0
	Oct 11	Oakwood Homes 500	27	11	334	329	0	Running	15,190	130	0
1988	May 29	Coca-Cola 600	34	7	400	399	0	Running	17,050	146	0
	Oct 9	Oakwood Homes 500	36	8	334	334	0	Running	13,825	142	0
1989	May 28	Coca-Cola 600	9	10	400	397	0	Running	16,925	134	0
	Oct 8	All Pro Auto Parts 500	16	21	334	331	0	Running	10,480	100	0
1990	Apr 8	Valleydale Meats 500	34	28	400	320	0	DNF - Camshaft	7,450	79	0
	Oct 7	Mello Yello 500	16	6	334	334	0	Running	18,425	150	0
1991	May 26	Coca-Cola 600	17	9	400	399	0	Running	21,500	138	0
	Oct 6	Mello Yello 500	10	32	334	232	0	DNF - Crash	10,550	67	0
1992	May 24	Coca-Cola 600	3	9	400	398	33	Running	30,100	143	5
	Oct 22	Mello Yello 500	5	5	334	334	0	Running	35,550	155	0
1993	May 30	Coca-Cola 600	20	37	400	164	0	DNF - Engine	11,310	52	0
	Oct 10	Mello Yello 500	8	8	334	333	0	Running	24,500	142	0
1994	May 29	Coca-Cola 600	13	6	400	400	10	Running	28,700	155	5
	Oct 9	Mello Yello 500	16	29	334	324	0	DNF - Crash	10,420	76	0
1995	May 28	Coca-Cola 600	18	5	400	399	3	Running	49,000	160	5
	Oct 8	UAW-GM 500	1	4	334	334	107	Running	90,200	170	10
1996	May 26	Coca-Cola 600	30	15	400	396	0	Running	30,620	118	0
	Oct 6	UAW-GM 500	39	13	334	333	0	Running	26,250	124	0
1997	May 25	Coca-Cola 600	18	10	333	333	0	Running	70,550	134	0
	Oct 5	UAW-GM Quality 500	22	41	334	102	0	DNF - Crash	28,880	40	0
1998	May 24	Coca-Cola 600	35	31	400	396	0	Running	59,025	70	0
	Oct 4	UAW-GM Quality 500	14	37	334	231	0	DNF - Crash	32,235	52	0
1999	May 30	Coca-Cola 600	23	28	400	395	0	Running	40,640	79	0
	Oct 10	UAW-GM Quality 500	21	38	334	278	0	Running	26,695	49	0
2000	May 28	Coca-Cola 600	20	17	400	399	0	Running	50,395	112	0
	Oct 8	UAW-GM Quality 500	6	3	334	334	98	Running	104,950	175	10
2001	May 27	Coca-Cola 600	21	7	400	400	0	Running	102,572	146	0
	Oct 7	UAW-GM Quality 500	19	21	334	331	0	Running	69,772	100	0

Lowe's Motor Speedway has been a hard-luck track for Rudd, who didn't win in his first 51 Charlotte starts.

The Tide crew tends to Rudd's No. 10 Ford during the Coca-Cola 600 at Charlotte in 1999.

Martinsville Speedway

Located 205 miles west of his hometown of Chesapeake, Virginia, Martinsville Speedway quickly became one of Ricky Rudd's best tracks. In 45 Martinsville starts through 2001, he had three victories and four poles. Only Dover and Sears Point have been as accommodating.

Rudd's greatest success at Martinsville came during the early 1980s. Between 1981 and 1986, he started 11 straight races in the Top 10, winning two poles, and finish in the Top 5 eight times. In that stretch, he won twice and had the most dominating day in his 26-year career. In the 1983 Goody's 500, he led 380 of 500 laps, the highest number of laps led in a single race during his career.

After that quick start, however, Rudd's relationship with Martinsville has cooled. Since 1987, the tiny track has become a troubling stop on the Winston Cup tour. In 30 races between 1987 and 2001, he finished outside of the Top 10 a total of 23 times. From the fall of 1994 through 1996, he didn't finish any better than 23rd.

But just when Rudd was ready to give up on the track, it rewarded his patient perseverance with a victory. In 1998, with just seven races left in the season, he pulled an unlikely win in the NAPA Autocare 500 and set the Modern Era record for most consecutive seasons with at least one victory. The win extended his streak to 16 seasons, breaking the record of 15 set by Darrell Waltrip and tied by Dale Earnhardt. In 2001, Rusty Wallace tied Rudd's mark.

Martinsville Stats Chart

Martinsville Record Book - Modern Era (min. 5 starts)

Category	Rudd's Total	Rudd's Rank	Modern Era Martinsville Leader
Money	$980,499	5th	Rusty Wallace -- 1,334,400
Starts	45	4th	Darrell Waltrip -- 52
Total Points[1]	5,490	4th	Darrell Waltrip -- 7,317
Avg. Start	10.6	12th	David Pearson -- 4.9
Avg. Finish	15.6	35th	Cale Yarborough -- 6.3
Wins	3	7th	Darrell Waltrip -- 11
Winning Pct.	6.7	13th	Cale Yarborough -- 29.4
Top 5s	12	6th	Darrell Waltrip -- 27
Top 10s	17	8th	Darrell Waltrip -- 31
DNFs	11	8th	Dave Marcis -- 16
Poles	4	3rd	Darrell Waltrip -- 8
Front Row Starts	7	4th	Darrell Waltrip -- 12
Laps Led	1,569	5th	Darrell Waltrip -- 3,616
Pct. Laps Led	7.0	15th	Cale Yarborough -- 40.0
Races Led	17	5th	Darrell Waltrip -- 32
Times Led	32	9th	Darrell Waltrip -- 79
Times Led Most Laps	4	6th	R. Wallace, C. Yarborough -- 9
Bonus Points[1]	105	5th	Darrell Waltrip -- 195
Laps Completed	19,884	3rd	Darrell Waltrip -- 23,727
Pct. Laps Completed	88.9	37th	Elliott Sadler -- 98.8
Points per Race[1]	122.0	28th	Cale Yarborough -- 156.8
Lead-Lap Finishes	12	5th	Darrell Waltrip -- 25

[1] -- Since implementation of current point system in 1975

Memorable Martinsville Moments

1981 Virginia 500—Driving the powerful No. 88 DiGard Racing Chevy, Rudd won his first career pole with a lap of 89.056 miles per hour. He accomplished the feat in his 96th start. After leading 24 laps, he finished third behind winner Morgan Shepherd and runner-up Neil Bonnett.

1983 Goody's 500—Rudd overpowered the field in his No. 3 Richard Childress Racing Chevy, leading 380 of 500 laps. The win was his first on a short track and the second victory of his career. It also marked his most dominant day in 700-plus Winston Cup starts. Only his 1987 victory at Dover, during which he led 373 laps, was as dominating.

1986 Sovran Bank 500—Rudd lapped the field en route to his second Martinsville win after most of the top contenders were eliminated by mechanical problems and wrecks. With 100 laps to go, Rudd had a full circuit advantage on second-place Joe Ruttman. He maintained that margin and became one of just four drivers since 1986 to win a race by a full lap. The last Winston Cup race to be decided by a lap or more was Geoffrey Bodine's victory in the fall North Wilkesboro race in 1994.

1998 NAPA Autocare 500—On a scorching late-September day, Rudd pulled out his first win at Martinsville in 25 tries. Not since 1986 had he visited the Virginia track's Victory Lane. The improbable victory allowed Rudd to set the Modern Era record for most consecutive seasons with at least one win. Glory came with a price, however. Rudd battled faulty cooling systems and a red-hot driver's seat throughout the race. With a relief driver—Hut Stricklin—waiting in his pit stall for 400 laps, Rudd soldiered on to lead the final 95 laps. He was treated in Victory Lane for a half-hour before recovering enough to join his team's celebration.

Martinsville Performance Chart

Martinsville Speedway
Martinsville, Va. — .526 miles — 12° banking

Year	Date	Race	St.	Fin.	Total Laps	Laps Completed	Laps Led	Condition	Money	Pts	Bonus Pts.
1977	Sep 25	Old Dominion 500	14	27	500	84	0	DNF - Rear End	$580	82	0
1979	Apr 22	Virginia 500	17	12	500	489	0	Running	2,470	127	0
	Sep 23	Old Dominion 500	10	6	500	491	0	Running	4,700	150	0
1981	Apr 26	Virginia 500	1	3	500	499	24	Running	15,250	170	5
	Sep 27	Old Dominion 500	2	8	500	486	1	Running	7,950	147	5
1982	Apr 25	Virginia National Bank 500	4	4	500	496	55	Running	8,520	165	5
	Oct 17	Old Dominion 500	1	2	500	500	77	Running	22,770	175	5
1983	Apr 24	Virginia National Bank 500	1	5	500	500	100	Running	9,670	160	5
	Sep 25	Goody's 500	2	1	500	500	380	Running	31,395	185	10
1984	Apr 29	Sovran Bank 500	9	18	500	487	121	Running	7,950	114	5
	Sep 23	Goody's 500	5	27	500	58	0	DNF - Engine	8,030	82	0
1985	Apr 28	Sovran Bank 500	7	2	500	500	1	Running	22,450	175	5
	Sep 22	Goody's 500	5	4	500	499	0	Running	12,350	160	0
1986	Apr 27	Sovran Bank 500	4	1	500	500	163	Running	40,850	185	10
	Sep 21	Goody's 500	10	28	500	319	0	DNF - Crash	8,345	79	0
1987	Apr 26	Sovran Bank 500	15	16	500	440	0	DNF - Rear End	9,050	115	0
	Sep 27	Goody's 500	15	21	500	387	1	DNF - Overheating	8,800	105	5
1988	Apr 24	Pannill Sweatshirts 500	1	18	500	446	37	DNF - Engine	8,555	114	5
	Sep 25	Goody's 500	14	24	500	423	237	DNF - Engine	6,025	101	10
1989	Apr 23	Pannill Sweatshirts 500	25	23	500	433	0	Running	3,945	94	0
	Sep 24	Goody's 500	7	8	500	499	0	Running	10,900	142	0
1990	Apr 29	Hanes Activewear 500	11	23	500	417	0	Running	5,100	94	0
	Sep 23	Goody's 500	16	28	500	289	85	DNF - Crash	6,200	89	10
1991	Apr 28	Hanes 500	22	11	500	496	0	Running	10,985	130	0
	Sep 22	Goody's 500	4	8	500	500	2	Running	15,300	147	5
1992	Apr 26	Hanes 500	5	23	500	426	0	Running	11,850	94	0
	Sep 28	Goody's 500	21	10	500	499	0	Running	17,200	134	0
1993	Apr 25	Hanes 500	14	29	500	310	0	Running	9,025	76	0
	Sep 26	Goody's 500	20	4	500	500	0	Running	25,250	160	0
1994	Apr 24	Hanes 500	19	12	500	498	0	Running	6,825	127	0
	Sep 25	Goody's 500	13	25	500	490	0	Running	10,975	88	0
1995	Apr 23	Hanes 500	8	30	356	313	0	DNF - Transmission	19,465	73	0
	Sep 24	Goody's 500	13	27	500	450	0	Running	19,700	82	0
1996	Apr 21	Goody's 500	30	23	500	490	0	Running	24,615	94	0
	Sep 22	Hanes 500	33	35	500	283	0	DNF - Rear End	24,050	58	0
1997	Apr 20	Goody's 500	5	13	500	500	0	Running	27,065	124	0
	Sep 28	Hanes 500	5	13	500	500	0	Running	27,065	124	0
1998	Apr 19	Goody's 500	4	14	500	499	0	Running	39,150	121	0
	Sep 27	NAPA Autocare 500	2	1	500	500	198	Running	102,575	180	5
1999	Apr 18	Goody's Body Pain 500	15	29	500	497	0	Running	32,100	76	0
	Oct 3	NAPA AutoCare 500	8	18	500	497	0	Running	34,155	109	0
2000	Apr 9	Goody's Body Pain 500	7	22	500	497	0	Running	36,325	97	0
	Oct 1	NAPA AutoCare 500	11	4	500	500	37	Running	59,275	165	5
2001	Apr 8	Virginia 500	4	2	500	500	50	Running	106,047	175	5
	Oct 14	Old Dominion 500	19	39	500	397	0	DNF - Engine	59,647	46	0

Rudd beat Jeff Gordon to the finish to win the 1998 NAPA Autocare 500. The victory extended Rudd's consecutive winning season streak to a Modern Era record 16.

Martinsville has been one of Rudd's best tracks. His first oval victory came there in 1983. He has three wins and four poles at Martinsville.

Michigan International Speedway

Circumstances and bad luck mask the fact that Michigan International Speedway is one of Ricky Rudd's most competitive tracks. Since 1994, he has led more laps at Michigan and Martinsville than any other tracks on the Winston Cup circuit. However, while he can point to a win at Martinsville (in 1998), he can only offer lengthy explanation for what happened at Michigan.

• In 1996, he climbed from his 14th starting position to take the lead at the midpoint of the race, but a lost cylinder ended his victory hopes shortly thereafter, and he fell to 31st, five laps down.

• In 1998, he started ninth and looked strong until throttle problems dropped him to 37th, five laps down.

• In the first race of 2000, the glass from the right-side window pops out when the jackman lowers his car after right-side tires were changed. Followed by a bout of loose lug nuts, he spends so much time on pit road that he falls back to 12th.

• In the second 2000 race, his comfortable lead with 22 laps to go was erased by a late caution for "debris." Rusty Wallace, who took on four tires while Rudd took two, gets by and pulls away to victory. Rudd finishes second.

• In 2001, he made a terrific move against Jeff Gordon in Turn 4 to make a pass for the lead but he did it a lap early. Gordon recovered with a terrific move on the outside going into Turn 1 and beat Rudd back to the finish line.

Rudd's Michigan performance has taken a decided turn for the better since he joined Robert Yates Racing in 2000. With Yates' horsepower pulling him down Michigan's long frontstretch, Rudd figures to turn his luck around soon.

Michigan Stats Chart

Michigan Record Book - All-Time (min. 5 starts)

Category	Rudd's Total	Rudd's Rank	All-Time Michigan Leader
Money	$1,115,096	7th	Bill Elliott --1,392,149
Starts	50	2nd	Dave Marcis -- 56
Total Points[1]	5,679	3rd	Bill Elliott -- 6,323
Avg. Start	13.8	24th	Bobby Isaac -- 3.1
Avg. Finish	17.9	31st	Jeff Gordon -- 6.7
Wins	1	14th	David Pearson -- 9
Winning Pct.	2.0	22nd	David Pearson -- 31.0
Top 5s	9	14th	Cale Yarborough -- 21
Top 10s	21	8th	Bill Elliott -- 29
DNFs	13	3rd	Dave Marcis -- 21
Poles	0	--	David Pearson -- 10
Front Row Starts	5	6th	Bill Elliott -- 12
Laps Led	344	13th	Cale Yarborough -- 1,308
Pct. Laps Led	3.5	24th	Jeff Gordon -- 18.5
Races Led	16	10th	Darrell Waltrip -- 33
Times Led	35	15th	Cale Yarborough -- 152
Times Led Most Laps	1	14th	Cale Yarborough -- 8
Bonus Points[1]	85	11th	Darrell Waltrip -- 190
Laps Completed	8,814	3rd	Dave Marcis -- 8,974
Pct. Laps Completed	88.5	47th	Matt Kenseth -- 99.9
Points per Race[1]	113.6	26th	Jeff Gordon -- 156.5
Lead-Lap Finishes	17	9th	Bill Elliott --26

[1] --Since implementation of current point system in 1975

1995 Miller 400—One of the hardest hits Ricky Rudd ever took while racing a stock car came at Michigan International Speedway in 1995. On lap 71 of the Miller 400, he made contact with Hut Stricklin and was sent into the wall in Turn 1. He nailed the wall driver's side first at 150 miles per hour, crumpling his car and forcing track safety officials to send him to a local hospital. Rudd was treated for bruised ribs, a sore right foot and amnesia. Luckily, Rudd survived the wreck without serious injury and was able to suit up for the race at Daytona two weeks later. But there have been many incidents Rudd would like to forget at Michigan. The 1995 crash ended what looked to be a promising day. He had started on the front row and led nearly half the race before his crash.

Michigan Breakout Charts

Longevity Record Watch

Michigan Starts		Michigan Laps Completed	
Driver	No. of Starts	Driver	Laps Completed
Dave Marcis	56	Dave Marcis	8,974
Ricky Rudd	50	Darrell Waltrip	8,884
Darrell Waltrip	48	Ricky Rudd	8,814
Bill Elliott	47	Richard Petty	8,695
Richard Petty	47	Bill Elliott	8,572

Michigan Performance Chart

Michigan Speedway
Brooklyn, Mich. — 2.0 miles — 18° banking

Rudd has one victory at Michigan, which came in 1993.

Year	Date	Race	St.	Fin.	Total Laps	Laps Completed	Laps Led	Condition	Money	Pts	Bonus Pts.
1977	Jun 19	Cam 2 Motor Oil 400	13	28	200	131	8	DNF - Engine	$950	84	5
	Aug 22	Champion Spark Plug 400	10	7	200	199	0	Running	2,000	146	0
1978	Jun 18	Gabriel 400	11	9	200	195	0	Running	5,400	138	0
	Aug 20	Champion Spark Plug 400	21	28	200	113	1	DNF - Engine	2,255	84	5
1979	Jun 17	Gabriel 400	8	8	200	199	0	Running	5,665	142	0
	Aug 19	Champion Spark Plug 400	16	7	200	199	0	Running	5,320	146	0
1980	Jun 15	Gabriel 400	22	32	200	111	0	DNF - Engine	740	67	0
	Aug 17	Champion Spark Plug 400	25	34	200	88	0	DNF - Transmission	1,220	61	0
1981	Jun 21	Gabriel 400	15	30	200	172	1	DNF - Engine	6,215	78	5
	Aug 16	Champion Spark Plug 400	9	3	200	200	0	Running	15,150	165	0
1982	Jun 20	Gabriel 400	8	5	200	200	1	Running	11,530	160	5
	Aug 22	Champion Spark Plug 400	3	14	200	195	0	Running	5,160	121	0
1983	Jun 19	Gabriel 400	14	6	200	200	0	Running	10,075	150	0
	Aug 21	Champion Spark Plug 400	9	27	200	188	0	Running	3,165	82	0
1984	Jun 17	Miller High Life 400	14	40	200	41	0	DNF - Engine	9,250	43	0
	Aug 12	Champion Spark Plug 400	10	12	200	198	0	Running	11,950	127	0
1985	Jun 16	Miller 400	5	7	200	199	0	Running	13,900	146	0
	Aug 11	Champion Spark Plug 400	4	31	200	128	0	DNF - Oil Leak	8,035	70	0
1986	Jun 15	Miller American 400	18	10	200	200	0	Running	15,150	134	0
	Aug 17	Champion Spark Plug 400	18	21	200	191	0	Running	10,195	100	0
1987	Jun 28	Miller American 400	17	14	200	199	0	Running	12,950	121	0
	Aug 16	Champion Spark Plug 400	27	25	200	180	0	Running	11,485	88	0
1988	Jun 26	Miller High Life 400	31	11	200	199	0	Running	10,425	130	0
	Aug 21	Champion Spark Plug 400	10	16	200	198	3	DNF - Engine	7,895	120	5
1989	Jun 25	Miller High Life 400	33	4	200	200	0	Running	24,575	160	0
	Aug 20	Champion Spark Plug 400	16	8	200	200	0	Running	15,050	142	0
1990	Jun 24	Miller Genuine Draft 400	13	9	200	200	0	Running	13,800	138	0
	Aug 19	Champion Spark Plug 400	39	5	200	200	0	Running	20,670	155	0
1991	Jun 23	Miller Genuine Draft 400	7	8	200	200	1	Running	18,600	147	5
	Aug 18	Champion Spark Plug 400	12	11	200	199	0	Running	15,850	130	0
1992	Jun 21	Miller Genuine Draft 400	12	5	200	200	0	Running	25,760	155	0
	Aug 16	Champion Spark Plug 400	11	36	200	55	0	DNF - Crash	13,765	55	0
1993	Jun 20	Miller Genuine Draft 400	2	1	200	200	19	Running	77,890	180	5
	Aug 15	Champion Spark Plug 400	3	35	200	125	86	DNF - Engine	14,590	68	10
1994	Jun 19	Miller 400	6	4	200	200	0	Running	31,430	160	0
	Aug 21	Goodwrench 400	15	10	200	199	0	Running	17,940	134	0
1995	Jun 18	Miller 400	2	38	200	70	31	DNF - Crash	24,780	54	5
	Aug 20	Goodwrench 400	2	30	200	160	46	DNF - Engine	23,615	78	5
1996	Jun 23	Miller 400	14	31	200	195	5	Running	35,540	75	5
	Aug 18	Goodwrench 400	23	8	200	200	6	Running	35,465	147	5
1997	Jun 15	Miller 400	34	13	200	200	0	Running	33,750	124	0
	Aug 17	DeVilbiss 400	27	29	200	198	0	Running	30,915	76	0
1998	Jun 14	Miller Lite 400	9	37	200	195	0	Running	35,390	52	0
	Aug 16	Pepsi 400	19	13	200	199	0	Running	39,490	124	0
1999	Jun 13	Kmart 400	35	38	200	196	0	Running	28,780	49	0
	Aug 22	Pepsi 400	6	38	200	186	0	Running	27,640	49	0
2000	Jun 11	Kmart 400	2	12	194	194	40	Running	41,050	132	5
	Aug 20	Pepsi 400	4	2	200	200	42	Running	94,530	175	5
2001	Jun 10	Kmart 400	2	2	200	200	3	Running	123,257	175	5
	Aug 19	Pepsi 400	3	42	162	120	51	DNF - Engine	64,957	42	5

Rudd started on the outside pole at Michigan twice since joining Robert Yates Racing. He also has two runner-up finishes in the No. 28 Ford.

Nashville Speedway USA

The banked .596-mile Nashville Speedway offered more proof of Rudd's innate short-track talents. He raced at the Tennessee track 12 times, finishing in the Top 10 eight times. Similar to his experience at Bristol and Martinsville, he achieved a comfort level at the track immediately. In his first three Nashville starts, he scored Top 10 finishes. In his fifth start, he won the pole and led half the race.

Before the track was removed from the Winston Cup Grand National schedule in 1984, Rudd claimed two poles, four front row starts and five Top 5 finishes. Interestingly, he finished only one race on the lead lap. Getting lapped was not an unusual phenomenon at Nashville. In the track's 25 Modern Era races, only 50 of the 737 drivers who started Nashville races ever finished on the lead lap. Eleven of those 25 races ended with the winner lapping the rest of the field.

Rudd's failure to win at Nashville wasn't unusual, either. Of the 134 drivers who took the green flag at the half-mile track during the Modern Era, only eight drivers ever visited Victory Lane. Darrell Waltrip and Cale Yarborough were especially jealous of Nashville's checkered flag, winning a combined 15 times. The two short-track geniuses also led a combined 6,326 of the track's 10,500 Modern Era laps.

In other words, Rudd's inability to get to Victory Lane at Nashville was a shared experience.

Nashville Stats Chart

Nashville Record Book - Modern Era (min. 5 starts)

Category	Rudd's Total	Rudd's Rank	Modern Era Nashville Leader
Money	$55,275	17th	Darrell Waltrip -- 238,120
Starts	12	16th	R. Petty, D. Waltrip -- 25
Total Points[1]	1,628	14th	Darrell Waltrip -- 3,241
Avg. Start	7.4	9th	Cale Yarborough -- 2.5
Avg. Finish	10.8	9th	Cale Yarborough -- 4.2
Wins	0	--	Darrell Waltrip -- 8
Winning Pct.	0.0	--	Cale Yarborough -- 43.8
Top 5s	5	7th	Darrell Waltrip -- 19
Top 10s	8	9th	Richard Petty -- 20
DNFs	2	41st	Richard Childress -- 11
Poles	2	5th	Darrell Waltrip -- 7
Front Row Starts	4	5th	Darrell Waltrip -- 9
Laps Led	246	10th	Cale Yarborough -- 3,633
Pct. Laps Led	4.9	11th	Cale Yarborough -- 54.1
Races Led	2	10th	Darrell Waltrip -- 20
Times Led	4	11th	Darrell Waltrip -- 40
Times Led Most Laps	1	4th	Cale Yarborough -- 11
Bonus Points[1]	15	9th	D. Waltrip, C. Yarborough -- 130
Laps Completed	4,689	15th	Richard Petty -- 10,019
Pct. Laps Completed	93.0	7th	Cale Yarborough -- 96.7
Points per Race[1]	135.7	11th	Cale Yarborough -- 173.4
Lead-Lap Finishes	1	8th	Darrell Waltrip -- 12

[1]—Since implementation of current point system in 1975

Memorable Nashville Moment

1981 Melling Tool 420—Driving the No. 88 Gatorade Chevy, Rudd won his first Nashville pole, then led the first 210 laps of the 420-lap race. He gave up the lead on 211 and eventually finished fifth. It marked the first time in Rudd's career that he led the most laps in an event. But as impressive as his run was, it was neither a track record nor, in term of miles led to start a race, a personal best. In 1978, Cale Yarborough led all 420 laps at Nashville to win the Music City USA 420. From a personal standpoint, Rudd had a better start at Talladega when he started on the outside pole for the 1992 DieHard 500 and led the first 50 laps. In terms of distance, his Talladega lead lasted 133 miles, while his 1981 Nashville lead lasted 125 miles.

Nashville Performance Chart

Nashville Speedway USA
Nashville, Tenn. — .596 miles

Year	Date	Race	St.	Fin.	Total Laps	Laps Completed	Laps Led	Condition	Money	Pts	Bonus Pts.
1977	May 7	Music City USA 420	12	10	420	401	0	Running	$1,815	134	0
	Jun 16	Nashville 420	17	10	420	404	0	Running	1,565	134	0
1979	May 12	Sun-Drop Music City USA 420	12	10	420	410	0	Running	1,850	134	0
1980	Jul 12	Busch Nashville 420	9	28	420	164	0	DNF - Engine	640	79	0
1981	May 9	Melling Tool 420	1	5	420	419	210	Running	7,375	165	10
	Jul 11	Busch Nashville 420	2	4	420	419	0	Running	7,450	160	0
1982	May 8	Cracker Barrel 420	8	19	420	393	0	DNF - Engine	1,885	106	0
	Jul 10	Busch Nashville 420	16	4	420	419	0	Running	5,360	160	0
1983	May 7	Marty Robbins 420	3	14	420	410	0	Running	2,540	121	0
	Jul 16	Busch Nashville 420	6	5	420	417	0	Running	4,770	155	0
1984	May 12	Coors 420	2	4	420	420	0	Running	10,450	160	0
	Jul 14	Pepsi 420	1	16	420	413	36	Running	9,575	120	5

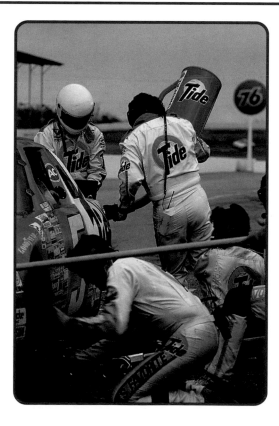

Rudd's crew tends to the No. 5 Tide car during the TranSouth 500 at Darlington.

New Hampshire International Speedway

Ricky Rudd's flat-track success at Martinsville transferred immediately to New Hampshire International Speedway. The level 1-mile track joined the Winston Cup circuit in 1993, Rudd's final season with Hendrick Motorsports. He showed early flare on the New England oval, finishing in the Top 5 in each of its first three events. In 1994, he earned his first victory as a car owner at New Hampshire.

After his quick start, Rudd went into something of a slide. During a five-race stretch between 1997 and 1999, while his self-owned team slowly imploded, his NHIS performances slipped. He failed to finish inside of the Top 10 and, thanks to wrecks, ended in 42nd place twice. New Hampshire is the only track where Rudd has finished 42nd or worse more than once.

Since joining Robert Yates Racing, his consistent presence among the leaders has returned. Following a 10th-place finish in the No. 28 Ford in the first New Hampshire race in 2000, he enjoyed consecutive 3rd-place runs. In the second of those efforts—the 2001 New England 300—he led 61 laps near the end of the race before being passed by teammate Dale Jarrett with four laps to go.

New Hampshire Stats Chart

New Hampshire Record Book - All-Time (min. 5 starts)

Category	Rudd's Total	Rudd's Rank	All-Time New Hampshire Leader
Money	$819,194	7th	Jeff Gordon -- 1,367,044
Starts	14	T-1st	15 Others with 14 Starts
Total Points	1,787	7th	Mark Martin -- 2,043
Avg. Start	19.4	16th	Ken Schrader -- 7.8
Avg. Finish	13.7	9th	Tony Stewart -- 7.7
Wins	1	3rd	Jeff Burton -- 4
Winning Pct.	7.1	5th	Jeff Burton -- 28.6
Top 5s	6	4th	Jeff Gordon -- 8
Top 10s	9	4th	Mark Martin -- 11
DNFs	2	11th	J. Andretti, T. Labonte -- 5
Poles	0	--	Jeff Gordon -- 4
Front Row Starts	1	8th	Jeff Gordon -- 6
Laps Led	123	11th	Jeff Gordon -- 912
Pct. Laps Led	2.9	12th	Jeff Gordon -- 21.9
Races Led	3	13	Jeff Gordon -- 10
Times Led	7	8th	Jeff Gordon -- 30
Times Led Most Laps	0	--	Jeff Gordon -- 5
Bonus Points	15	14th	Jeff Gordon -- 75
Laps Completed	3,927	9th	(Mark Martin -- 4,156)
Pct. Laps Completed	94.1	20th	Tony Stewart -- 99.8
Points per Race	127.6	9th	Tony Stewart -- 151.3
Lead-Lap Finishes	9	5th	Mark Martin -- 12

Memorable New Hampshire Moment

1994 Slick 50 300—In one of the most exciting NASCAR races ever run at New Hampshire, Rudd survived a multlap side-by-side battle with Dale Earnhardt to win for the first time as a Winston Cup car owner. Rudd raced his own cars beginning in 1994 after a four-year stint with Hendrick Motorsports. His NHIS victory came in his 16th race as an independent. Crew chief Bill Ingle made the call that contributed to Rudd's win, instructing the Tide crew to put two fresh tires on the No. 10 Ford rather than four. Given improved track position, Rudd ducked under leader Earnhardt with six laps to go. The fact that the two long-time rivals raced close without taking each other out was further confirmation that their late-1980s slugfest was over. Earnhardt and Rudd had taken turns putting each other in the wall or ruining each other's victorious runs. At Richmond in 1991, they appeared to bury the hatchet in another close battle that Earnhardt ended up winning. At New Hampshire, it was Rudd who emerged as the winner.

New Hampshire Performance Chart

New Hampshire International Speedway
Loudon, N.H. — 1.058 miles — 12° banking

Year	Date	Race	St.	Fin.	Total Laps	Laps Completed	Laps Led	Condition	Money	Pts	Bonus Pts.
1993	Jul 11	Slick 50 300	10	5	300	300	0	Running	$25,375	155	0
1994	Jul 10	Slick 50 300	3	1	300	300	55	Running	91,875	180	5
1995	Jul 9	Slick 50 300	7	5	300	300	0	Running	35,125	155	0
1996	Jul 14	Jiffy Lube 300	20	3	300	300	6	Running	49,825	170	5
1997	Jul 13	Jiffy Lube 300	18	9	300	300	0	Running	38,325	138	0
	Sep 14	CMT 300	37	42	300	233	0	DNF - Crash	37,400	37	0
1998	Jul 12	Jiffy Lube 300	33	19	300	299	0	Running	48,400	106	0
	Aug 30	New Hampshire 300	35	10	300	300	0	Running	59,500	134	0
1999	Jul 11	Jiffy Lube 300	26	27	300	298	0	Running	48,000	82	0
	Sep 19	Dura-Lube/Kmart 300	33	42	300	125	0	DNF - Crash	39,775	37	0
2000	Jul 9	Jiffy Lube 300	14	10	273	273	0	Running	68,925	134	0
	Sep 17	New Hampshire 300	19	3	300	300	0	Running	94,950	165	0
2001	Jul 22	New England 300	14	3	300	300	62	Running	105,097	170	5
	Nov 23	New Hampshire 300	2	13	300	299	0	Running	76,622	124	0

Rudd has one victory at New Hampshire. Here he battles Chad Little during the 1997 Jiffy Lube 300.

Since joining the powerful Robert Yates Racing team, Rudd has finished third at New Hampshire two times.

North Carolina Speedway

Ricky Rudd started his NASCAR career at North Carolina Speedway in 1975 as an 18-year-old without stock car experience. A go-kart and motorcross champion looking for a sustainable racing career, he purchased a ride in Bill Champion's Ford. When Rudd finished a solid 11th (after starting 26th), he gave the first indication that talent, not family fortune, would continue his racing career.

Though a racer never forgets his first race track, Rudd has tried to put "Rockingham" out of his mind on more than one occasion. The banked 1-mile oval has shown little sentimentality toward the Chesapeake, Virginia, native. Rudd has more DNFs at The Rock than at any other track. After his career-launching start in 1975, he failed to finish 11 of his next 20 NCS races.

His consecutive crashes in Rockingham's two 1979 races indicate just how much NASCAR history Rudd has witnessed during his long career. In the 1979 spring race, he got caught up in a Donnie Allison-Cale Yarborough wreck just after the drop of the green flag. Rockingham was the first race following the famous 1979 Daytona 500 race that ended with the Allisons and Yarborough fighting on the apron grass near Turn 3. Donnie Allison and Yarborough wrecked each other on the backstretch going for the Daytona 500 win. Bobby Allison, nearly a lap down, came back around and joined in the brawl to help his brother. At Rockingham, in his first chance following Daytona, Donnie Allison took out his frustrations by spinning Yarborough in Turn 3. Rudd was the innocent victim, getting collected in the melee. He had qualified 6th—then a career best—but saw his hopes dashed after just nine laps. Later in 1979, when the series returned to Rockingham, Rudd was involved in a crash with another Allison—this time Bobby—and ended the race back in 20th.

Even when his finishes became more consistent starting in 1988, Rudd never found the same strength of performance he had on other 1-mile and short tracks on the circuit. He broke through in 1996 to win his first Rockingham race. However, in the 28 events between 1988 and 2001, he managed just 13 Top 10s and suffered eight finishes outside of the Top 20. Though finishing has been difficult, Rudd has had success qualifying at the Rock; he has three poles and six front row starts.

Memorable Rockingham Moments

1989 Goodwrench 500—In an early skirmish in his war with Dale Earnhardt, Rudd crashed while trying to put Earnhardt a lap down with 130 laps to go. The race leader for 104 laps, Rudd tried repeatedly to make his pass on the No. 3 car. Earnhardt ignored the move-over flag from NASCAR and continued to block Rudd's every move. Coming out of Turn 2, Rudd got inside of Earnhardt but was hit when Earnhardt attempted to block him. The contact sent Rudd's car spinning into the inside wall where he was plowed into by Harry Gant, who was following close behind. As a result of the mishap, Rudd dropped 42 laps off the pace and finished 32nd. Earnhardt, meanwhile, never fell a lap down and ended the race in 3rd. The two drivers continued to trade shots until 1991.

Longevity Record Watch

Rockingham Starts / Rockingham Laps Completed

Driver	No. of Starts	Driver	Laps Completed
Dave Marcis	61	Darrell Waltrip	24,031
Darrell Waltrip	56	Dave Marcis	22,960
Richard Petty	54	Richard Petty	21,626
Ricky Rudd	49	Ricky Rudd	19,365
Terry Labonte	46	Terry Labonte	19,154

Rockingham Stats Chart

Rockingham Record Book - All-Time (min. 5 starts)

Category	Rudd's Total	Rudd's Rank	All-Time Rockingham Leader
Money	$1,033,430	7th	Rusty Wallace -- 1,167,735
Starts	49	4th	Dave Marcis -- 61
Total Points[1]	5,806	4th	Darrell Waltrip -- 6,443
Avg. Start	10.7	15th	Jeff Gordon -- 6.1
Avg. Finish	16.5	30th	Tony Stewart -- 7.7
Wins	1	15th	Richard Petty -- 11
Winning Pct.	2.0	29th	Jeff Gordon -- 22.2
Top 5s	12	9th	B. Allison, R. Petty -- 23
Top 10s	19	8th	Darrell Waltrip -- 29
DNFs	14	7th	Buddy Baker -- 25
Poles	3	6th	M. Martin, K. Petty, D. Pearson, C. Yarborough -- 5
Front Row Starts	6	6th	Richard Petty -- 11
Laps Led	478	19th	Cale Yarborough -- 3,733
Pct. Laps Led	2.1	43rd	Cale Yarborough -- 18.9
Races Led	17	8th	Richard Petty -- 32
Times Led	38	15th	Cale Yarborough -- 131
Times Led Most Laps	0	--	Cale Yarborough -- 11
Bonus Points[1]	85	11th	R. Petty, C. Yarborough -- 200
Laps Completed	19,365	4th	Darrell Waltrip -- 24,031
Pct. Laps Completed	84.9	46th	Tony Stewart -- 99.9
Points per Race[1]	118.5	25th	Tony Stewart -- 145.2
Lead-Lap Finishes	12	6th	D. Earnhardt, R. Petty -- 16

[1] -- Since implementation of current point system in 1975

Rockingham Performance Chart

North Carolina Speedway
Rockingham, N.C. — 1.017 miles — 22-25° banking

Year	Date	Race	St.	Fin.	Total Laps	Laps Completed	Laps Led	Condition	Money	Pts	Bonus Pts.
1975	Mar 2	Carolina 500	26	11	492	436	0	Running	$2,000	130	0
1977	Mar 13	Carolina 500	19	19	492	396	0	DNF - Engine	970	106	0
	Oct 23	American 500	16	25	492	234	0	DNF - Engine	920	88	0
1978	Oct 22	American 500	6	25	492	262	0	DNF - Engine	2,225	88	0
1979	Mar 4	Carolina 500	6	34	492	9	0	DNF - Crash	1,030	61	0
	Oct 21	American 500	13	20	492	420	0	DNF - Crash	2,480	103	0
1980	Mar 9	Carolina 500	11	12	492	472	0	Running	3,640	127	0
1981	Mar 1	Carolina 500	5	31	492	224	1	DNF - Crash	6,045	75	5
	Nov 1	American 500	3	18	492	434	16	Running	7,000	114	5
1982	Mar 28	Warner W. Hodgdon Carolina 500	10	15	492	437	0	Running	3,960	118	0
	Oct 31	Warner W. Hodgdon American 500	6	28	492	242	0	DNF - Engine	2,610	79	0
1983	Mar 13	Warner W. Hodgdon Carolina 500	1	6	492	489	30	Running	8,465	155	5
	Oct 30	Warner W. Hodgdon American 500	8	3	492	491	57	Running	11,370	170	5
1984	Mar 4	Warner W. Hodgdon Carolina 500	3	7	492	488	0	Running	11,415	146	0
	Oct 21	Warner W. Hodgdon American 500	21	23	492	389	0	DNF - Engine	9,950	94	0
1985	Mar 3	Carolina 500	3	32	492	162	0	DNF - Engine	7,975	67	0
	Oct 20	Nationwise 500	9	7	492	492	0	Running	11,150	146	0
1986	Mar 2	Goodwrench 500	14	28	492	315	0	DNF - Engine	9,715	79	0
	Oct 19	Nationwise 500	4	2	492	492	0	Running	26,550	170	0
1987	Mar 1	Goodwrench 500	5	2	492	492	70	Running	28,135	175	5
	Oct 25	AC-Delco 500	7	31	492	342	3	DNF - Engine	9,985	75	5
1988	Mar 6	Goodwrench 500	3	17	492	487	0	Running	7,120	112	0
	Oct 23	AC-Delco 500	9	2	492	492	8	Running	26,985	175	5
1989	Mar 5	Goodwrench 500	11	32	492	450	104	Running	5,825	72	5
	Oct 22	AC-Delco 500	8	28	492	456	66	Running	10,700	84	5
1990	Mar 4	GM Goodwrench 500	25	31	492	302	15	DNF - Oil Pan	6,600	75	5
	Oct 21	AC-Delco 500	11	7	492	491	0	Running	10,925	146	0
1991	Mar 3	GM Goodwrench 500	5	4	492	491	0	Running	20,250	160	0
	Oct 20	AC-Delco 500	5	12	492	489	0	Running	13,800	127	0
1992	Mar 1	GM Goodwrench 500	23	28	492	437	0	Running	12,950	79	0
	Oct 25	AC-Delco 500	7	3	492	491	0	Running	31,225	165	0
1993	Feb 28	GM Goodwrench 500	12	12	492	490	0	Running	15,735	127	0
	Oct 24	AC-Delco 500	5	14	492	490	0	Running	15,350	121	0
1994	Feb 27	Goodwrench 500	34	11	492	489	0	Running	12,885	130	0
	Oct 23	AC-Delco 500	1	4	492	492	2	Running	28,076	165	5
1995	Feb 26	Goodwrench 500	2	4	492	492	3	Running	33,480	165	5
	Oct 22	AC-Delco 400	7	13	393	392	0	Running	21,950	124	0
1996	Feb 25	Goodwrench 400	25	4	393	393	3	Running	35,810	165	5
	Oct 20	AC-Delco 400	2	1	393	393	81	Running	90,025	180	5
1997	Feb 23	Goodwrench Service 400	10	4	393	393	0	Running	39,210	160	0
	Oct 27	AC-Delco 400	13	40	393	241	0	DNF - Crash	26,550	43	0
1998	Feb 22	Goodwrench Service Plus 400	30	43	393	90	0	DNF - Engine	30,615	34	0
	Nov 1	AC-Delco 400	7	10	393	393	0	Running	43,150	134	0
1999	Feb 21	Dura-Lube/Big Kmart 400	1	30	393	389	3	Running	38,325	78	5
	Oct 24	Pop Secret Popcorn 400	15	19	393	391	0	Running	36,150	106	0
2000	Feb 27	Dura-Lube/Kmart 400	2	6	393	392	0	Running	47,010	150	0
	Oct 22	Pop Secret Popcorn 400	13	3	393	393	13	Running	65,300	170	5
2001	Feb 25	Dura-Lube 400	4	39	393	355	3	Running	63,462	51	5
	Nov 4	Pop Secret Popcorn 400	37	8	393	393	0	Running	75,572	142	0

Rudd leads the field to the green flag at Rockingham in 1999. He has three poles at the 1-mile track.

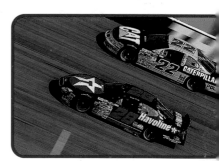

Rudd battles Ward Burton (No. 22) on Rockingham's high banks during the Pop Secret Popcorn 400 in October of 2000.

North Wilkesboro Speedway

Even more than Bristol, North Wilkesboro Speedway witnessed some of the most intense chase scenes in Ricky Rudd's career. He pursued victories and bad guys with equal gusto at the now-defunct .626-mile track. And though he never snagged a win, he got into a few classic showdowns with his fellow competitors.

For a good chunk of his career, no track was as friendly to Rudd as North Wilkesboro. During a 14-race streak starting in 1983 and ending in 1990, he finished ninth or better 13 times. Though the track ranks 12th in his career in terms of the number of starts, it ranks 6th in terms of Top 10s.

Rudd's consistent excellence at North Wilkesboro usually took a back seat to his on-track brawls, however, especially with the late Dale Earnhardt. Their combat escalated in the 1988 Holly Farms 400, a race the two drivers dominated (leading a combined 304 laps). Rudd got things started by tapping Earnhardt out of the way with 40 laps to go and retaking the lead. But Rudd soon learned a fact of NASCAR life: if you messed with Earnhardt, he had to be removed completely from the race. Or else. Within a lap of the initial tap, Earnhardt recovered and returned the favor by spinning Rudd and taking him out of the lead. NASCAR flagged both drivers, pushing them to the back of the field. On the final lap, however, they battled again, with Earnhardt crossing the line in sixth place. Rudd finished seventh. After the race, NASCAR fined Rudd $6,000 for rough driving.

The Rudd-Earnhardt clash became more relevant in 1989, when last-lap contact took both drivers out. For Rudd, it prevented a first North Wilkesboro win. For Earnhardt, however, it caused a dramatic points swing that prevented him from winning his fourth Winston Cup title.

Rudd didn't confine his battles to Earnhardt, of course. In 1990, his periodic battles with Derrike Cope included a showdown at North Wilkesboro. While riding among the leaders, Rudd gave Cope a tap, though he was down a lap at the time. Cope, already out of the running and with nothing to lose, retaliated by putting Rudd into the wall. Rudd fell to 11th in the final running order.

Rudd had a similar back-and-forth fight with Brett Bodine. In the 1991 First Union 400, he took out Bodine while Bodine was in the lead. Two years later, after Bodine wrecked Rudd at Bristol, Rudd took a swing at Bodine in the garage area at North Wilkesboro. Bodine had just qualified for the pole for the 1993 First Union 400 when Rudd approached him to talk about the Bristol incident. Rudd threatened to put Bodine in the wall and then threw a punch.

The hard-nosed Rudd showed his toughness on every Winston Cup track, but few have highlighted his combativeness like North Wilkesboro.

North Wilkesboro Stats Chart

North Wilkesboro Record Book - Modern Era (min. 5 starts)

Category	Rudd's Total	Rudd's Rank	Modern Era North Wilkesboro Leader
Money	$415,675	10th	Dale Earnhardt -- 853,685
Starts	36	4th	Dave Marcis -- 46
Total Points[1]	4,987	4th	Darrell Waltrip -- 6,375
Avg. Start	11.1	17th	Cale Yarborough -- 3.9
Avg. Finish	10.1	8th	Cale Yarborough -- 5.7
Wins	0	--	Darrell Waltrip -- 10
Winning Pct.	0.0	--	Cale Yarborough -- 31.3
Top 5s	11	10th	Dale Earnhardt -- 21
Top 10s	23	5th	Dale Earnhardt -- 32
DNFs	4	15th	J.D. McDuffie -- 16
Poles	1	15th	Darrell Waltrip -- 9
Front Row Starts	4	9th	Darrell Waltrip -- 13
Laps Led	653	9th	Darrell Waltrip -- 2,923
Pct. Laps Led	4.5	14th	Cale Yarborough -- 25.2
Races Led	9	10th	D. Earnhardt, D. Waltrip -- 24
Times Led	19	10th	Darrell Waltrip -- 65
Times Led Most Laps	2	7th	Darrell Waltrip -- 8
Bonus Points[1]	55	9th	Darrell Waltrip -- 160
Laps Completed	12,987	6th	Darrell Waltrip -- 17,370
Pct. Laps Completed	90.2	39th	Ken Schrader -- 99.2
Points per Race[1]	138.5	8th	Cale Yarborough -- 158.3
Lead-Lap Finishes	14	4th	Dale Earnhardt -- 22

[1]—Since implementation of current point system in 1975

North Wilkesboro Performance Chart

North Wilkesboro Speedway
Wilkesboro, N.C. — .625 miles — 14° banking

Year	Date	Race	St.	Fin.	Total Laps	Laps Completed	Laps Led	Condition	Money	Pts	Bonus Pts.
1975	Apr 6	Gwyn Staley Memorial	22	28	400	3	0	DNF - Crash	$345	79	0
1977	Oct 2	Wilkes 400	14	7	400	388	0	Running	2,730	146	0
1979	Mar 25	Northwestern Bank 400	9	14	400	392	0	Running	1,945	121	0
	Oct 14	Holly Farms 400	8	5	400	398	0	Running	3,325	155	0
1981	Apr 5	Northwestern Bank 400	4	6	400	399	0	Running	6,550	150	0
	Oct 4	Holly Farms 400	15	25	400	112	0	DNF - Crash	5,085	88	0
1982	Apr 18	Northwestern Bank 400	7	9	400	398	0	Running	3,525	138	0
	Oct 3	Holly Farms 400	4	25	400	67	0	DNF - Engine	1,260	88	0
1983	Apr 17	Northwestern Bank 400	7	27	400	59	0	DNF - Crash	1,875	82	0
	Oct 2	Holly Farms 400	3	6	400	399	1	Running	4,675	155	5
1984	Apr 8	Northwestern Bank 400	1	3	400	400	290	Running	22,190	175	10
	Oct 14	Holly Farms 400	8	6	400	400	0	Running	9,475	150	0
1985	Apr 21	Northwestern Bank 400	13	4	400	400	0	Running	9,870	160	0
	Sep 29	Holly Farms 400	2	5	400	399	0	Running	9,500	155	0
1986	Apr 20	First Union 400	14	2	400	400	102	Running	20,075	175	5
	Sep 28	Holly Farms 400	7	7	400	399	0	Running	9,300	146	0
1987	Apr 5	First Union 400	11	5	400	399	0	Running	14,890	155	0
	Oct 4	Holly Farms 400	12	13	400	397	0	Running	8,720	124	0
1988	Apr 17	First Union 400	7	2	400	400	3	Running	21,025	175	5
	Oct 16	Holly Farms 400	4	7	400	400	154	Running	10,025	156	10
1989	Apr 16	First Union 400	8	6	400	400	0	Running	7,475	150	0
	Oct 15	Holly Farms 400	5	9	400	400	0	Running	8,630	138	0
1990	Apr 22	First Union 400	8	4	400	400	0	Running	12,775	160	0
	Sep 30	Tyson/Holly Farms 400	15	11	400	399	0	Running	6,650	130	0
1991	Apr 21	First Union 400	11	11	400	399	0	Running	10,175	130	0
	Sep 29	Tyson/Holly Farms 400	22	12	400	399	0	Running	9,950	127	0
1992	Apr 12	First Union 400	2	3	400	400	0	Running	23,465	165	0
	Oct 5	Tyson/Holly Farms 400	5	15	400	396	0	Running	12,275	118	0
1993	Apr 18	First Union 400	10	7	400	400	0	Running	14,960	146	0
	Oct 3	Tyson/Holly Farms 400	2	5	400	399	23	Running	21,235	160	5
1994	Apr 17	First Union 400	25	6	400	400	5	Running	8,390	155	5
	Oct 2	Tyson 400	26	11	400	397	0	Running	13,550	130	0
1995	Apr 9	First Union 400	12	29	400	392	0	Running	19,215	76	0
	Oct 1	Tyson 400	24	5	400	400	58	Running	31,640	160	5
1996	Apr 14	First Union 400	33	15	400	397	0	Running	24,140	118	0
	Sep 29	Tyson 400	21	7	400	400	17	Running	24,765	151	5

Before it was pushed off the Winston Cup schedule in 1996, Rudd had 11 Top 5s and 23 Top 10s at North Wilkesboro.

Phoenix International Raceway

Ricky Rudd can be forgiven if he reacts violently to the word "Phoenix." Since the oddly shaped 1-mile Arizona track joined the Winston Cup circuit in 1988, Rudd has been a consistently strong performer with consistently terrible luck. On four occasions, an apparent victory was foiled by circumstances:

• In the 1988 inaugural race, he led 183 laps and was cruising toward a sure victory when his engine failed with just 16 laps to go. The late Alan Kulwicki took advantage as Rudd slipped back to 26th. Rudd still holds the track record for most laps led in a single race without winning.

•In 1994, Rudd led 99 laps and appeared headed to victory when a broken air wrench on a late pit stop doomed his victory hopes. He finished seventh.

• Trying desperately to salvage his consecutive winning season streak at Phoenix in 1999, Rudd came on strong as the race reached its conclusion, climbing to third with 30 laps remaining. But during the race's final pit stop under caution, his crew stumbled through a 21-second stop. He dropped to seventh on the restart and managed to finish fifth. His 16-year winning streak ended two weeks later at Atlanta, where he finished seventh.

• Leading comfortably with 18 laps to go in the 2000 race, Rudd got caught up in a wreck involving the lapped cars of Mike Bliss and Rick Mast. The two drivers crashed while racing each other off of Turn 2. Rudd just happened to be the first car on the scene and had nowhere to go. He T-boned Bliss and hobbled to a 37th-place finish. It was one of five races in 2000 in which Rudd appeared to have victory in his grasp. He ended the season without a win.

Rudd resisted his ever-present bad luck in 1995 when he won the Dura-Lube 500. He set the record for lowest starting position for an eventual winner by starting the race in 29th. It also marked the lowest starting spot for any of Rudd's 22 career victories.

Phoenix Stats Chart

Phoenix Record Book - All-Time (min. 5 starts)

Category	Rudd's Total	Rudd's Rank	All-Time Phoenix Leader
Money	$537,452	4th	Mark Martin -- 688,636
Starts	14	T-1st	Eight Others with 14 Starts
Total Points	1,562	8th	Mark Martin -- 2,088
Avg. Start	13.4	8th	Rusty Wallace -- 4.9
Avg. Finish	18.9	18th	Alan Kulwicki -- 5.2
Wins	1	3rd	D. Allison, J. Burton -- 2
Winning Pct.	.7.1	7th	Davey Allison -- 40.0
Top 5s	3	8th	Mark Martin -- 7
Top 10s	5	8th	Mark Martin -- 11
DNFs	2	12th	Dick Trickle -- 5
Poles	0	--	Rusty Wallace -- 3
Front Row Starts	0	--	Rusty Wallace -- 5
Laps Led	387	3rd	Rusty Wallace -- 868
Pct. Laps Led	9.0	7th	Rusty Wallace -- 20.1
Races Led	5	3rd	Rusty Wallace -- 10
Times Led	10	6th	Rusty Wallace -- 24
Times Led Most Laps	1	4th	Rusty Wallace -- 3
Bonus Points	30	3rd	Rusty Wallace -- 65
Laps Completed	4,192	3rd	Terry Labonte -- 4,307
Pct. Laps Completed	97.2	14th	Alan Kulwicki -- 100.0
Points per Race	111.6	16th	Alan Kulwicki -- 160.0
Lead-Lap Finishes	4	12th	Mark Martin -- 12

Memorable Phoenix Moments

1995 Dura-Lube 500—Rudd overcame a poor qualifying effort to claim his first Phoenix victory. The 39-year-old veteran started the race in 29th, but overwhelmed the field late in the race to grab the win. He was in 6th place with 31 laps to go on a restart. Within eight laps, he moved into the lead and led the remaining 23 circuits. With his victory, he extended his consecutive winning season streak to 13 years. The 1995 Phoenix race was the next-to-last event of the season, qualifying it as the second closest call in his efforts to keep the streak alive. In 1985, the streak's third season, he waited until the final race at Riverside before winning.

Overcoming the Odds

In 1995, Ricky Rudd set the Phoenix track record for worst start by an eventual race winner.

Driver	Year	Starting Pos.
Ricky Rudd	1995	29
Alan Kulwicki	1988	21
Terry Labonte	1994	19
Bobby Hamilton	1996	17

Phoenix Performance Chart

Phoenix International Raceway
Phoenix, Ariz. — 1.0 mile — 9-11° banking

Year	Date	Race	St.	Fin.	Total Laps	Laps Completed	Laps Led	Condition	Money	Pts	Bonus Pts.
1988	Nov 6	Checker Auto Parts 500	4	26	312	296	183	DNF - Engine	$17,350	95	10
1989	Nov 5	Autoworks 500	11	29	312	272	1	DNF - Radiator	10,930	81	5
1990	Nov 4	Checker Auto Parts 500	9	32	312	293	0	Running	5,780	67	0
1991	Nov 3	Pyroil 500	14	11	312	311	0	Running	13,250	130	0
1992	Nov 1	Pyroil 500K	4	30	312	288	0	Running	12,885	73	0
1993	Oct 31	Slick 50 500	4	6	312	312	0	Running	21,120	150	0
1994	Oct 30	Slick 50 300	4	7	312	311	99	Running	20,220	151	5
1995	Oct 29	Dura-Lube 500K	29	1	312	312	63	Running	78,260	180	5
1996	Oct 27	Dura-Lube 500K	3	14	312	311	0	Running	26,855	121	0
1997	Nov 2	Dura-Lube 500	39	36	312	308	0	Running	26,495	55	0
1998	Oct 25	Dura-Lube 500	21	27	257	254	0	Running	31,895	82	0
1999	Nov 7	Checker Auto Parts/Dura-Lube 500	7	5	312	312	0	Running	86,240	155	0
2000	Nov 5	Checker Auto Parts/Dura-Lube 500	17	37	312	300	41	Running	46,375	57	5
2001	Oct 28	Checker Auto Parts/Dura-Lube 500	21	3	312	312	0	Running	139,797	165	0

Phoenix has been a tough-luck track for Rudd. On four separate occasions, he has seen bad luck take away apparent victories.

Rudd's lone Phoenix win came in 1995. After starting 29th, he led 63 laps en route to the win.

Pocono Raceway

Ricky Rudd's relationship with Pocono Raceway goes way back. Driving for Junie Donlavey, Rudd participated in the fourth Winston Cup race ever run on the 2.5-mile track, back in 1979. When he finished that race in fifth place, it marked the first time he had finished on the lead lap.

Rudd has been in the line-up for every Pocono race since then. His 45 starts are a track record, though Rudd has done more than just show up. He's made Pocono one of his best big tracks. In his first 16 starts, he finished 10th or better 11 times. His nine Top 5s match his best performance on any Winston Cup track longer than 1.5 miles. In 2001, he picked up his first Pocono victory and passed Darrell Waltrip as the track's all-time leader in championship points earned. Heading into 2002, Rudd had collected 5,319 point at Pocono, topping Waltrip's 5,286.

Truth be told, Waltrip owes Rudd a few of his points. In 1979, Waltrip crashed his DiGard Racing Chevy beyond repair in practice and was in need of an intact car to run the race. At the time, Waltrip was the series points leader. Missing a race was not an option. He negotiated and purchased a ride in Rudd's family-owned Chevy and was officially driving the No. 22 Al Rudd Chevrolet when the green flag flew on the Coca-Cola 500. Waltrip nearly won the race, but was done in by NASCAR's decision to allow the event to end under caution. Waltrip ended up in seventh place. He eventually lost the championship race by 11 points to Richard Petty, who won his seventh and final Winston Cup title.

Rudd made history of his own at Pocono in 1986, when he and Tim Richmond closed the Summer 500 with a photo finish. Richmond led Rudd by two-tenths of a second coming off of Turn 3 on the final lap, before Rudd was able to pull even down the long frontstretch in his Bud Moore Thunderbird. Unfortunately, Rudd didn't have quite enough to get by. Richmond won the race by five-hundredths, or .05, of a second, the closest finish in Pocono history.

Memorable Pocono Moment

2001 Pocono 500—For the first time in his long career, Rudd won a race after starting on the pole. He achieved that mark in his 721st career start. He earned the victory by making a cool three-wide pass on race leader Dale Jarrett and Dale Earnhardt Jr. (who was a lap down) as they headed into Pocono's treacherous tunnel turn with 24 laps to go. Rudd pulled away to a 1.1-second win over Jarrett. The victory was Rudd's first in nearly three years (89 races), his first in 44 Pocono starts and his first with Robert Yates Racing. He and the No. 28 crew had endured seven near-wins in 2000 and 2001 before finding the right combination at Pocono. It was the 28 car's first visit to Victory Lane since June of 1997, when Ernie Irvan drove to a win at Michigan.

Pocono Stats Chart

Pocono Record Book - All-Time (min. 5 starts)

Category	Rudd's Total	Rudd's Rank	All-Time Pocono Leader*
Money	$1,104,379	5th	Jeff Gordon -- 1,297,649
Starts	45	1st	(Darrell Waltrip -- 44)
Total Points[1]	5,319	1st	(Darrell Waltrip -- 5,286)
Avg. Start	11.2	13th	David Pearson -- 4.7
Avg. Finish	16.4	22nd	Tony Stewart -- 8.7
Wins	1	16th	B. Elliott, T. Richmond, R. Wallace, D. Waltrip -- 4
Winning Pct.	2.2	21st	Tim Richmond -- 28.6
Top 5s	9	9th	Mark Martin -- 15
Top 10s	20	4th	D. Earnhardt, M. Martin -- 22
DNFs	10	7th	Dave Marcis -- 15
Poles	1	13th	Ken Schrader -- 5
Front Row Starts	5	5th	Ken Schrader -- 8
Laps Led	132	24th	Geoffrey Bodine -- 809
Pct. Laps Led	1.5	31st	David Pearson -- 27.8
Races Led	12	16th	Dale Earnhardt -- 24
Times Led	17	22nd	Darrell Waltrip -- 106
Times Led Most Laps	0	--	Geoffrey Bodine -- 6
Bonus Points[1]	60	17th	Geoffrey Bodine -- 145
Laps Completed	7,722	2nd	Terry Labonte -- 7,889
Pct. Laps Completed	86.5	43rd	Tony Stewart -- 99.9
Points per Race[1]	118.2	25th	Jeff Gordon -- 148.3
Lead-Lap Finishes	19	7th	Mark Martin -- 24

[1] -- Since implementation of current point system in 1975

* -- Second-place driver listed in parentheses if Rudd is category leader

Pocono Longevity Record Watch (All-Time)

Pocono Starts		Pocono Laps Completed		Pocono Total Points (Since 1975)	
Driver	No. of Starts	Driver	Laps Completed	Driver	Total Points
Ricky Rudd	45	Terry Labonte	7,889	Ricky Rudd	5,319
Darrell Waltrip	44	Ricky Rudd	7,722	Darrell Waltrip	5,286
Terry Labonte	43	Darrell Waltrip	7,404	Dale Earnhardt	5,230
Dave Marcis	41	Kyle Petty	7,288	Terry Labonte	5,142
Dale Earnhardt	41	Bill Elliott	7,064	Bill Elliott	4,854

Pocono Performance Chart

Pocono Raceway
Long Pond, Penn. — 2.5 miles — 6-14° banking

Year	Date	Race	St.	Fin.	Total Laps	Laps Completed	Laps Led	Condition	Money	Pts	Bonus Pts.
1977	Jul 31	Coca-Cola 500	12	7	200	198	0	Running	$3,300	146	0
1978	Jul 30	Coca-Cola 500	17	6	200	197	0	Running	5,745	150	0
1979	Jul 30	Coca-Cola 500	6	5	200	200	0	Running	6,215	155	0
1980	Jul 27	Coca-Cola 500	10	10	200	196	0	Running	4,890	134	0
1981	Jul 26	Mountain Dew 500	7	6	200	199	0	Running	8,665	150	0
1982	Jul 6	Van Scoy Diamond Mine 500	15	6	200	199	0	Running	7,150	150	0
	Jul 25	Mountain Dew 500	3	31	200	62	0	DNF - Engine	2,050	70	0
1983	Jun 12	Van Scoy Diamond Mine 500	2	31	200	100	8	DNF - Engine	2,550	75	5
	Jul 24	Like Cola 500	6	7	200	200	0	Running	7,460	146	0
1984	Jun 10	Van Scoy Diamond Mine 500	14	18	200	197	0	Running	10,490	109	0
	Jul 22	Like Cola 500	21	39	200	23	0	DNF - Engine	9,675	46	0
1985	Jun 9	Van Scoy Diamond Mine 500	9	7	200	198	0	Running	12,130	146	0
	Jul 21	Summer 500	10	14	200	197	0	Running	9,765	121	0
1986	Jun 8	Miller High Life 500	14	4	200	200	3	Running	18,375	165	5
	Jul 20	Summer 500	13	2	150	150	0	Running	29,500	170	0
1987	Jun 14	Miller High Life 500	23	7	200	200	5	Running	14,825	151	5
	Jul 19	Summer 500	8	26	200	142	4	DNF - Engine	10,620	90	5
1988	Jun 19	Miller High Life 500	10	30	200	105	0	DNF - Engine	4,935	73	0
	Jul 24	AC Spark Plug 500	25	12	200	200	2	Running	7,875	132	5
1989	Jun 18	Miller High Life 500	13	20	200	197	0	Running	11,225	103	0
	Jul 23	AC Spark Plug 500	18	31	200	111	0	DNF - Engine	9,575	70	0
1990	Jun 17	Miller Genuine Draft 500	15	32	200	169	0	Running	6,275	67	0
	Jul 22	AC Spark Plug 500	13	7	200	200	0	Running	12,650	146	0
1991	Jun 16	Champion Spark Plug 500	4	20	200	199	16	Running	13,025	108	5
	Jul 21	Miller Genuine Draft 500	7	20	179	177	0	Running	12,725	103	0
1992	Jun 14	Champion Spark Plug 500	9	36	200	22	0	DNF - Engine	12,515	55	0
	Jul 19	Miller Genuine Draft 500	2	4	200	200	0	Running	24,695	160	0
1993	Jun 13	Champion Spark Plug 500	12	9	200	200	1	Running	15,765	143	5
	Jul 18	Miller Genuine Draft 500	3	11	200	200	0	Running	15,615	130	0
1994	Jun 12	UAW-GM 500	2	21	200	198	11	Running	10,850	105	5
	Jul 17	Miller 500	6	6	200	200	0	Running	17,260	150	0
1995	Jun 11	UAW-GM 500	4	13	200	200	0	Running	23,655	124	0
	Jul 16	Miller 500	13	3	200	200	0	Running	41,010	165	0
1996	Jun 16	UAW-GM 500	9	2	200	200	11	Running	52,900	175	5
	Jul 21	Miller 500	7	2	200	200	9	Running	56,615	175	5
1997	Jun 8	Pocono 500	6	21	200	199	0	Running	26,505	100	0
	Jul 20	Pennsylvania 500	19	36	200	192	0	Running	25,640	55	0
1998	Jun 21	Pocono 500	33	41	200	49	0	DNF - Engine	29,315	40	0
	Jul 26	Pennsylvania 500	13	42	200	136	0	DNF - Radiator	37,450	37	0
1999	Jun 20	Pocono 500	16	15	200	200	0	Running	46,355	118	0
	Jul 25	Pennsylvania 500	35	27	200	199	0	Running	36,565	82	0
2000	Jun 18	Pocono 500	3	3	200	200	0	Running	95,870	165	0
	Jul 23	Pennsylvania 500	14	38	200	111	0	DNF - Crash	35,150	49	0
2001	Jun 17	Pocono 500	1	1	200	200	39	Running	158,427	180	5
	Jul 29	Pennsylvania 500	2	11	200	200	23	Running	73,612	135	5

Rudd rushed back to his pits after sustaining a flat left-front tire during the 1999 Pennsylvania 500. He finished 15th.

Rudd holds the all-time Pocono record in starts and total points.

Richmond International Raceway

If there's anything like a home track for Ricky Rudd on Winston Cup circuit, Richmond International Raceway must be it. Judging by his performance at the current track and its predecessor, he has made himself at home. It's easy to see why: the track is a 90-minute drive from his hometown of Chesapeake.

Midway through the 1988 season, the former Richmond Fairgrounds Raceway, a .542-mile oval, was replaced by the current Richmond International Raceway, a .75-mile D-shaped oval. Rudd didn't seem to mind the switch. He won a race and a pole on the older, shorter track. In time, he won a pole and a race on the newer track. If anything, Rudd's performance became even more consistent after the new track opened.

Rudd stumbled in the new track's first race—falling to 26th with engine trouble—but quickly rebounded with an eight-race string of Top 8 finishes. Combined, the Richmond tracks account for more Top 5 finishes in Rudd's career than any other track. Since joining Robert Yates Racing, his results have returned to among the best in the series. In his first four Richmond races in the No. 28 Ford, he has three Top 10s and a victory.

Memorable Richmond Moments

1984 Miller High Life 400—Any arguments about Ricky Rudd's toughness begin and end with the 1984 Richmond spring race. Just two weeks after a tumbling wreck at Daytona in the Busch Clash—which left his face so swollen he used duct tape to help keep his blackened eyes open—he raced to victory on the .542-mile oval. Adding to the legend, Rudd beat one of the best short-track racers in history. He passed Darrell Waltrip with 20 laps to go and won by half a straightaway. It was his first victory at Richmond, and it gave him wins at both Virginia tracks.

2001 Chevrolet Monte Carlo 400—Severely underestimating the old man's willingness to trade paint, 25-year-old rookie Kevin Harvick booted Rudd out of the lead with 18 laps to go. Turned sideways on the backstretch, Rudd recovered quickly and, 12 laps later, taught the youngster the secret to doing it right: if you mess with a veteran, make sure to take him out completely. Or else. It was a lesson Rudd learned the hard way from Dale Earnhardt during their short-track wars in the late-1980s. Harvick, who took over the Goodwrench car after Earnhardt's fatal crash at Daytona, learned the same lesson with six laps to go. In a textbook move, Rudd approached Harvick in Turn 3 and knocked him out of the way as they exited Turn 4. Rudd got Harvick so loose, the rookie couldn't get back into contention. Rudd went on to an easy eight car-length victory over Harvick.

Richmond Stats Chart

Richmond Record Book - Modern Era (min. 5 starts)

Category	Rudd's Total	Rudd's Rank	Modern Era Richmond Leader
Money	$1,121,229	3rd	Rusty Wallace -- 1,279,150
Starts	46	4th	Darrell Waltrip -- 51
Total Points[1]	6,135	3rd	Darrell Waltrip -- 7,011
Avg. Start	14.7	32nd	Benny Parsons -- 5.2
Avg. Finish	12.1	14th	Tony Stewart -- 6.3
Wins	2	8th	B. Allison, R. Petty, R. Wallace, D. Waltrip -- 6
Winning Pct.	4.3	18th	Tony Stewart -- 33.3
Top 5s	19	5th	Dale Earnhardt -- 25
Top 10s	26	3rd	D. Earnhardt, D. Waltrip -- 33
DNFs	7	13th	J.D. McDuffie -- 12
Poles	2	9th	Bobby Allison -- 8
Front Row Starts	3	11th	Darrell Waltrip -- 14
Laps Led	762	9th	Rusty Wallace -- 3,024
Pct. Laps Led	4.2	19th	Rusty Wallace -- 21.
Races Led	15	7th	Darrell Waltrip -- 27
Times Led	35	6th	Rusty Wallace -- 76
Times Led Most Laps	2	7th	Rusty Wallace -- 9
Bonus Points[1]	85	7th	R. Wallace, D. Waltrip -- 165
Laps Completed	16,642	5th	Darrell Waltrip -- 18,741
Pct. Laps Completed	92.0	29th	Tony Stewart -- 100.0
Points per Race[1]	133.4	12th	Tony Stewart -- 155.2
Lead-Lap Finishes	21	3rd	D. Earnhardt, R. Wallace -- 25

[1] -- Since implementation of current point system in 1975

Richmond Longevity Record Watch (Modern Era)

Richmond Starts		Richmond Laps Completed	
Driver	No. of Starts	Driver	Laps Completed
Darrell Waltrip	51	Darrell Waltrip	18,741
Dave Marcis	50	Dave Marcis	18,706
Terry Labonte	47	Terry Labonte	17,146
Ricky Rudd	46	Dale Earnhardt	16,808
Dale Earnhardt	44	Ricky Rudd	16,642

Most Top 5s

Richmond has produced more Top 5 finishes in Ricky Rudd's career than any other Winston Cup track

Track	Top 5s
Richmond	19
Dover	14
Bristol	13
Martinsville	12
Rockingham	12

Richmond Performance Chart

Richmond International Raceway
Richmond, Va. — .75 miles — 14° banking

Year	Date	Race	St.	Fin.	Total Laps	Laps Completed	Laps Led	Condition	Money	Pts	Bonus Pts.
1977	Feb 27	Richmond 400	18	26	245	187	0	DNF - Rear End	$400	85	0
	Sep 11	Capital City 400	15	11	400	384	0	Running	2,540	130	0
1979	Mar 11	Richmond 400	15	11	400	390	0	Running	2,245	130	0
	Sep 9	Capital City 400	10	3	400	399	1	Running	5,650	170	5
1981	Feb 22	Richmond 400	8	2	400	400	7	Running	13,400	175	5
	Sep 13	Wrangler Sanfor-Set 400	12	12	400	392	0	Running	5,550	127	0
1982	Feb 21	Richmond 400	14	22	250	242	0	Running	2,450	97	0
	Sep 12	Wrangler Sanfor-Set 400	5	4	400	399	0	Running	7,930	160	0
1983	Feb 27	Richmond 400	1	28	400	177	26	DNF - Engine	3,615	84	5
	Sep 11	Wrangler Sanfor-Set 400	13	2	400	400	133	Running	19,025	175	5
1984	Feb 26	Miller High Life 400	4	1	400	400	36	Running	31,775	180	5
	Sep 9	Wrangler Sanfor-Set 400	4	2	400	400	68	Running	22,325	175	5
1985	Feb 24	Miller High Life 400	21	25	400	108	0	DNF - Engine	7,155	88	0
	Sep 8	Wrangler Sanfor-Set 400	3	5	400	400	53	Running	9,900	160	5
1986	Feb 23	Miller High Life 400	8	30	400	17	0	DNF - Crash	7,715	73	0
	Sep 7	Wrangler Jeans Indigo 400	8	24	400	350	113	DNF - Crash	8,235	101	10
1987	Mar 8	Miller High Life 400	8	28	400	143	0	DNF - Crash	8,215	79	0
	Sep 13	Wrangler Jeans Indigo 400	6	3	400	400	0	Running	20,050	165	0
1988	Feb 21	Pontiac Excitement 400	22	2	400	400	0	Running	25,660	170	0
	Sep 11	Miller High Life 400	12	26	400	349	14	DNF - Engine	5,010	90	5
1989	Mar 26	Pontiac Excitement 400	18	4	400	400	0	Running	13,600	160	0
	Sep 10	Miller High Life 400	7	4	400	399	0	Running	16,450	160	0
1990	Feb 25	Pontiac Excitement 400	1	3	400	400	40	Running	25,050	170	5
	Sep 9	Miller Genuine Draft 400	14	8	400	399	0	Running	8,350	142	0
1991	Feb 24	Pontiac Excitement 400	4	2	400	400	154	Running	45,675	180	10
	Sep 7	Miller Genuine Draft 400	7	5	400	400	1	Running	18,125	160	5
1992	Mar 8	Pontiac Excitement 400	27	6	400	400	0	Running	16,050	150	0
	Sep 12	Miller Genuine Draft 400	2	6	400	400	1	Running	18,205	155	5
1993	Mar 7	Pontiac Excitement 400	15	15	400	398	0	Running	13,035	118	0
	Sep 11	Miller Genuine Draft 400	17	4	400	400	0	Running	26,505	160	0
1994	Mar 6	Pontiac Excitement 400	34	18	400	398	0	Running	7,250	109	0
	Sep 10	Miller 400	32	5	400	400	0	Running	26,705	155	0
1995	Mar 5	Pontiac Excitement 400	30	21	400	395	0	Running	23,150	100	0
	Sep 9	Miller 400	12	8	400	399	0	Running	25,455	142	0
1996	Mar 3	Pontiac Excitement 400	34	9	400	400	0	Running	27,875	138	0
	Sep 7	Miller 400	37	12	400	399	0	Running	29,405	127	0
1997	Mar 26	Pontiac Excitement 400	6	6	400	399	0	Running	30,770	150	0
	Sep 6	Exide Batteries 400	35	28	400	395	0	Running	30,320	79	0
1998	Jun 6	Pontiac Excitement 400	26	11	400	400	0	Running	41,900	130	0
	Sep 12	Exide Batteries 400	25	34	400	383	0	Running	36,035	61	0
1999	May 15	Pontiac Excitement 400	9	36	400	345	0	Running	28,825	55	0
	Sep 11	Exide Batteries 400	31	27	400	396	0	Running	33,255	82	0
2000	May 6	Pontiac Excitement 400	6	4	400	400	0	Running	63,025	160	0
	Sep 9	Chevrolet Monte Carlo 400	26	9	400	400	0	Running	42,580	138	0
2001	May 5	Pontiac Excitement 400	3	5	400	400	27	Running	93,297	160	5
	Sep 8	Chevrolet Monte Carlo 400	9	1	400	400	88	Running	158,427	180	5

The second of Rudd's two Richmond wins came in the 2001 Chevrolet Monte Carlo 400.

Rudd's crew tends to the No. 28 Ford during the Chevrolet Monte Carlo 400 in September 2001.

Riverside International Raceway

During the first six years of Ricky Rudd's career, bare-bones budgets dictated the number of races in which he could compete. A 3,000-mile trip to California to race on a road course was never an option. Building a special car for a non-oval track and then transporting it and a crew across the country simply cost too much.

Consequently, Rudd's natural road course ability remained hidden until 1981, when he made his first start at Riverside International Raceway. Driving for the big-bucks, high-powered DiGard Racing team, he qualified third in his first attempt at right turns. In his second road course start, he recorded a Top 5. Two years later, in just his sixth non-oval start, he picked up his first-ever Winston Cup win.

Before the California track disappeared from NASCAR in 1988, it was one of Rudd's favorites. He won twice on the 2.63-mile track and finished in the Top 5 in half of his 16 starts. Of the 28 tracks he has competed on in 26 years of Winston Cup racing, none was better for qualifying. Rudd's average start was 5.9 at Riverside. In the track's final race—the Budweiser 400 in June 1988—Rudd won the pole with a track-record lap of 118.484. Because Riverside was ripped up shortly after it closed, that record will stand forever.

Riverside Stats Chart

Riverside Record Book - Modern Era (min. 5 starts)

Category	Rudd's Total	Rudd's Rank	Modern Era Riverside Leader
Money	$225,500	7th	Bobby Allison -- 390,350
Starts	16	20th	Bobby Allison -- 34
Total Points[1]	2,094	13th	Richard Petty -- 3,846
Avg. Start	5.9	4th	Cale Yarborough -- 3.8
Avg. Finish	13.8	17th	Cale Yarborough -- 7.4
Wins	2	7th	Bobby Allison -- 5
Winning Pct.	12.5	7th	Tim Richmond -- 28.6
Top 5s	8	8th	Bobby Allison -- 15
Top 10s	9	10th	Richard Petty -- 23
DNFs	4	38th	Hershel McGriff -- 19
Poles	1	7th	Darrell Waltrip -- 9
Front Row Starts	3	7th	Darrell Waltrip -- 15
Laps Led	147	9th	Bobby Allison -- 820
Pct. Laps Led	8.6	10th	Cale Yarborough -- 33.6
Races Led	9	6th	Bobby Allison -- 22
Times Led	18	8th	Bobby Allison -- 69
Times Led Most Laps	1	8th	Bobby Allison -- 8
Bonus Points[1]	50	7th	Bobby Allison -- 150
Laps Completed	1,395	20th	Bobby Allison -- 3,754
Pct. Laps Completed	81.5	28th	Jody Ridley -- 97.8
Points per Race[1]	130.9	10th	David Pearson -- 165.9
Lead-Lap Finishes	8	9th	Bobby Allison -- 18

[1] -- Since implementation of current point system in 1975

Memorable Riverside Moments

1983 Budweiser 400—In his 161st start, Rudd led the final 41 laps and picked up the first victory of his Winston Cup career. The win was also the first for his car owner, Richard Childress, who had never visited Victory Lane in his 13-year career as a driver. Rudd, who led a race-high 57 laps, passed Harry Gant on lap 54. He cruised to a seven-second victory over Bill Elliott.

1985 Winston Western 500—Though not obvious at the time, Rudd's victory at Riverside in the final race of the 1985 season helped save his 16-year consecutive winning season streak before it really got started. After wins in 1983 and 1984, Rudd endured a 56-race winless streak. He ended that stretch by passing Terry Labonte with 24 to go. He beat Labonte to the finish line by five car lengths. Over the next 13 years of Rudd's famous winning streak, he never again waited until the final race of the season.

Best Qualifying Tracks (min. 5 starts)

Rudd qualified better at Riverside than any other track in his Winston Cup career.

Track	Average Start
Riverside	5.9
Sears Point	6.7
Nashville	7.4
Watkins Glen	10.1
Martinsville	10.7

Riverside Performance Chart

Riverside International Raceway
Riverside, Calif. — 2.63 miles — Road Course

Year	Date	Race	St.	Fin.	Total Laps	Laps Completed	Laps Led	Condition	Money	Pts	Bonus Pts.
1981	Jan 11	Winston Western 500	3	19	119	98	19	DNF - Engine	$6,950	111	5
	Jun 14	Warner W. Hodgdon 400	6	5	95	95	0	Running	8,900	155	0
	Nov 22	Winston Western 500	13	40	119	2	0	DNF - Engine	6,150	43	0
1982	Jun 13	Budweiser 400	22	29	95	39	0	DNF - Oil Leak	1,785	76	0
	Nov 21	Winston Western 500	5	2	119	119	1	Running	16,980	175	5
1983	Jun 5	Budweiser 400	4	1	95	95	57	Running	24,530	185	10
	Nov 20	Winston Western 500	2	37	119	32	1	Running	1,900	57	5
1984	Jun 3	Budweiser 400	7	9	95	94	0	Running	10,100	138	0
	Nov 18	Winston Western 500	6	15	119	117	0	Running	11,000	118	0
1985	Jun 2	Budweiser 400	5	4	95	95	0	Running	11,825	160	0
	Nov 17	Winston Western 500	4	1	119	119	27	Running	37,875	180	5
1986	Jun 1	Budweiser 400	8	3	95	95	0	Running	18,650	165	0
	Nov 16	Winston Western 500	3	19	119	115	2	Running	9,855	111	5
1987	Jun 21	Budweiser 400	4	2	95	95	5	Running	28,450	175	5
	Nov 8	Winston Western 500	2	31	119	90	5	DNF - Engine	9,600	75	5
1988	Jun 12	Budweiser 400	1	3	95	95	30	Running	20,950	170	5

Sears Point Raceway

Sears Point Raceway showed up just in time for Ricky Rudd. He got his first taste for California road course racing at Riverside International Raceway, winning twice in 1983 and 1985. When the track closed in 1988, NASCAR replaced it with Sears Point in 1989.

The sanctioning body never did a bigger favor for Rudd. Few tracks have been more productive for the long-time Winston Cup driver. He won Sears Point's inaugural race and never finished lower than fourth in the track's first five seasons. Starting hasn't been much of a problem, either. Rudd is the track's all-time leading pole winner with four. He won three straight poles from 1990 through 1992.

Rudd's mastery at Sears Point was so complete that even his feet became famous. During the mid-1990s, ESPN regularly rigged Rudd's car with cameras to show his foot work as his steered through the track's multiple left and right turns. Fancy footwork couldn't prevent Rudd's slide from the top during the late-1990s, however. As his self-owned team's competitiveness degraded, his road course performance also fell off. He finished 34th, 28th, and 28th during his "dark years" between 1997 and 1999.

Since joining the No. 28 Robert Yates Racing team, his road course program has regained its former strength. He finished in the Top 5 in 2000 and 2001.

Sears Point Stats Chart

Sears Point Record Book - All-Time (min. 5 starts)

Category	Rudd's Total	Rudd's Rank	All-Time Sears Point Leader*
Money	$554,937	4th	Jeff Gordon -- 736,742
Starts	13	T-1st	8 Others with 13 Starts
Total Points	1,801	2nd	Mark Martin -- 1,892
Avg. Start	6.7	2nd	Jeff Gordon -- 4.8
Avg. Finish	11.3	4th	Jeff Gordon -- 7.2
Wins	1	4th	Jeff Gordon -- 3
Winning Pct.	7.7	8th	Jeff Gordon -- 33.3
Top 5s	8	T-1st	(Rusty Wallace—8)
Top 10s	9	2nd	Mark Martin -- 11
DNFs	1	19th	Hershel McGriff -- 4
Poles	4	1st	(Jeff Gordon—3)
Front Row Starts	6	1st	(Rusty Wallace -- 4)
Laps Led	114	4th	Jeff Gordon -- 238
Pct. Laps Led	10.2	6th	Jeff Gordon -- 29.1
Races Led	6	2nd	Rusty Wallace -- 8
Times Led	9	4th	Rusty Wallace -- 15
Times Led Most Laps	1	4th	Jeff Gordon -- 4
Bonus Points	35	3rd	Rusty Wallace -- 55
Laps Completed	1,100	2nd	Michael Waltrip -- 1,108
Pct. Laps Completed	98.7	10th	Johnny Benson Jr. -- 100.
Points per Race	138.5	4th	Jeff Gordon -- 155.8
Lead-Lap Finishes	11	T-1st	(D. Earnhardt, M. Martin, R. Wallace, M. Waltrip -- 11)

* -- Second-place driver listed in parentheses if Rudd is category leader

Memorable Sears Point Moments

1991 Banquet Frozen Foods 300—In one of the most controversial rulings in NASCAR history, Rudd was stripped of an apparent victory after a bumping incident with Davey Allison, who at the time drove Yates' No. 28 Havoline For. On the next-to-last lap, Rudd tagged Allison's rear bumper in Sears Point's hairpin Turn 11. Allison got turned around, allowing Rudd to assume the lead. Rudd led the final lap and finished four seconds ahead of Allison. However, the flag waving as Rudd crossed the finish line was black rather than checkered. NASCAR deemed that Rudd used "unnecessary roughness" to make his final pass and slapped a five-second penalty on the No. 5 Tide Chevy. The penalty put Rudd behind Allison in the final running order and Allison was declared the winner by a margin of victory of one second. NASCAR claimed that the location of Rudd's tap determined the penalty. Had he hit Allison in the right-rear quarter panel, the contact between the two cars would likely been deemed a "racing incident." Instead, because Rudd slammed Allison's bumper, the "unnecessary roughness" call was made. Rudd, his crew chief, Waddell Wilson, and team owner, Rick Hendrick, pointed to a similar incident between Mark Martin and Tommy Kendall a few laps earlier, which did not draw a penalty. Their protests were unsuccessful.

1989 Banquet Frozen Foods 300—Rudd survived a race-ending duel with Rusty Wallace to win the inaugural Sears Point race. Among Winston Cup drivers at that time, Rudd and Wallace were the top Winston Cup road course racers. In the first race on the northern California track, Rudd led 61 of the race's 74 laps. Wallace won the pole and led the first 10 laps. In the closing laps, Rudd made his No. 26 Buick wide enough to hold off Wallace's challenges. With four laps to go, Wallace made his final move in the horseshoe-shaped Turn 11. Rudd knocked Wallace off course and went on to win by more than a second.

Sears Point Performance Chart

Sears Point Raceway
Sonoma, Calif. — 1.949 miles — Road Course

Year	Date	Race	St.	Fin.	Total Laps	Laps Completed	Laps Led	Condition	Money	Pts	Bonus Pts.
1989	Jun 11	Banquet Frozen Foods 300	4	1	74	74	61	Running	$62,350	185	10
1990	Jun 10	Banquet Frozen Foods 300	1	3	74	74	13	Running	28,675	170	5
1991	Jun 9	Banquet Frozen Foods 300	1	2	74	74	13	Running	41,975	175	5
1992	Jun 7	Save Mart 300K	1	4	74	74	9	Running	25,710	165	5
1993	May 16	Save Mart Supermarkets 300K	2	3	74	74	0	Running	29,590	165	0
1994	May 15	Save Mart 300	3	14	74	74	0	Running	9,155	121	0
1995	May 7	Save Mart 300	1	4	74	74	4	Running	39,870	165	5
1996	May 5	Save Mart 300	2	7	74	74	0	Running	31,195	146	0
1997	May 5	Save Mart Supermarkets 300	10	34	74	66	0	Running	45,890	61	0
1998	Jun 28	Save Mart/Kragen 300K	15	28	112	112	14	Running	41,455	84	5
1999	Jun 27	Save Mart/Kragen 350K	15	38	112	106	0	DNF - Crash	32,320	49	0
2000	Jun 25	Save Mart/Kragen 300K	10	5	112	112	0	Running	67,915	155	0
2001	Jun 24	Dodge/Save Mart 350	22	4	112	112	0	Running	98,847	160	0

The road course at Sears Point is one of Rudd's best tracks. In the track's first five races, he started and finished each race fourth or better.

Rudd won the inaugural Sears Point race in 1989, and he holds the track record with four poles.

Talladega Superspeedway

Talladega SuperSpeedway was the fifth track Ricky Rudd ever raced on in his Winston Cup career. In May 1976, he strapped into his dad's car—the No. 22 Al Rudd Chevrolet—and held on tight before mechanical problem forced him from the race in 23rd place. His willingness to take on the longest, fastest track in NASCAR in just his fifth stock car race says a lot about his competitiveness and toughness. Most 19-year-olds could have been excused if they preferred to cut their teeth on slower, safer short tracks.

Rudd has raced in nearly every Talladega race since. Of NASCAR's older tracks, none has been tougher on the veteran than Talladega. Though it was the site of his first-ever Top 5 (in 1977), he is approaching three decades of competition on the imposing 2.66-mile track without a victory or a pole to his credit. His 20.3 average finish is the worst of his career on any track. In his first 50 starts, he never put together a Top 10 string longer than two races.

The introduction of restrictor plates in 1988 had a negligible affect on Rudd. A look at the 44 Daytona and Talladega races before the implementation of the plate and the 56 races since reveal approximately similar performances. His average start inched up by nearly two spots, while his average finish bumped up one slot. If Rudd's oft-repeated claim is true that Talladega and Daytona success is directly related to money, he has shown that he hasn't been able to overcome that disadvantage with his skill, toughness or competitiveness.

Memorable Talladega Moments

1995 Winston 500—An early round of inspections exposed a highly illegal hydraulic device on Rudd's car and prompted one of the largest monetary fines in NASCAR history. Rudd was fined $45,000 as driver and team owner and his crew chief Bill Ingle was fined $5,000 for the infraction. The device allowed Rudd to use his clutch to control the height of the rear of his car. Ingle set up the car to naturally lower under the weight of gravity and G-forces. On the cool-down lap, Rudd could use the clutch to raise the rear end back to regulation height. Without the device, he started 26th and finished a lap down in 22nd.

1999 Winston 500—Rudd received help from his new Robert Yates Racing team and cruised to the best restrictor-plate finish of his career. A month after signing a three-year contract to drive Yates' No. 28 Ford starting in 2000, RYR donated an engine and aerodynamic and chassis expertise to Rudd's Tide team in preparation for the Talladega 500-miler. He reacted by qualifying on the front row and finishing third. Rudd's previous best restrictor-plate performance was fourth place at Daytona on four separate occasions.

Talladega Stats Chart

Talladega Record Book - All-Time (min. 5 starts)

Category	Rudd's Total	Rudd's Rank	All-Time Talladega Leader
Money	$1,063,326	9th	Dale Earnhardt -- 2,081,045
Starts	50	3rd	Dave Marcis -- 61
Total Points[1]	5,258	5th	Bill Elliott -- 6,259
Avg. Start	16.9	32nd	Bobby Isaac -- 3.6
Avg. Finish	20.3	47th	Pete Hamilton -- 5.6
Wins	0	--	Dale Earnhardt -- 10
Winning Pct.	0.0	--	Dale Earnhardt -- 22.7
Top 5s	9	12th	Dale Earnhardt -- 23
Top 10s	12	14th	Dale Earnhardt -- 27
DNFs	15	6th	Darrell Waltrip -- 23
Poles	0	--	Bill Elliott -- 8
Front Row Starts	2	18th	Bill Elliott -- 13
Laps Led	79	32nd	Dale Earnhardt -- 1,377
Pct. Laps Led	0.8	59th	Pete Hamilton -- 22.9
Races Led	10	24th	Dale Earnhardt -- 38
Times Led	14	32nd	Buddy Baker -- 228
Times Led Most Laps	1	16th	Dale Earnhardt -- 11
Bonus Points[1]	55	24th	Dale Earnhardt -- 245
Laps Completed	7,818	4th	Dave Marcis -- 9,777
Pct. Laps Completed	83.8	49th	Buckshot Jones -- 99.7
Points per Race[1]	105.2	42nd	Dale Earnhardt -- 138.3
Lead-Lap Finishes	12	14th	Dale Earnhardt -- 27

[1] -- Since implementation of current point system in 1975

Before & After Restrictor Plates

A look at Ricky Rudd's career at Talladega and Daytona before and after the introduction of restrictor plates.

Period	Starts	Avg. Start	Avg. Finish	Wins	Top 5s	Top 10s	Poles	Laps Led
Before (1976-1987)	44	16.3	17.8	0	7	15	1	20
After (1988-2001)	56	18.3	19.2	0	8	17	0	105

Talladega Performance Chart

Talladega Superspeedway
Talladega, Ala. — 2.66 miles — 33° banking

Year	Date	Race	St.	Fin.	Total Laps	Laps Completed	Laps Led	Condition	Money	Pts	Bonus Pts.
1976	May 2	Winston 500	20	23	188	159	0	DNF - Mechanical	$2,035	94	0
1977	May 1	Winston 500	36	28	188	110	0	DNF - Engine	1,585	79	0
	Aug 7	Talladega 500	13	4	188	186	0	Running	8,000	160	0
1978	May 14	Winston 500	13	27	188	150	1	DNF - Engine	3,355	87	5
	Aug 6	Talladega 500	7	39	188	22	0	DNF - Engine	2,580	46	0
1979	May 6	Winston 500	18	27	188	38	0	DNF - Steering	2,655	82	0
	Aug 5	Talladega 500	11	3	188	186	0	Running	13,920	165	0
1980	Aug 3	Talladega 500	28	20	188	150	0	Running	4,185	103	0
1981	May 3	Winston 500	10	4	188	188	8	Running	18,750	165	5
	Aug 2	Talladega 500	12	23	188	133	0	Running	7,575	94	0
1982	May 2	Winston 500	3	24	188	116	1	Running	4,470	96	5
	Aug 1	Talladega 500	6	9	188	188	0	Running	8,250	138	0
1983	May 1	Winston 500	4	8	188	187	0	Running	10,865	142	0
	Jul 31	Talladega 500	17	16	188	182	0	Running	5,750	115	0
1984	May 6	Winston 500	10	22	188	165	0	DNF - Valve	11,000	97	0
	Jul 29	Talladega 500	24	14	188	188	0	Running	11,870	121	0
1985	May 5	Winston 500	15	5	188	187	0	Running	21,025	155	0
	Jul 28	Talladega 500	12	18	188	180	0	Running	11,050	109	0
1986	May 4	Winston 500	20	36	188	85	0	DNF - Engine	10,500	55	0
	Jul 27	Talladega 500	20	3	188	188	0	Running	29,255	165	0
1987	May 3	Winston 500	17	30	178	89	0	DNF - Crash	11,745	73	0
	Jul 26	Talladega 500	27	15	188	187	0	Running	12,975	118	0
1988	May 1	Winston 500	14	29	188	177	0	DNF - Engine	6,345	76	0
	Jul 31	Talladega DieHard 500	9	41	188	45	0	DNF - Engine	5,135	40	0
1989	May 7	Winston 500	32	31	188	169	0	DNF - Crash	6,445	70	0
	Jul 30	Talladega DieHard 500	24	17	188	187	0	Running	12,220	112	0
1990	May 6	Winston 500	14	33	188	104	0	DNF - Crash	7,285	64	0
	Jul 19	DieHard 500	25	5	188	188	0	Running	22,050	155	0
1991	May 6	Winston 500	6	13	188	186	2	Running	15,860	129	5
	Jul 28	DieHard 500	18	4	188	188	2	Running	29,400	165	5
1992	May 3	Winston 500	4	26	188	186	0	Running	16,005	85	0
	Jul 26	DieHard 500	2	4	188	187	54	Running	32,195	170	10
1993	May 2	Winston 500	26	41	188	12	0	DNF - Camshaft	12,120	40	0
	Jul 25	DieHard 500	5	24	188	186	1	Running	14,155	96	5
1994	May 1	Winston 500	33	25	188	180	0	Running	9,045	88	0
	Jul 24	DieHard 500	28	7	188	188	1	Running	19,350	151	5
1995	Apr 30	Winston 500	26	22	188	187	0	Running	25,115	97	0
	Jul 23	DieHard 500	6	41	188	68	0	DNF - Engine	24,175	40	0
1996	Apr 28	Winston Select 500	18	28	188	175	0	Running	27,480	79	0
	Jul 28	DieHard 500	28	37	129	113	0	Running	27,406	52	0
1997	May 10	Winston 500	29	11	188	188	0	Running	34,295	130	0
	Oct 12	DieHard 500	41	34	188	153	0	Running	36,745	61	0
1998	Apr 26	DieHard 500	13	24	188	179	0	Running	40,985	91	0
	Oct 11	Winston 500	17	18	188	187	0	Running	44,155	109	0
1999	Apr 25	DieHard 500	7	19	188	188	0	Running	44,045	106	0
	Oct 17	Winston 500	2	3	188	188	7	Running	82,235	170	5
2000	Apr 16	DieHard 500	10	27	188	182	0	Running	46,570	82	0
	Oct 15	Winston 500	11	11	188	188	0	Running	52,930	130	0
2001	Apr 22	Talladega 500	32	14	188	188	2	Running	83,407	126	5
	Oct 21	Alabama 500	23	26	188	187	0	DNF - Crash	73,742	85	0

Rudd hasn't had much luck at Talladega. He has yet to win at the 2.66-mile track.

Texas Motor Speedway

After six years of independence and self-ownership, Ricky Rudd had to get used to teammates again when he joined Robert Yates Racing in 2000. The last time Rudd had to share resources and information was in 1993 when he drove for Rick Hendrick. His strong comments about in-fighting at Hendrick Motorsports, and his down-to-the-wire efforts to save his team from folding in 1999 seemed to indicate unequivocally that Rudd simply didn't trust multicar teams. When he joined Yates, however, the positive side of teamwork was readily apparent: he could draw on the experience and stunning success of his new teammate, Dale Jarrett. Texas Motor Speedway is a prime example of how Rudd can capitalize on the data-sharing possibilities of his new situation. Jarrett has made Texas a second home, leading or being near the top of every major statistical category at the track. He finished three of the first five races in first or second place.

Rudd has a lot to learn from Jarrett. Besides a fifth-place finish in the inaugural race in 1997, he has had difficulty getting a handle on the high-speed 1.5-mile track. He settled for 27th in 1998, then 19th in 1999. In his first Yates race at Texas, he earned a 10th-place finish. In 2001, his dropped out in 37th after engine trouble.

Texas Stats Chart

Texas Record Book - All-Time (min. 2 starts)

Category	Rudd's Total	Rudd's Rank	All-Time Texas Leader
Money	$606,197	6th	Dale Jarrett -- 1,089,477
Starts	5	T-1st	21 Others with 5 Starts
Total Points	539	12th	Terry Labonte -- 776
Avg. Start	17.6	14th	Dale Earnhardt, Jr. -- 2.5
Avg. Finish	19.6	20th	Dale Earnhardt Jr. -- 4.5
Wins	0	--	J. Burton, D. Earnhardt Jr., D. Jarrett, T. Labonte, M. Martin --1
Winning Pct.	0.0	--	Dale Earnhardt Jr. -- 50.
Top 5s	1	7	D. Jarrett, B. Labonte -- 3
Top 10s	2	6	B. Labonte, T. Labonte -- 4
DNFs	2	4th	E. Irvan, J. Nemechek, J. Spencer -- 3
Poles	0	--	5 Drivers with 1 Pole
Front Row Starts	0	--	Bobby Labonte -- 2
Laps Led	35	13	Dale Jarrett -- 272
Pct. Laps Led	2.1	15	Dale Earnhardt Jr. -- 31.9
Races Led	2	7	Dale Jarrett -- 5
Times Led	3	9	Dale Jarrett -- 18
Times Led Most Laps	0	--	Terry Labonte -- 2
Bonus Points	10	8	Dale Jarrett -- 30
Laps Completed	1,580	9	Terry Labonte -- 1,670
Pct. Laps Completed	94.6	21	D. Earnhardt Jr., T. Labonte -- 100.0
Points per Race	107.8	20	Dale Earnhardt Jr. -- 166.0
Lead-Lap Finishes	2	9	Terry Labonte -- 5

Texas Performance Chart

Texas Motor Speedway
Ft. Worth, Texas — 1.5 miles — 24° banking

Year	Date	Race	St.	Fin.	Total Laps	Laps Completed	Laps Led	Condition	Money	Pts	Bonus Pts.
1997	Apr 6	Interstate Batteries 500	8	5	334	334	26	Running	$118,775	160	5
1998	Apr 5	Texas 500	20	27	334	315	0	DNF - Handling	65,900	82	0
1999	Mar 28	Primestar 500	34	19	334	333	0	Running	73,400	106	0
2000	Apr 2	DirecTV 500	20	10	334	334	9	Running	105,125	139	5
2001	Apr 1	Harrah's 500	6	37	334	264	0	DNF - Engine	73,097	52	0

The No. 28 crew tends to Rudd's car at Texas in 2000.

Watkins Glen International

In 1988, Rudd proved that his road course talents were bicoastal. After success at Riverside International Raceway, he added a victory at Watkins Glen International, the 2.45-mile track in upstate New York. Though his performance at WGI has not been as dominant as Riverside and Sears Point, Rudd can boast a productive record nonetheless.

Rudd is one of four drivers who have started every Watkins Glen race since 1986, when the track rejoined the NASCAR circuit. It arrived just as his road course skills were reaching their early peak. He finished the first two races in the Top 10 before scoring his 1988 victory. After a blown engine ruined a strong run in 1989, he returned with another victory in 1990.

More recently, Watkins Glen has been less kind to Rudd. Between 1996 and 2000, he failed to crack the Top 10. In 1997, he suffered one of the worst crashes of his career during prequalifying practice. Traveling 160 miles per hour, he went off the track and slammed into the Turn 10 wall. He was able to spin his car to avoid a head-on collision and was helped by the Styrofoam cushions placed in front of the guard rails. Rudd escaped injury, but had to go to a back-up car that lasted just 24 laps three days later in the race. He finished 40th, tying the worst road course performance of his career.

Rudd seemed to regain his footing in 2001. He started on the outside pole, next to his teammate, Dale Jarrett. He survived a late-race skirmish with Boris Said and finished the race in fourth, his best effort in six years.

Memorable Watkins Glen Moments

1988 Budweiser at The Glen—Rudd staged a miraculous comeback to win his first Watkins Glen event. In the race's opening laps, he made a costly and unscheduled pit stop to replace a bad set of tires. Dropping to 38th in the field, he slowly climbed back into contention, thanks to eight caution periods. With four laps to go, he passed race leader Darrell Waltrip and then battled road-course nemesis Rusty Wallace to the finish line. Rudd topped Wallace by less than two-tenths of a second.

1990 Budweiser at The Glen—Rudd claimed the fifth road-course win of his career despite a rash of bad luck. He survived a spin after contact from Geoffrey Bodine, then watched a 12-second lead late in the race disappear due to a caution. Rudd still was able to pull away to a seven-second win over Bodine. After an amazing run on NASCAR's road courses, the 1990 Watkins Glen win was his last nonoval victory. Through 2001, Rudd has not visited Victory Lane at Sears Point or Watkins Glen since his 1990 win.

Watkins Glen Stats Chart

Watkins Glen Record Book - All-Time (min. 5 starts)

Category	Rudd's Total	Rudd's Rank	All-Time Watkins Glen Leader
Money	$520,857	4th	Mark Martin -- 816,311
Starts	16	T-1st	(K. Schrader, R. Wallace, M. Waltrip -- 16)
Total Points	2,049	2nd	Mark Martin -- 2,211
Avg. Start	10.1	6th	Rusty Wallace -- 6.6
Avg. Finish	14.1	7th	Mark Martin -- 5.9
Wins	2	3rd	Jeff Gordon -- 4
Winning Pct.	12.5	4th	Jeff Gordon -- 44.4
Top 5s	7	2nd	Mark Martin -- 11
Top 10s	8	3rd	Mark Martin -- 12
DNFs	2	16th	Derrike Cope -- 6
Poles	0	--	D. Earnhardt, M. Martin -- 3
Front Row Starts	1	8th	M. Martin, D. Jarrett -- 4
Laps Led	55	7th	Mark Martin -- 204
Pct. Laps Led	3.9	14th	Jeff Gordon -- 19.8
Races Led	7	4th	Rusty Wallace -- 9
Times Led	9	6th	M. Martin, R. Wallace -- 16
Times Led Most Laps	0	--	J. Gordon, M. Martin -- 3
Bonus Points	35	6th	Rusty Wallace -- 55
Laps Completed	1,289	5th	Michael Waltrip -- 1,360
Pct. Laps Completed	92.0	28th	Darrell Waltrip -- 100.0
Points per Race	128.1	5th	Mark Martin -- 157.9
Lead-Lap Finishes	11	5th	D. Earnhardt, D. Waltrip -- 14

Watkins Glen Performance Chart

Watkins Glen International
Watkins Glen, N.Y. — 2.45 miles — Road Course

Year	Date	Race	St.	Fin.	Total Laps	Laps Completed	Laps Led	Condition	Money	Pts	Bonus Pts.
1986	Aug 10	The Budweiser at the Glen	7	7	90	90	0	Running	$14,090	146	0
1987	Aug 10	The Budweiser at the Glen	7	4	90	90	0	Running	20,135	160	0
1988	Aug 14	The Budweiser at the Glen	6	1	90	90	4	Running	49,625	180	5
1989	Aug 13	The Budweiser at the Glen	8	29	90	69	12	DNF - Engine	9,145	81	5
1990	Aug 12	The Budweiser at the Glen	12	1	90	90	20	Running	55,000	180	5
1991	Aug 11	The Budweiser at the Glen	22	2	90	90	11	Running	37,325	175	5
1992	Aug 9	The Budweiser at the Glen	4	13	51	51	0	Running	14,400	124	0
1993	Aug 8	The Budweiser at the Glen	9	24	90	87	0	Running	10,910	91	0
1994	Aug 14	The Bud at the Glen	7	5	90	90	3	Running	20,875	160	5
1995	Aug 13	The Bud at the Glen	7	4	90	90	0	Running	34,320	160	0
1996	Aug 11	The Bud at the Glen	3	34	90	69	0	Running	24,370	61	0
1997	Aug 10	The Bud at the Glen	31	40	90	24	0	DNF - Handling	27,865	43	0
1998	Aug 9	The Bud at the Glen	3	14	90	90	0	Running	24,900	121	0
1999	Aug 15	Frontier at the Glen	24	32	90	89	0	Running	29,285	67	0
2000	Aug 13	Global Crossing at the Glen	9	11	90	90	3	Running	40,580	135	5
2001	Aug 12	Global Crossing at the Glen	2	4	90	90	2	Running	96,322	165	5

Rudd is one of the best road course racers in the Winston Cup series. He had seven Top 5s in his first 16 Watkins Glen starts.

Watkins Glen has been one of Rudd's best tracks. He won twice there, in 1988 and 1990.

Major Races

Chapter 5

Ricky Rudd's Performance in the Winston Cup Series' Biggest Events

On the Winston Cup schedule, there are races, and then there are events. In the NASCAR world, the biggest events are the season-opening Daytona 500, the Memorial Day Coca-Cola 600, and the Labor Day Southern 500. While other races are popular or important to the Winston Cup schedule—races such as the Brickyard 400, the Bristol night race and the Talladega races—none has yet reached the prestige of the Big Three. This section details Rudd's career in the major races, listing career statistics, season-by-season totals, and individual race performances.

Daytona 500	**143**
Coca-Cola 600	**145**
Southern 500	**146**

Rudd and the rest of the field visit pit road early during the 1996 Daytona 500. In his first 25 Daytona 500 starts, Rudd's best finish was third place (1981).

Daytona 500

Ricky Rudd has yet to win a "major" on the Winston Cup circuit. At Daytona, he is quickly approaching record territory for most Modern Era Daytona 500 starts without a victory, trailing only Dave Marcis with 24 winless 500s. Not surprisingly, Rudd's best chances came when he occupied powerful cars. While driving the stout No. 88 DiGard Racing Chevy in 1981, he finished third—a finish that remains the best Daytona 500 performance of his career. He nearly matched that effort in 2000, when he piloted his No. 28 Robert Yates Racing Ford to a fourth-place finish. He also finished fourth while driving the No. 5 Hendrick Motorsports Chevy in 1990.

Perhaps the most satisfying 500 in Rudd's career came in 1984 when he drove Bud Moore's No. 15 Ford. A week after his spectacular and violent wreck in the Busch Clash, he rebounded with a solid fifth-place finish in the 500. Though battered and bruised from the crash—during which his car flipped seven times along the infield near the entrance to pit road—he raced in the Top 10 for most of the race before earning the second Daytona 500 Top 5 of his career.

Another Daytona highlight was his "pole" in 1983 while driving for Richard Childress. Rudd ran a lap of 198.864 miles per hour, but was easily outpaced by Cale Yarborough, whose first lap reached just over 200 miles per hour. Yarborough, however, crashed during his second lap and tore up his car so badly that he had to go to a back-up car for the race. Under NASCAR rules at the time, a driver had to race the car he qualified. Otherwise, his qualifying time was erased and he was forced to start at the back of the field. The turn of events left Rudd as the fastest qualifier and gave him his only career Daytona pole. Unfortunately for Rudd, he led just one lap and went out early with mechanical problems. He finished 24th.

Daytona 500 Stats Chart

Daytona 500 Record Book - Modern Era (min. 5 starts)

Category	Rudd's Total	Rudd's Rank	Modern Era Daytona 500 Leader
Starts	24	3rd	D. Marcis, D. Waltrip -- 28
Total Points[1]	2,689	5th	Dale Earnhardt -- 3,238
Avg. Start	18.3	31st	Mike Skinner -- 5.8
Avg. Finish	18.0	25th	Jody Ridley -- 9.7
Wins	0	--	Richard Petty -- 4
Winning Pct.	0.0	--	Dale Jarrett -- 23.1
Top 5s	4	10th	Dale Earnhardt -- 12
Top 10s	10	5th	Dale Earnhardt -- 16
DNFs	7	14th	A.J. Foyt -- 13
Poles	1	7th	Bill Elliott -- 4
Front Row Starts	2	9th	Bill Elliott -- 5
Laps Led	14	36th	Dale Earnhardt -- 686
Pct. Laps Led	0.3	56th	Buddy Baker -- 15.9
Races Led	5	21st	Dale Earnhardt -- 19
Times Led	6	31st	Dale Earnhardt -- 92
Times Led Most Laps	0	--	B. Allison, B. Baker, D. Earnhardt -- 3
Bonus Points[1]	25	23rd	Dale Earnhardt -- 110
Laps Completed	4,001	6th	Darrell Waltrip -- 4,726
Pct. Laps Completed	83.4	36th	Rick Mast -- 99.1
Points per Race[1]	112.0	20th	Dale Earnhardt -- 140.8
Lead-Lap Finishes	10	3rd	Dale Earnhardt -- 14

[1] -- Since implementation of current point system in 1975

Daytona 500 Performance Chart

Daytona 500
Daytona International Speedway

Year	Date	St.	Fin.	Total Laps	Laps Completed	Laps Led	Condition	Money	Pts	Bonus Pts.
1977	Feb 20	21	22	200	135	0	DNF - Rear End	$2,935	97	0
1978	Feb 19	36	37	200	21	0	DNF - Handling	4,375	52	0
1979	Feb 18	11	31	200	79	0	DNF - Engine	4,110	70	0
1981	Feb 15	5	3	200	200	9	Running	53,115	170	5
1982	Feb 14	16	35	200	51	0	DNF - Engine	6,050	58	0
1983	Feb 20	1	24	200	182	1	DNF - Mechanical	16,515	96	5
1984	Feb 19	14	7	200	199	0	Running	38,700	146	0
1985	Feb 17	9	5	200	199	0	Running	52,900	155	0
1986	Feb 16	22	11	200	198	0	Running	32,690	130	0
1987	Feb 15	31	9	200	200	0	Running	38,425	138	0
1988	Feb 14	27	17	200	200	0	Running	20,125	112	0
1989	Feb 19	36	19	200	197	2	Running	19,120	111	5
1990	Feb 18	19	4	200	200	1	Running	77,050	165	5
1991	Feb 17	9	9	200	199	0	Running	52,600	138	0
1992	Feb 16	8	40	200	79	0	DNF - Engine	34,350	43	0
1993	Feb 14	12	30	200	177	0	Running	31,285	73	0
1994	Feb 20	20	8	200	200	0	Running	56,465	142	0
1995	Feb 19	18	13	200	200	0	Running	60,620	124	0
1996	Feb 18	10	9	200	200	0	Running	79,987	138	0
1997	Feb 16	13	9	200	200	0	Running	88,590	138	0
1998	Feb 15	40	42	200	117	0	DNF - Valve Spring	86,480	37	0
1999	Feb 14	29	30	200	168	0	Running	102,226	73	0
2000	Feb 20	2	15	200	200	1	Running	119,475	123	5
2001	Feb 18	30	4	200	200	0	Running	517,831	160	0

No Satisfaction

A look at Winston Cup drivers who have the most Daytona 500 starts in the Modern Era without a victory

Driver	No. of Starts	Closest Call
Dave Marcis	28	6th in 1975, 1978
Ricky Rudd	24	3rd in 1981
Terry Labonte	23	2nd in 1986, 1990, 1997
Kyle Petty	20	6th in 1992
Rusty Wallace	19	3rd in 2001

Rudd leads the field to the green flag for the 2000 Twin 125s.

Coca-Cola 600

In his first 25 Coca-Cola 600 starts, Ricky Rudd finished on the lead lap just three times. Getting lapped in a 600-mile race is neither unusual nor embarrassing. But Rudd's almost intractable habit of getting passed by the leader of the race has made top finishes rare.

While he has 13 Top 10 finishes in 25 starts, Rudd can point to just two finishes in the Top 5. Since 1995, even Top 10s have become rare. His 10th-place finish in 1997 and his 7th-place effort in 2001 are his only Top 10s in the last seven years.

Bill Elliott is the only driver besides Rudd to start as many 600s in the Modern Era and not win. Rudd's best finish was fourth in 1981, though he was three laps behind race winner Bobby Allison. His best chances for a win in the Memorial Day marathon came in 1994 and 1995. In the 1994, he led with 10 laps to go before pulling down pit lane for a final fuel stop. He gave the lead to Jeff Gordon, who went on to win. In 1995, another late fuel stop prevented a Rudd win. He led midway through the event, but got knocked off the lead lap and finished fourth.

Falling Short

A look at Winston Cup drivers who have the most Coca-Cola 600 starts in the Modern Era without a victory

Driver	No. of Starts	Closest Call
Ricky Rudd	25	4th in 1981
Bill Elliott	25	2nd in 1982, 1990
Dave Marcis	24	6th in 1974
Terry Labonte	23	2nd in 1995

Coca-Cola 600 Stats Chart

Coca-Cola 600 Record Book - Modern Era (min. 5 starts)

Category	Rudd's Total	Rudd's Rank	Modern Era Coca-Cola 600 Leader
Starts	25	2nd	Darrell Waltrip -- 28
Total Points[1]	3,007	3rd	Darrell Waltrip -- 3,370
Avg. Start	18.1	32nd	David Pearson -- 2.8
Avg. Finish	15.2	12th	Bobby Labonte -- 9.9
Wins	0	--	Darrell Waltrip -- 5
Winning Pct.	0.0	--	Jeff Gordon -- 33.3
Top 5s	2	24th	Darrell Waltrip -- 11
Top 10s	13	3rd	Darrell Waltrip -- 15
DNFs	3	48th	Dave Marcis -- 15
Poles	0	--	David Pearson -- 6
Front Row Starts	0	--	David Pearson -- 9
Laps Led	48	36th	Dale Earnhardt -- 975
Pct. Laps Led	0.5	47th	Davey Allison -- 15.2
Races Led	4	23rd	Dale Earnhardt -- 16
Times Led	6	31st	Dale Earnhardt -- 72
Times Led Most Laps	0	--	Bobby Allison -- 4
Bonus Points[1]	20	26th	Dale Earnhardt -- 95
Laps Completed	9,179	2nd	Darrell Waltrip -- 10,317
Pct. Laps Completed	92.4	13th	Mike Skinner -- 97.7
Points per Race[1]	120.3	29th	Bobby Labonte -- 145.2
Lead-Lap Finishes	3	18th	Dale Earnhardt -- 10

[1] -- Since implementation of current point system in 1975

Coca-Cola 600 Performance Chart

Coca-Cola 600
Charlotte Motor Speedway

Year	Date	St.	Fin.	Total Laps	Laps Completed	Laps Led	Condition	Money	Pts	Bonus Pts.
1977	May 29	18	17	400	384	2	Running	$2,960	117	5
1978	May 28	20	28	400	331	0	Running	3,430	79	0
1979	May 27	10	6	400	397	0	Running	14,845	150	0
1980	May 27	13	9	400	394	0	Running	7,425	138	0
1981	May 24	13	4	400	397	0	Running	18,975	160	0
1982	May 30	10	7	400	397	0	Running	11,130	146	0
1983	May 29	9	32	400	245	0	Running	3,425	67	0
1984	May 27	10	11	400	395	0	Running	14,025	130	0
1985	May 26	17	13	400	391	0	Running	13,255	124	0
1986	May 25	13	8	400	399	0	Running	18,200	142	0
1987	May 24	25	25	400	254	0	DNF - Crash	11,950	88	0
1988	May 29	34	7	400	399	0	Running	17,050	146	0
1989	May 28	9	10	400	397	0	Running	16,925	134	0
1990	May 27	34	28	400	320	0	DNF - Camshaft	7,450	79	0
1991	May 26	17	9	400	399	0	Running	21,500	138	0
1992	May 24	3	9	400	398	33	Running	30,100	143	5
1993	May 30	20	37	400	164	0	DNF - Engine	11,310	52	0
1994	May 29	13	6	400	400	10	Running	28,700	155	5
1995	May 28	18	5	400	399	3	Running	49,000	160	5
1996	May 26	30	15	400	396	0	Running	30,620	118	0
1997	May 25	18	10	333	333	0	Running	70,550	134	0
1998	May 24	35	31	400	396	0	Running	59,025	70	0
1999	May 30	23	28	400	395	0	Running	40,640	79	0
2000	May 28	20	17	400	399	0	Running	50,395	112	0
2001	May 27	21	7	400	400	0	Running	102,572	146	0

Southern 500

Fairly or unfairly, Ricky Rudd developed a "good, but conservative" reputation as he established himself among the top Winston Cup drivers. That characterization is laughable considering his all-out attack on road courses and his willingness to mix it up with Earnhardt and the rest on short tracks. Where the reputation may hold true is on the larger ovals (that is, tracks greater than a mile). Usually driving for smaller-budget teams, tearing up equipment was a sure way to raise the ire of the owner.

Rudd's performance in the Southern 500 may be the best illustration of his cautious approach. He has more Top 10 finishes in the Labor Day race than any driver besides Bill Elliott during the Modern Era. Though he started more Southern 500s than any other active driver, he has yet to visit Victory Lane. With just four Top 5 finishes, his ability to lead the field in the 500 is amazing for its minimalism. In 8,789 possible Southern 500 laps, he led just 135.

Of course, not all Darlington difficulties are Rudd's fault. He led 76 laps in 1983 and looked promising until a blown engine 100 laps from the finish ruined his day. In 1995, he started second, led 37 laps, and finished 6th. He finished 3rd in 1989, the best Southern 500 finish of his career. Otherwise, Rudd's performance has been good but not great. Since 1983, he has finished outside of the Top 15 just three times. On the other hand, he has finished inside the Top 5 just four times.

Southern 500 Stats Chart

Southern 500 Record Book - Modern Era (min. 5 starts)

Category	Rudd's Total	Rudd's Rank	Modern Era Southern 500 Leader
Starts	25	2nd	Darrell Waltrip -- 27
Total Points[1]	3,175	2nd	Bill Elliott -- 3,481
Avg. Start	14.7	23rd	David Pearson -- 4.7
Avg. Finish	13.6	8th	Jeff Gordon -- 5.7
Wins	0	--	J. Gordon, C. Yarborough -- 4
Winning Pct.	0.0	--	Jeff Gordon -- 44.4
Top 5s	4	13th	Bill Elliott -- 11
Top 10s	16	2nd	Bill Elliott -- 17
DNFs	5	22nd	H.B. Bailey, B. Baker -- 9
Poles	0	--	David Pearson -- 5
Front Row Starts	1	15th	B. Elliott, D. Pearson -- 6
Laps Led	135	25th	Dale Earnhardt -- 1,138
Pct. Laps Led	1.5	31st	Cale Yarborough -- 17.0
Races Led	9	8th	Bill Elliott -- 17
Times Led	14	17th	Darrell Waltrip -- 56
Times Led Most Laps	0	--	Dale Earnhardt -- 5
Bonus Points[1]	45	10th	B. Elliott, D. Waltrip -- 95
Laps Completed	7,996	3rd	Darrell Waltrip -- 8,252
Pct. Laps Completed	91.0	17th	Jeff Gordon -- 99.8
Points per Race[1]	127.0	12th	Jeff Gordon -- 160.7
Lead-Lap Finishes	9	3rd	Bill Elliott -- 13

[1] -- Since implementation of current point system in 1975

Southern 500 Performance Chart

Southern 500
Darlington Raceway

Year	Date	St.	Fin.	Total Laps	Laps Completed	Laps Led	Condition	Money	Pts	Bonus Pts.
1977	Sep 5	18	7	367	360	0	Running	$7,400	146	0
1978	Sep 4	13	36	367	122	1	DNF - Crash	3,025	60	5
1979	Sep 3	14	8	367	361	0	Running	7,105	142	0
1980	Sep 3	16	34	367	201	0	DNF - Steering	2,025	61	0
1981	Sep 7	7	23	367	343	0	DNF - Crash	7,850	94	0
1982	Sep 6	6	31	367	168	1	DNF - Engine	4,175	75	5
1983	Sep 5	8	25	367	272	76	DNF - Engine	7,415	93	5
1984	Sep 2	11	5	367	364	0	Running	17,050	155	0
1985	Sep 1	11	6	367	366	0	Running	13,450	150	0
1986	Aug 31	15	6	367	367	0	Running	15,735	150	0
1987	Sep 6	12	7	202	202	0	Running	15,055	146	0
1988	Sep 4	29	10	367	366	6	Running	13,130	139	5
1989	Sep 3	8	3	367	367	0	Running	26,865	165	0
1990	Sep 2	5	7	367	367	6	Running	12,755	151	5
1991	Sep 1	18	15	367	363	0	Running	14,100	118	0
1992	Sep 6	18	10	298	297	3	Running	18,470	139	5
1993	Sep 5	16	6	351	350	0	Running	16,940	150	0
1994	Sep 4	18	4	367	367	3	Running	24,715	165	5
1995	Sep 3	2	6	367	367	37	Running	34,865	155	5
1996	Sep 1	18	16	367	365	2	Running	27,805	120	5
1997	Aug 31	21	5	367	367	0	Running	39,345	155	0
1998	Sep 6	14	22	367	362	0	Running	38,095	97	0
1999	Sep 5	26	34	270	237	0	Running	32,840	61	0
2000	Sep 3	17	8	328	328	0	Running	52,475	142	0
2001	Sep 2	26	7	367	367	0	Running	85,657	146	0

Still Waiting

A look at Winston Cup drivers who have the most Southern 500 starts in the Modern Era without a victory

Driver	No. of Starts	Closest Call
Ricky Rudd	25	3rd in 1989
Dave Marcis	25	3rd in 1981
Richard Petty	21	2nd in 1975, 1976, 1982
Kyle Petty	20	7th in 1992
Geoffrey Bodine	19	3rd in 1985

Good, Not Great

A look at Winston Cup drivers with the most Top 10 finishes in the Southern 500 during the Modern Era

Driver	Top 10s
Bill Elliott	17
Ricky Rudd	16
Dale Earnhardt	14
Terry Labonte	12
Bobby Allison	11
Darrell Waltrip	11

Ricky Rudd's Performance in All-Star Events

Adding spice to the Winston Cup schedule are two high-stakes shoot-outs that, despite having no direct effect on the championship, are run with an unbridled urgency sometimes missing from regular events. To race in these two all-star events—the Bud Shootout and the Winston—a driver must perform at a top level. The field for the Bud Shootout at Daytona is dependent on winning a pole during the previous season. The Winston at Charlotte is reserved for race winners over the previous season. This section details Rudd's career performance in these races.

The 2000 Bud Shootout was memorable for Robert Yates Racing. Dale Jarrett won the race, while Ricky Rudd finished on his roof. Rudd was looking for a Top 5 finish when his car was bumped and sent into the wall. It flipped on its roof and slid down the track, coming to rest in the infield grass. Rudd, unhurt in the flip, joined his teammate in Victory Lane.

Bud Shootout

Crashes, not quality finishes, have marked Ricky Rudd's efforts in the annual Bud Shootout. Staged on the Sunday before the Daytona 500 every year since 1979, the sprint race formerly known as the Busch Clash pits pole winners from the previous season. As one of the best qualifiers on the circuit through the 1980s, Rudd has been a regular participant. His 13 starts rank fourth in the event's history.

Unfortunately for Rudd, he ranks first in Bud Shootout history in DNFs. His propensity to get into trouble has resulted in a race-record six early exits, including four via crashes. Two of those wrecks are especially memorable. In 1984, 16 laps into his first race in the No. 15 Bud Moore Ford Thunderbird, Rudd lost control coming off of Turn 4 and began a harrowing end-over-end tumble near the entrance to pit road. Miraculously, he emerged without serious injury, though his face was severely bruised and swollen. The 27-year-old used duct tape to help keep his eyes open three days later when he returned to practice for the Twin 125 qualifying races. Proving his toughness, he raced the Daytona 500 (finishing seventh) and won at Richmond 14 days after his accident.

Sixteen years later, Rudd endured a similar fate in his first race for Robert Yates. Racing for a Top 3 finish in the 2000 Bud Shootout, he was again involved in a spectacular wreck, this time just a few hundred yards from the finish line on the race's last lap. Rudd's No. 28 Ford was flipped on its top as it slid into the infield grass. Though much less banged up than after his 1984 incident, he was left once again without a top finish. In his 13 starts, Rudd has never finished better than fifth place.

Bud Shootout Stats Chart

Bud Shootout Record Book - All-Time (min. 5 starts)

Category	Rudd's Total	Rudd's Rank	All-Time Bud Shootout Leader*
Money	196,722	12th	Dale Earnhardt -- 601,222
Starts	13	4th	Bill Elliott -- 16
Avg. Finish	9.6	22nd	Dale Earnhardt -- 2.8
Wins	0	--	Dale Earnhardt -- 6
Winning Pct.	0.0	--	Dale Earnhardt -- 50.0
Top 5s	1	23rd	Dale Earnhardt -- 11
Top 10s	8	9th	Bill Elliott -- 14
DNFs	6	1st	(6 Drivers with 2 DNFs)
Laps Led	4	20	Dale Earnhardt -- 98
Pct. Laps Led	1.3	24	Tony Stewart -- 37.9
Races Led	2	12	Dale Earnhardt -- 9
Times Led	2	15	Dale Earnhardt -- 15
Times Led Most Laps	0	--	Dale Earnhardt -- 6
Laps Completed	270	6	Bill Elliott -- 375
Pct. Laps Completed	85.7	23	12 Drivers with 100 percent
Lead-Lap Finishes	7	10	Bill Elliott -- 16

* -- Second-place drivers in parentheses if Rudd is category leader

Bud Shootout Performance Chart

Bud Shootout
Daytona International Speedway

Year	Date	Race	St.	Fin.	Total Laps	Laps Completed	Laps Led	Condition	Money
1982	Feb 7	Busch Clash	2	12	20	13	3	DNF - Engine	$10,000
1983	Feb 14	Busch Clash	7	13	20	16	0	DNF - Cut Tire	10,000
1984	Feb 12	Busch Clash	6	10	20	15	0	DNF - Crash	10,000
1985	Feb 10	Busch Clash	1	6	20	20	0	Running	11,500
1987	Feb 8	Busch Clash	6	10	20	0	0	DNF - Crash	10,000
1989	Feb 12	Busch Clash	2	13	20	20	0	Running	10,000
1991	Feb 10	Busch Clash	14	13	20	12	0	DNF - Crash	13,000
1992	Feb 8	Busch Clash	5	9	20	20	0	Running	12,000
1993	Feb 7	Busch Clash	11	5	20	20	0	Running	16,000
1995	Feb 12	Busch Clash	13	6	20	20	1	Running	12,500
1996	Feb 11	Busch Clash	6	6	20	20	0	Running	18,000
2000	Feb 13	Bud Shootout	9	13	25	24	0	DNF - Crash	26,000
2001	Feb 11	Bud Shootout	11	9	70	70	0	Running	37,722

The Winston

It's just a midseason all-star event, but for Ricky Rudd, The Winston must feel a lot like a major race. In his first 75 attempts to win the Daytona 500, the Coca-Cola 600, and the Southern 500—the biggest races in NASCAR—Rudd has failed to find Victory Lane. His luck isn't much better in the Winston.

Designed to pit recent winners and champions in a sprint race, The Winston is often a lively event that features unexpected results. Rudd's performance has been depressingly predictable. In his first 15 starts, he has not won, hasn't led a lap (of 1,258 possible laps) and finished in the Top 5 just three times. His best finish came in 1995, when he started sixth and ended third.

Unfortunately for Rudd, his most memorable Winston all-star race was also his most painful. In 1988, he slammed into the Turn 1 wall at Charlotte after cutting a tire. The wreck left him with severe ligament damage in his left knee. Forced to wear a cast and change his driving style, he sought relief in the Coca-Cola 600 the following week. Two weeks later, despite the continuing pain, he set a track qualifying record at Riverside.

The Winston Performance Chart

The Winston
Charlotte Motor Speedway

Year	Date	Race	St.	Fin.	Total Laps	Laps Completed	Laps Led	Condition	Money
1985	May 25	The Winston	10	8	70	70	0	Running	$12,500
1986	May 11	The Winston	7	8	83	82	0	Running	15,500
1987	May 17	The Winston	18	11	135	135	0	Running	10,650
1988	May 22	The Winston	8	15	135	96	0	DNF - Crash	10,000
1989	May 21	The Winston	13	8	135	135	0	Running	19,000
1990	May 20	The Winston	13	12	70	70	0	Running	20,000
1991	May 19	The Winston	11	11	70	70	0	Running	20,500
1992	May 16	The Winston	9	4	70	70	0	Running	30,000
1993	May 2	The Winston	11	16	70	43	0	DNF - Engine	18,000
1994	May 22	The Winston	6	5	70	70	0	Running	27,000
1995	May 20	The Winston	6	3	70	70	0	Running	65,000
1996	May 18	The Winston	8	6	70	70	0	Running	25,000
1997	May 17	The Winston	12	9	70	70	0	Running	20,500
1998	May 16	The Winston	12	15	70	31	0	DNF - Crash	18,000
1999	May 22	The Winston	19	21	70	11	0	DNF - Crash	18,000

The Winston Stats Chart

The Winston Record Book - All-Time (min. 5 starts)

Category	Rudd's Total	Rudd's Rank	All-Time The Winston Leader
Money	329,650	17th	Jeff Gordon -- 1,335,610
Starts	15	5th	Elliott, Earnhardt, T. Labonte, D. Waltrip -- 16
Avg. Start	10.9	13th	D. Allison, B. Labonte -- 3.9
Avg. Finish	10.1	12th	Ken Schrader -- 5.1
Wins	0	--	Dale Earnhardt -- 3
Winning Pct.	0.0	--	Jeff Gordon -- 37.5
Top 5s	3	11th	Dale Earnhardt -- 9
Top 10s	8	5th	B. Elliott, D. Earnhardt -- 12
DNFs	4	2nd	Rusty Wallace -- 5
Poles	0	--	Bill Elliott -- 4
Front Row Starts	0	--	B. Elliott, R. Wallace -- 5
Laps Led	0	--	Bill Elliott -- 267
Pct. Laps Led	0.0	--	Jeff Gordon -- 25.9
Races Led	0	--	Dale Earnhardt -- 11
Times Led	0	--	Dale Earnhardt -- 13
Times Led Most Laps	0	--	B. Elliott, J. Gordon -- 3
Laps Completed	1,093	6th	Bill Elliott -- 1,327
Pct. Laps Completed	86.9	15th	Sterling Marlin -- 100.0
Lead-Lap Finishes	10	6th	Bill Elliott -- 15

Ricky Rudd's Performance in the International Race of Champions Series

For 26 years, the International Race of Champions (IROC) has been staged as an exhibition series. Designed to pit the champions of various series together in identically prepared cars, the series attempts to isolate driver talent by removing any mechanical advantage and thereby determine which driver from which series is truly the best. This section details Rudd's IROC career, listing career statistics, season-by-season totals, and individual race performances.

Ricky Rudd made the most of his first opportunity to race in the IROC series in 1992. Fresh off of his second-place finish in the Winston Cup standings in 1991, he was invited to participate in the annual four-race series. Racing one of 12 identically prepared Dodge Daytonas, he charged to the front in each of the circuit's four races and won the 1992 IROC championship by 5.5 points over Dale Earnhardt.

The title was the first (and only) major series championship of Rudd's racing career. He became one of just five drivers in the series' 26-year history to win the title in his first season. The other drivers to accomplish the same feat were Geoffrey Bodine in 1987, Al Unser Jr. in 1986, Harry Gant in 1985, and Mark Donohue by default in 1974, the series' first season. Making Rudd's championship even sweeter, he defeated Earnhardt, the same driver who had defeated Rudd in the Winston Cup championship chase the season before.

Rudd also became just the fourth driver in IROC history to win the title without winning a race during the season (A.J. Foyt did the same twice in 1976 and 1977, while Bobby Allison went without a win in 1980). Though he didn't win, Rudd certainly earned his championship. He started each of the four events in 10th or worse, but finished each race 3rd or better. He made an immediate splash in his first career IROC race—at Daytona in February of 1992. He, Earnhardt, and Gant crossed the finish line three-wide with Earnhardt taking the victory by a fender. Rudd and Gant, meanwhile, finished in a dead heat—the first official tie for a position in the series' history.

Rudd followed Daytona with third-place runs at Talladega and Michigan and trailed Earnhardt in the standings by 1.5 points as the series headed into its fourth and final race (which was also run at Michigan). In the final race, he passed Earnhardt and bump-drafted Unser Jr. to the finish line. Al Jr. won the race, with Rudd finishing a close second. Earnhardt dropped back to fifth, giving the 36-year-old Rudd a six-point edge in the final standings.

Rudd also raced in the IROC series in 1993, 1995 and 2001, though he couldn't repeat as champion. He had three Top 5s en route to a fourth-place finish in the 1993 title chase. In 2001, he matched his career-best IROC finish at Daytona with another second-place. In both 1995 and 2001, however, he fell from championship contention early.

IROC Standings

Rudd's position in the final standings during his four IROC seasons

Year	Final Standing	Total Points	Money	Season Champion (Points)*
1992	1st	68.5	$175,000	*Dale Earnhardt (63)*
1993	4th	49	50,000	Davey Allison (63)
1995	10th	28	40,000	Dale Earnhardt (61)
2001	6th	45	65,000	Bobby Labonte (68)

* -- Second-place driver listed in italics.

IROC Stats Chart

IROC Record Book - All-Time (min. 8 starts)

Category	Rudd's Total	Rudd's Rank	All-Time IROC Leader
Championships	1	5th	D. Earnhardt, M. Martin -- 4
Money	$330,000	10th	Dale Earnhardt -- 1,286,960
Starts	17	23rd	Dale Earnhardt -- 59
Wins	0	--	D. Earnhardt, A. Unser Jr. -- 11
Winning Pct.	0.0	--	Neil Bonnett -- 37.5
Total Points	178	19th	Dale Earnhardt -- 693
Avg. Finish	5.7	18th	Mark Martin -- 3.7
Top 5s	10	15th	Al Unser Jr. -- 38
Top 10s	16	21st	Dale Earnhardt -- 53
DNFs	1	39th	Al Unser Jr. -- 8
Laps Led	64	14th	Mark Martin -- 426
Pct. Led	8.3	13th	Mark Martin -- 28.5
Races Led	7	12th	Dale Earnhardt -- 26
Times Led	14	9th	Dale Earnhardt -- 70
Laps Completed	728	17th	Dale Earnhardt -- 2,321
Pct. Completed	94.3	19th	B. Labonte, K. Brack -- 100.0

Rudd and Ricky Craven check on Johnny Benson's condition after the three were involved in a wreck at Atlanta in 1996.

Career IROC Results

Year	Date	Track	St	Fin	Laps	Laps Completed	Laps Led	Condition
1992	Feb 16	Daytona International Speedway	11	2	40	40	17	Running
	May 4	Talladega SuperSpeedway	10	3	38	38	0	Running
	Aug 3	Michigan International Speedway	10	3	50	50	13	Running
	Aug 17	Michigan International Speedway	10	2	50	50	0	Running
1993	Feb 14	Daytona International Speedway	8	5	40	40	21	Running
	Mar 29	Darlington Raceway	7	5	60	60	0	Running
	May 3	Talladega SuperSpeedway	10	4	38	38	4	Running
	Aug 2	Michigan International Speedway	9	7	50	50	0	Running
1995	Feb 19	Daytona International Speedway	1	4	40	40	1	Running
	Mar 27	Darlington Raceway	8	11	60	17	0	DNF - Crash
	May 1	Talladega SuperSpeedway	4	8	38	38	3	Running
	Jul 31	Michigan International Speedway	4	10	50	49	0	Running
1996	Aug 19	Michigan International Speedway[1]	8	10	50	50	0	Running
2001	Feb 17	Daytona International Speedway	10	2	40	40	5	Running
	Apr 23	Talladega SuperSpeedway	10	4	38	38	0	Running
	Jun 11	Michigan International Speedway	10	10	50	50	0	Running
	Aug 6	Indianapolis Motor Speedway	7	6	40	40	0	Running

[1] -- Drove for Dale Earnhardt, who was injured in a Winston Cup race at Talladega.

INDEX

Dale Jarrett
ISBN 0-7603-1324-5
134980

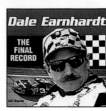

**Dale Earnhardt:
The Final Record**
ISBN 0-7603-0953-1

Jeff Gordon
ISBN 0-7603-0952-3

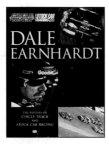

**Dale Earnhardt:
23 Years With the Intimidator**
ISBN 0-7603-1186-2

The American Stock Car
ISBN 0-7603-0977-9

NASCAR Transporters
ISBN 0-7603-0816-0

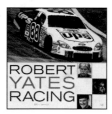

Robert Yates Racing
ISBN 0-7603-0865-9

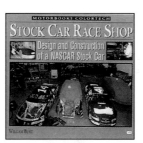

**Stock Car Race Shop: Design and
Construction of a NASCAR Stock Car**
ISBN 0-7603-0905-1
131566

Stock Cars of the 1990s
ISBN 0-7603-1019-X
133373